T0291554

An Accessible Past

ABOUT THE SERIES

The American Association for State and Local History Book Series addresses issues critical to the field of state and local history through interpretive, intellectual, scholarly, and educational texts. To submit a proposal or manuscript to the series, please request proposal guidelines from AASLH headquarters: AASLH Editorial Board, 2021 21st Ave. South, Suite 320, Nashville, Tennessee 37212. Telephone: (615) 320-3203. Website: www.aaslh.org.

ABOUT THE ORGANIZATION

The American Association for State and Local History (AASLH) is a national history membership association headquartered in Nashville, Tennessee, that provides leadership and support for its members who preserve and interpret state and local history in order to make the past more meaningful to all people. AASLH members are leaders in preserving, researching, and interpreting traces of the American past to connect the people, thoughts, and events of yesterday with the creative memories and abiding concerns of people, communities, and our nation today. In addition to sponsorship of this book series, AASLH publishes *History News* magazine, a newsletter, technical leaflets and reports, and other materials; confers prizes and awards in recognition of outstanding achievement in the field; supports a broad education program and other activities designed to help members work more effectively; and advocates on behalf of the discipline of history. To join AASLH, go to www.aaslh.org or contact Membership Services, AASLH, 2021 21st Ave. South, Suite 320, Nashville, TN 37212.

An Accessible Past

Making Historic Sites Accessible

Edited by

Heather Pressman

ROWMAN & LITTLEFIELD
Lanham • Boulder • New York • London

Published by Rowman & Littlefield
An imprint of The Rowman & Littlefield Publishing Group, Inc.
4501 Forbes Boulevard, Suite 200, Lanham, Maryland 20706
www.rowman.com

86-90 Paul Street, London EC2A 4NE

British Library Cataloguing in Publication Information Available

Library of Congress Cataloging-in-Publication Data

Names: Pressman, Heather, 1980- editor.
Title: An accessible past : making historic sites accessible / edited by
   Heather Pressman.
Description: Lanham : Rowman & Littlefield Publishers, 2023. | Series:
   American association for state and local history | Includes
   bibliographical references and index. | Summary: "An Accessible Past:
   Making Historic Sites Accessible helps historic sites and house
   museums understand what they need to do in order to be legally
   compliant, and then, going beyond legal compliance, find creative ways
   in which to make their sites and museums accessible to visitors with a
   variety of types of disabilities"— Provided by publisher.
Identifiers: LCCN 2023035484 (print) | LCCN 2023035485 (ebook) | ISBN
   9781538168257 (cloth) | ISBN 9781538168271 (ebook)
Subjects: LCSH: Historic sites—Law and legislation—United States. |
   Museums—Law and legislation—United States. | Museums and people with
   disabilities—United States. | Museum buildings—Barrier-free
   design—United States. | People with disabilities—Legal status, laws,
   etc.—United States.
Classification: LCC KF4310 .A93 2023 (print) | LCC KF4310 (ebook)
LC record available at https://lccn.loc.gov/2023035484
LC ebook record available at https://lccn.loc.gov/2023035485

♾️™ The paper used in this publication meets the minimum requirements of American National Standard for Information Sciences—Permanence of Paper for Printed Library Materials, ANSI/NISO Z39.48-1992.

This book is dedicated to my mom and the other strong women in my life who continue to inspire me to be more.

Contents

Part III: Diving Deeper

Acknowledgments

This book would not have been possible without the help, support, and expertise of many people. I would like to thank everyone who took time out of their busy lives to contribute to this volume.

Thank you to the American Association for State and Local History and Rowman & Littlefield for the opportunity to contribute to this important work and field of study. A special thanks to my editor Charles Harmon and his staff for helping guide me through the process once again.

A special thank you to my colleagues and friends at Historic Denver's Molly Brown House Museum, especially our fearless leader Andrea Malcomb. Thanks for letting me always push you to be more accessible and for being open to all of my wild ideas!

Thank you too to Jay for being my historic preservation sounding board in an attempt to balance the museum educator in me.

Finally, to my kids who continue to inspire me to do this work and make the world just a little bit kinder for everyone.

A Few Notes on Language

Throughout this book, you will notice the use of person-first language (sometimes also called people-first language), which places the person before their disability, for example, a man who is Deaf as opposed to a Deaf man. The use of identity-first language, where some people with disabilities are embracing language that is more inclusive of their disability, is on the rise. Because some people prefer person-first versus identity-first language (or vice versa), person-first language is used throughout the book because it is considered more neutral. Never be afraid to ask how someone prefers to be called though! Person-first versus identity-first language is a personal choice, and however someone identifies should be respected.

You will also notice that the authors use d/Deaf, as opposed to deaf. When referencing d/Deaf and hard of hearing in written form it is important to acknowledge there are two different communities. Deaf, written with an uppercase "D," is used by people who are culturally deaf (typically born Deaf) and whose native language is American Sign Language (ASL). When deaf is written with a lowercase "d," it refers to the medical condition of losing your hearing. Many people who are deaf become so later in life and ASL is not their native language. Just like how person-first/identity-first language is a personal choice, using deaf versus Deaf is also a personal choice. In written form, d/Deaf allows for greater inclusion whether someone considers themselves to be deaf or Deaf.

Preface

An Accessible Past is designed to help historic sites overcome barriers to accessibility by clarifying what they must do to be legally compliant. It also provides sites with inspiration for how they can make their historic properties accessible. This book focuses on how organizations can support visitors and potential visitors of differing ages and abilities to feel welcome. In addition to covering the basics of the laws, this volume contains a number of case studies of historic sites that have gotten creative when it comes to making their sites accessible to individuals with different types of disabilities (physical, intellectual, sensory, etc.). Hopefully these case studies will give sites the guidance and inspiration they need to start making changes and expanding access.

This book is meant to be a useful tool for anyone who is a practitioner or student in the public history and museum fields who works, volunteers, or has an interest in historic sites. Access touches all aspects of public history, and it is vital that every member of these (frequently small) staffs understand the laws and the importance of accessibility. The book is broken into three parts.

Part I covers why access is important, what access is, a brief history of disability laws, what the ADA means for historic sites, and steps to take to make historical sites accessible.

A variety of case studies in part II cover programmatic and physical accessibility solutions from a diverse selection of historic sites. These case studies offer creative ways visitors can engage with the museum while retaining the historical integrity of the places in question.

Part III is for those who are ready to ask, what comes next? Also included in this section is appendix A, which contains a list of resources to help you continue on your accessibility journey.

Editor's Note: *An Accessible Past* differs from my previous book, *The Art of Access: A Practical Guide to Museum Accessibility*, coauthored with Danielle Schulz, in that this edited volume dives more deeply into how historic sites can comply with the laws as well as provides numerous case studies as examples for museums and historic sites to draw inspiration from. *The Art of Access* touches on historic sites, but only very briefly, whereas *An Accessible Past* expands on the content in that book. While some of the information contained herein is similar to *The Art of Access*, the content is specific to historic sites/museums. If you are looking for a more general guide to museum accessibility, I recommend reading *The Art of Access: A Practical Guide to Museum Accessibility*.

Part I

Beginning with Access

In this section, dive into why access is important for your historic house, site, or museum. Learn what access is and what the ADA means for historic sites (yes, you must still comply) and explore steps you can take to make historical sites accessible. This section also covers a brief history of disability laws in the United States.

1

Setting the Stage

AN INTRODUCTION TO ACCESS AT HISTORIC SITES

There are over 16,500 history museums in the United States.[1] History institutions—historic houses, history museums, and historic sites—comprise about 55.5 percent of the total of all US museums.[2] History museums and historic sites are one of the most visited types of museums in the United States, but what is the experience like for visitors with disabilities? Are they able to get in the front door? If they can, do they feel welcome? Visitors with disabilities, particularly those with physical disabilities, may only be able to access a portion of your site of significance, meaning that they are only getting part of the story you are trying to tell. So what can you do to help ensure that visitors are able to experience the whole story? The answer is simple: make your historic site accessible. Now you may be thinking that sounds easier said than done. In some cases yes, but in most cases no. The majority of historic sites and museums are physically inaccessible to people with physical disabilities, but designing for accessibility is more than just physical access to sites and museums.

WHAT IS ACCESS?

If you are new to the world of access work, you may be asking, what is access? What does it mean to a historic site or museum? When talking about access and accessibility at historic sites and museums, we are primarily talking about access for people with disabilities. The Americans with Disabilities Act (ADA) defines a disability as "physical or mental impairment that substantially limits one or more major life activity."[3] According to the American Alliance of Museums (AAM), "Accessibility is giving equitable access to everyone along the continuum of human ability and experience."[4] The American Association for

State and Local History (AASLH) notes that "access to historical resources gives preservation activities their meaning. Providing and promoting equitable access to historical resources through exhibitions, tours, educational programs, publications, electronic media, and research is critical in fulfilling the public trust and mission of history organizations."[5] In short, everyone deserves equitable access to our shared history.

Results of the 2010 census showed that nearly 20 percent of Americans had a disability.[6] As of 2019, that number increased to just under 27 percent, according to the Centers for Disease Control and Prevention.[7] That means that one out of every three to four members in your community has a disability, whether visible or not.[8] This number will undoubtedly continue to grow as the population ages. The US Census Bureau estimates that by 2030, Americans over the age of sixty-five will make up approximately 21 percent of the population and that by 2060, this number will increase to nearly one in four. By 2060, it is estimated that the number of Americans over the age of eighty-five will triple.[9] As the population ages, age-related disabilities, such as vision loss, hearing loss, and dementias, will also increase.

When public history practitioners hear talk of making sites accessible, their reaction is often that these two things are opposed and that in order to make a site accessible, major physical changes to historic buildings and landscapes will be required. But this is not the case. There is no need to render the historic integrity of a site null by making drastic changes to the physical structure, but there are creative ways to work around the physical challenges historic sites present. It is important to remember that physical disabilities only account for

"In planning for accessibility, it is important to remember that disabilities are far from uniform. In addition to mobility, physical impairments may affect sight or hearing. Cognitive abilities may be diminished by dementia. Sensory sensitivities may result from autism. Mental illness may cause anxiety or phobias that make public places difficult to navigate. . . . Although a common symbol for accessibility is a schematic of a person in a wheelchair, the reality is that impairments are often invisible and do not have to involve recognizable assistive devices.'

—Cynthia Falk, *The Inclusive Historian's Handbook*

Figure 1.1. From https://inclusivehistorian.com/accessibility/.
Courtesy Heather Pressman.

about 13 percent of people with disabilities in the United States, and by ensuring that your site is welcoming to people with a diversity of abilities, you will be able to invite more visitors to your site.[10] Access can at first, especially for historic sites, seem daunting; however, fortunately for practitioners in the museum field, it can be easily broken down into smaller, more easily accomplished chunks. But why is it important to do this work?

WHY DO WE DO WHAT WE DO?

History museums are "the most trusted source of history, outperforming history professors, history teachers, and even history books."[11] Despite the fact that more than twenty years have passed since this finding was first published by Roy Rosenzweig and David Thelen in *The Presence of the Past: Popular Uses of History in American Life*, over 80 percent of Americans still "trust what they hear and see from history museums."[12] A 2021 report from AAM confirmed that museums are regarded as "highly trustworthy," more so than the government, news organizations, researchers/scientists, NGOs, and social media. Museums ranked second only to friends and family.[13]

If you look at prepandemic numbers, annual visitation numbers to US historic sites and museums were increasing. History organizations as a whole saw an increase of more than 5 percent (by comparison, the US population increased by only about 4 percent during this same period of time).[14] Breaking this number down further, between 2013 and 2018, as a segment of museums, historic houses saw an increase of nearly 9 percent in average visitation, while historic sites saw an increase of just over 10 percent. These increases in visitation occurred regardless of budget level or region.[15] The pandemic obviously impacted visitation numbers, but sites around the country are expecting numbers to rise once again as we approach semiquincentennial celebrations.[16]

In 2026, the United States will commemorate its two-hundred-fiftieth anniversary. In advance of this historic moment, marking the longest continuous democracy, a commission was formed to plan and orchestrate "the largest and most inclusive anniversary."[17] The question is, how can it be inclusive unless it is accessible? If historic sites and house museums with ties to the Revolutionary War remain inaccessible, how can this commemoration be truly inclusive? This anniversary has the opportunity to have an impact on inspiring future historians, public history practitioners, and museologists. In order to diversify the fields of history and historic preservation, these sites, and others like them, need to be welcoming to people of all kinds. We know from research that visiting a museum has long-term impacts on children. According to a 2014 paper, "children who visited a museum during kindergarten had higher achievement scores in reading, mathematics, and science than children who did not."[18] One thing to keep in mind is that kids with a low socioeconomic status (low levels of income and parental education) are less likely to go visit museums than peers from higher socioeconomic groups, losing out on the benefits of visiting a museum at an early age.[19] People with disabilities are overwhelmingly unemployed and underemployed, making them part of the low socioeconomic status group; however, additional barriers exist for people with disabilities.

ACCESS AND HISTORIC SITES

To understand the importance of accessibility at historic sites, it is essential to first have an understanding of the history of disability. The history of disability in the United States goes back as far as the founding of the country.[20] The first federal programs for people with disabilities occurred with the Vocational Rehabilitation Act of 1918.[21] Disabled veterans returning to the United States from World War I pressured the government to provide rehabilitation and vocational training.[22] Despite this action on the part of the government, generally speaking, people with disabilities continued to be marginalized and overlooked. In fact, it was not until the 1960s that housing, transportation, and public facilities became more accessible. The first steps toward access were made when the US Congress passed the Architectural Barriers Act in 1968. This act stated that "all future public buildings and

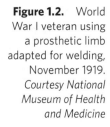

Figure 1.2. World War I veteran using a prosthetic limb adapted for welding, November 1919. *Courtesy National Museum of Health and Medicine*

those buildings significantly altered with federal funds needed to be accessible to all citizens."[23] The law applied only to public buildings, and it lacked an enforcement arm. This meant that privately owned commercial spaces, public transportation, housing, and recreational facilities were still exempt from being required to be accessible.

Five years later, in September 1973, the United States enacted what is widely considered to be the first civil rights disability law. The Rehabilitation Act, intended to establish rehabilitation programs, particularly for returning servicemen, supported equal access for people with disabilities through one section in particular. Arguably one of the most important parts of the Rehabilitation Act of 1973 is Section 504, which prohibits discrimination against people with disabilities. Section 504 outlines that individuals with disabilities cannot "be excluded from participation in, be denied the benefits of, or be subjected to discrimination under any program or activity receiving federal financial assistance" due to having a disability.[24] For museums and historic sites this means that "all programs, projects, and activities that receive financial assistance from the federal government are to operate in accordance with the laws outlined in the Act."[25] The Rehabilitation Act of 1973 only applied to federally funded programs and activities, so further action was called for.

Landmark disability rights legislation was finally passed nearly two decades later, in 1990. The ADA was born out of a need for people with disabilities to physically access spaces and places, whether or not they were federally funded. ADA legislation covers "all areas of public life" from transportation to schools to jobs to museums and more.[26] The ADA was built on the foundations laid by the Architectural Barriers Act of 1968, the Rehabilitation Act of 1973, and other similar disability laws, focusing on bringing awareness to the environmental concerns people with disabilities face daily. These federal laws are one step in creating inclusive spaces by outlining a baseline that museums and other spaces must comply with. However, considerations were made for historic buildings and sites of significance.

In an effort to provide a tool to help people working at historic sites and houses, in 1993 the National Park Service published a preservation brief titled *Making Historic Properties Accessible*. The brief "provides guidance on making historic properties accessible while preserving their historic character" and stresses that both historic preservation and accessibility experts should be consulted before any "permanent physical changes" are made to a historic structure.[27] The brief outlines the steps for planning accessible modifications, suggests solutions to common physical accessibility issues, and discusses federal accessibility laws. While *Making Historic Properties Accessible* is helpful, it should be noted that it was published thirty years ago and has not been updated; the focus of the brief is on physical accessibility, and updated changes to the laws are not addressed.

AN ACCESSIBLE PAST

So what does the ADA mean for historic sites? Are historic properties and landscapes bound by the same laws as nonhistoric sites? Yes and no. The passage of the ADA made access to historic properties a civil right, however, provisions were left in to preserve sites for future generations. The law challenges property owners to find ways to make their sites accessible through alternative solutions. As *Making Historic Properties Accessible* notes, "Most historic buildings are not exempt from providing accessibility, and with careful planning, historic properties can be made more accessible, so that all citizens can enjoy our Nation's diverse heritage."[28]

So once again, we ask what is access and what does it mean for your historic site? Accessibility is simply creating a welcoming and equitable experience for visitors to your historic property. History organizations are trusted by people with and without disabilities, so we need to do our best to make everyone feel welcome and included at our sites. It took nearly one hundred years from the passage of the first disability legislation to get where we are today, and we should not let it take us another one hundred years to make visitors with disabilities feel welcome. The next chapter dives into the specifics of what the ADA Titles (sections) mean to historic houses and sites, starting by clarifying what historic properties must do in order to be legally compliant.

NOTES

1. Institute for Museum and Library Services, "Museum Data Files," November 2018, https://www.imls.gov/sites/default/files/museum_data_file_documentation_and _users_guide.pdf.
2. Bob Beatty, "Running the Numbers on Attendance at History Museums in the US," *Hyperallergic*, March 1, 2018, https://hyperallergic.com/429788/running-the-num bers-on-attendance-at-history-museums-in-the-us/
3. ADA National Network, "What Is the Definition of Disability under the ADA?," accessed October 4, 2022, https://adata.org/faq/what-definition-disability-under-ada.
4. American Alliance of Museums, "DEIA Definitions," accessed January 2, 2022, https://www.aam-us.org/wp-content/uploads/2018/04/AAM-DEAI-Defini tions-Infographic.pdf.
5. American Association for State and Local History, "AASLH Statement of Standards and Ethics," accessed January 2, 2022, http://download.aaslh.org/AASLH+State ment+of+Standards+and+Ethics+-+Revised+2018.pdf.
6. US Census Bureau Public Information Office, "Nearly 1 in 5 People Have a Disability in the U.S., Census Bureau Reports—Miscellaneous—Newsroom—U.S. Census Bureau." US Census Bureau, May 19, 2016, accessed January 3, 2022, https://www .census.gov/newsroom/releases/archives/miscellaneous/cb12-134.html.
7. Center for Disease Control and Prevention, "Disability & Health Data System," accessed January 3, 2022, https://www.cdc.gov/ncbddd/disabilityandhealth/dhds/index.html.
8. Visible disabilities are frequently physical disabilities that require the use of some sort of assistive device such as a wheelchair or cane. Invisible disabilities are actu-

ally more common and less obvious. They include things such as anxiety, sensory processing disorders, autism spectrum, ADHD, etc.

9. Jonathan Vespa, "The Graying of America: More Older Adults than Kids by 2035," Center for Disease Control and Prevention, March 13, 2018, accessed January 3, 2022, https://www.census.gov/library/stories/2018/03/graying-america.html.
10. Centers for Disease Control and Prevention, "Disability Impacts All of Us Infographic," September 16, 2020, https://www.cdc.gov/ncbddd/disabilityandhealth/infographic-disability-impacts-all.html.
11. John Dichtl, "Most Trust Museums as Sources of Historical Information," AASLH, August 12, 2020, https://aaslh.org/most-trust-museums/.
12. Dichtl, "Most Trust Museums as Sources of Historical Information."
13. American Alliance of Museums, "Museums and Trust," accessed January 5, 2022, https://www.aam-us.org/2021/09/30/museums-and-trust-2021/.
14. AASLH National Visitation Report Summary 2019, no page.
15. John Garrison Marks and W. Maclane Hull, "Visitation at Historic House Museums," AASLH, January 9, 2020, https://aaslh.org/visitation-at-historic-house-museums/.
16. At the time of this writing, the effects of the COVID-19 pandemic were still ongoing so it is hard to say what the long-term impacts on historic sites and house museums will be.
17. America250, "About," accessed January 2, 2022, https://america250.org/about/.
18. Deanne W. Swan, "The Effect of Informal Learning Environments on Academic Achievement during Elementary School," paper presented to the American Educational Research Association, Philadelphia, Pennsylvania, 2014, https://www.imls.gov/blog/2014/04/children-who-visit-museums-have-higher-achievement-reading-math-and-science.
19. Swan, "The Effect of Informal Learning Environments on Academic Achievement during Elementary School."
20. This is a very condensed history of disability civil rights laws and history. For a longer, albeit brief, history of disability in the United States, see chapter 1 of *The Art of Access* by Heather Pressman and Danielle Schulz; for a more in-depth history, see *A Disability History of the United States* by Kim Nielsen, which covers disability history from pre-1492 through the late twentieth century.
21. Department of Veteran's Affairs, "VA History in Brief," accessed January 3, 2022, https://www.va.gov/opa/publications/archives/docs/history_in_brief.pdf.
22. Anti-Defamation League, "A Brief History of the Disability Rights Movement," accessed January 3, 2022, https://www.adl.org/education/resources/backgrounders/disability-rights-movement.
23. Nielsen, *A Disability History of the United States*, 165.
24. US Department of Labor, "Section 504, Rehabilitation Act of 1973," accessed September 14, 2023, https://www.dol.gov/agencies/oasam/centers-offices/civil-rights-center/statutes/section-504-rehabilitation-act-of-1973.
25. Pressman and Schulz, *The Art of Access*, 6.
26. ADA National Network, "What Is the Americans with Disabilities Act (ADA)?," accessed January 12, 2022, https://adata.org/learn-about-ada.
27. Thomas C. Jester and Sharon C. Park, *Making Historic Properties Accessible* (Washington, DC: US National Park Service, Heritage Preservation Services, 1993), https://www.nps.gov/tps/how-to-preserve/briefs/32-accessibility.htm.
28. Jester and Park, *Making Historic Properties Accessible*.

2

Getting Started

The first step to making visitors with disabilities feel welcome at your historic property is to understand what you are legally required to do. At its most basic level, the ADA "is a civil rights law that prohibits discrimination against individuals with disabilities in all areas of public life, including jobs, schools, transportation, and all public and private places that are open to the general public. The purpose of the law is to make sure that people with disabilities have the same rights and opportunities as everyone else."[1] The law is broken into five sections, called Titles, that cover different aspects of life. They are

- Title I—Employment,
- Title II—State and Local Governments (physical and program accessibility in state/local government entities),
- Title III—Public Accommodations and Commercial Facilities (physical and program accessibility in restaurants, hotels, stores, museums, and other places of business),
- Title IV—Telecommunications, and
- Title V—Miscellaneous.

The full act as we know it today did not immediately go into effect: Title I became law when the ADA was signed in July 1990, Titles II and III were enacted the following July, Title IV was added in 1993, and Title V was added later.

The ADA applies to all places of public accommodation, including historic sites, history museums, and historic houses. Generally speaking, the ADA applies to businesses and organizations with fifteen or more employees, government agencies (whether they are federally funded or not), and privately operated commercial entities (including museums). Religious organizations and private clubs are exempt. Titles II and III are the ones that most directly impact museums and historic sites. According to Title II, state and local governments, and sites such as museums that are funded by them, "must remove accessibility barriers either by shifting services and programs to accessible buildings, or by making alterations to existing buildings."[2] Under Title III, privately owned public accommodations are required to make "readily achievable" changes to be accessible, but what exactly does this mean?[3] In short, accessibility should be increased whenever possible; however, a historic property's spaces, features, and significant materials should not be destroyed in the pursuit of accessibility.

WITH HERITAGE SO RICH

A marriage of preservation and accessibility is not impossible, it just takes a bit of creativity and a thorough understanding of accessibility laws and how they apply to historic sites and structures. As writer, professor, and endurance athlete Susan Lacke (who happens to be d/Deaf) put it, "Though accessibility wasn't integrated into the original design of most historic buildings, bringing such structures up to today's standards doesn't have to run counter to the goals of historic preservation."[4] But what is historic preservation?

Historic preservation "is a movement in planning designed to conserve old buildings and areas in an effort to tie a place's history to its population and culture."[5] The preservation movement in the United States began in the 1850s when Ann Pamela Cunningham fought to save Washington's Mount Vernon from ruin.[6] Today, the scope of the field has broadened from "saving the homes of prominent Americans" to include everything from sites of triumph or loss to the birthplaces of leaders and everything in between.[7] America's historic sites are "physical remind-

Figure 2.1. Mount Vernon had badly deteriorated by 1858 when it was purchased by the Mount Vernon Ladies' Association with the express purpose of preserving the mansion. *Courtesy Mount Vernon Ladies' Association*

Chapter 2

ers of the diversity of our experiences and the history we share."[8] Preserving these sites and making them more accessible can bring us together in our shared past.

How did we get from Mount Vernon to where we are today? In 1933, the Historic American Buildings Survey (HABS) was begun. The survey was the United States' first federal preservation program and set out to document the country's architectural heritage. The program was "motivated primarily by the perceived need to mitigate the negative effects upon our history and culture of rapidly vanishing architectural resources."[9] In 1935, the Historic Sites Act (HSA) was signed into law. The law declared, "It is a national policy to preserve for public use historic sites, buildings and objects of national significance for the inspiration and benefit of the people of the United States."[10] Around this same time, other early preservation efforts were just starting. For example, the development of the first National Historic Sites and historic parks were being developed by the National Park Service. The first National Historic Site established was Salem Maritime National Historic Site on March 17, 1938.[11] Another important preservation project of the time was the restoration of what is now known as Colonial Williamsburg.[12]

By 1965, HABS had documented twelve thousand sites in the country, and the number of sites that had been destroyed or damaged beyond repair in the thirty-two years since its inception numbered close to half. The HABS committee urged the federal government to intervene to save further loss of the

Figure 2.2.   Historic American Buildings Survey team, measuring the Kentucky School for the Blind in Louisville, Kentucky in March 1934. *Courtesy Library of Congress, Prints & Photographs Division, KY-20-19-7*

Getting Started   **13**

nation's historic fabric. A special committee was formed by President Lyndon B. Johnson to determine the extent of the situation. Their report confirmed that preservation needed to become a priority. In 1966, the National Historic Preservation Act was passed by Congress, which established "permanent institutions and created a clearly defined process for historic preservation in the United States."[13] The new law "was the most comprehensive preservation law the nation had ever known."[14]

WITH HERITAGE SO RICH . . . AND ACCESSIBLE

To be included under the ADA's definition of historic, a site must be listed or eligible for listing on the National Register of Historic Places or designated as historic under state or local law.[15] Buildings that do not meet these criteria do not fall under the ADA exception. Historic buildings are required to be as accessible as nonhistoric structures as thoroughly as possible, provided it does not cause undue financial hardship to the organization running the site. At a very minimum, historic sites must meet at least the following requirements:

- At least one accessible route from a site access point to an accessible entrance. A ramp with less than a 1:6 slope for a run of under two feet may be used as part of an accessible route to an entrance.
- At least one accessible entrance. If a public entrance does not work, a nonpublic unlocked entrance may be used with directional signage at the main entrance. Remote monitoring may be used where security is a problem.
- At least one toilet (if provided) along an accessible route. Toilet facilities may be all gender in design.
- An accessible route, at the level of entry, must be provided to all public spaces. Whenever possible, access to all parts of the building, facility, or site should be provided.
- Exhibits, displays, and other written information (for example, books or other documents) should be viewable by a seated person at a height of no more than forty-four inches from the floor surface.[16]

Keep in mind that these are the *minimum* requirements and any time you can provide more to your visitors with disabilities it helps create a sense of welcome at your site for this audience. Exceptions to the requirements listed previously should only occur "when it is formally and properly determined that meeting the standard requirements for alterations to buildings would destroy the historic nature of the structure."[17]

Many of the things that you can do to improve accessibility at your site are simple fixes and can be accomplished for very little money as well. In addition to programmatic and digital access (which are covered in part II of this book), you can adapt or retrofit existing elements and structures at your site. For example, if you have an elevator on site, consider adding Braille or raised markings to the elevator buttons. If you are looking for ways to widen a doorway to allow easier access (or access at all) for mobility devices, consider installing offset hinges. Add a ramp in place of a few steps. Reposition furniture or exhibit displays. Under the ADA, you are required to provide accessible parking spaces. To make your site more accessible, consider providing more than the minimum required number of spaces or relocating accessible parking spaces closer to the entrance.

If physical accessibility seems impossible without threatening or destroying the historic integrity and significance of a site, the ADA Accessibility Guidelines (ADAAG) outline how to approach these situations. Property owners whether public or private "are required to consult with people with disabilities, disability organizations and their State Historic Preservation Officer (SHPO) to determine if the special accessibility provisions for historic properties may be used."[18] If, through this consultation process, it is determined that physical modifications would "threaten or destroy" the significance of the property, then equitable access through other means is an option. Accessibility is never impossible to achieve, to some degree or another. If physical access is impossible, create a virtual tour of your space, add a tactile 3-D model, invest in virtual reality technology, or some other alternative (again, the second part of this book provides you with a variety of creative ideas to get started).

READY AND ACHIEVABLE

The ADA "takes into account the national interest in preserving significant historic structures."[19] Barrier removal in historic buildings is required by the ADA if it is "readily achievable." The term "readily achievable" means that it is

"Historic preservation is a conversation with our past about our future. It provides us with opportunities to ask, 'What is important in our history?' and 'What parts of our past can we preserve for the future?' Through historic preservation, we look at history in different ways, ask different questions of the past, and learn new things about our history and ourselves. Historic preservation is an important way for us to transmit our understanding of the past to future generations."

Figure 2.3. From https://www.nps.gov/subjects/historicpreservation/what-is -historic-preservation.htm. *Courtesy Heather Pressman*

easy to accomplish and can be done without too much difficulty or expense. If the barrier removal threatens or destroys the historical significance or integrity of the building or facility, it is not considered "readily achievable." According to the Title III Technical Assistance Manual, "Public accommodations must remove architectural barriers and communication barriers that are structural in nature in existing facilities, when it is readily achievable to do so."[20] Architectural barriers are defined as "physical elements of a facility that impede access by people with disabilities," such as steps and curbs, but also things like paper towel dispensers, drinking fountains, and mirrors that are mounted too high for people of short stature or who use a wheelchair or other mobility device.[21]

So how do you determine what barriers to remove (if possible) and how? The first thing you should do is conduct a review of the historical significance of the property. Identify any character-defining features of the building and site. Contact your certified local government, local State Historic Preservation Office, or other local preservation organizations for assistance with this step. These preservation professionals and organizations can help identify appropriate barriers for removal.

DEFINING CHARACTER

When determining what barriers to remove (if any) to make your historic site more accessible, one of the first things you need to do is to review the historical significance of the property and identify any character-defining features. But what does that mean?

Character-defining features exist on both the interior and exterior of historic sites and buildings. According to the Secretary of the Interior (SOI), "Every old building is unique, with its own identity and its own distinctive character. Character refers to all those visual aspects and physical features that comprise the appearance of every historic building. Character-defining elements include the overall shape of the building, its materials, craftsmanship, decorative details, interior spaces and features, as well as the various aspects of its site and environment."[1] The SOI recommends a three-step process to determine a building's character-defining features. First, study the structure from a distance to better understand the architectural context and setting (look at the shape, any openings, the general setting, materials, etc.). Second, examine the building up close (look at materials and craftsmanship). Finally, determine the visual character of the interior spaces.

---

1. Lee H. Nelson, *Architectural Character: Identifying the Visual Aspects of Historic Buildings as an Aid to Preserving Their Character,* accessed May 14, 2023, https://www.nps.gov/orgs/1739/upload/preservation-brief-17-architectural-character.pdf.

Determining a building's exterior "historic character" will likely take less time than surveying its interior "because so much of the exterior can be seen at one time and it is possible to grasp its essential character rather quickly."[2] Preservation Brief 17, *Architectural Character: Identifying the Visual Aspects of Historic Buildings as an Aid to Preserving Their Character*, offers some examples as well as a checklist to guide you through determining what may or may not be character-defining features of your site such as shape, openings, or projections, among others.

When examining interior spaces, you want to look for any tangible architectural features or elements that convey the building's sense of time and place. "The careful identification and evaluation of interior architectural elements, after undertaking research on the building's history and use, is critically important before changes to the building are contemplated."[3] The goal of assessing interior spaces is "to identify which elements contribute to the building's character and which do not."[4] It is vital to know the building's history before starting this process as sometimes rooms are associated with an important event or historical figure, although they are not "architecturally distinguished," and therefore should be kept or restored. Preservation Brief 18, *Rehabilitating Interiors in Historic Buildings Identifying and Preserving Character-Defining Elements*, offers examples and recommendations to help you in your interior survey work.

---

2. Nelson, *Architectural Character*.
3. H. Ward Jandl, *Rehabilitating Interiors in Historic Buildings Identifying and Preserving Character-Defining Elements*, accessed May 14, 2023, https://www.nps.gov/orgs/1739/upload/preservation-brief-18-interiors.pdf.
4. Jandl, *Rehabilitating Interiors in Historic Buildings Identifying and Preserving Character-Defining Elements*.

Changes made to the site without consultation with preservation professionals are highly discouraged and could result in negative long-term impacts. Consulting with preservation professionals will ensure that the integrity of the site is maintained, whereas, by not doing so, it could be lost or damaged, making it impossible to seek out preservation grants, historic tax credits, and other such benefits in the future. Preservation professionals will ensure that any changes made follow the standards set forth by the Secretary of the Interior's Standards for the Treatment of Historic Properties.[22] This is especially important as the Standards for Rehabilitation that are included therein are used as criteria to determine whether or not a property qualifies for the Federal Historic Preservation Tax Incentives program.[23]

After determining your building's historic significance/history and character-defining features, the next step is to determine your current level of accessibility by conducting an accessibility audit. An audit examines your spaces, programs, services, and policies. The point is to identify any existing barriers that may be preventing people with disabilities from visiting your museum or site of significance. If your museum or historic site falls under Title II of the ADA, then you are required by law to conduct an audit and self-evaluate the accessibility of your site or museum. Once you have completed the audit you can compare it to the required level of accessibility based on the ADA. Audits and the transition plans (described shortly) that result from them are discussed further in the next chapter.

Finally, create your transition plan for changes, within a preservation context. A transition plan lays out how your site will address the barriers to access that were identified as a part of the audit, including reasonable timelines and specific solutions. Again, as with conducting an audit or self-evaluation, Title II organizations are required by law to also complete a transition plan. Everyone else is highly encouraged to complete one as well.

After you have created your transition plan, begin the work. Just as with nonhistoric sites, you will want to review your plan periodically to ensure that the changes you are planning to implement are still needed and feasible within the budget. You may not be able to do as much to your site as a nonhistoric or protected site, but remember, the goal is to provide a high level of accessibility by selecting appropriate solutions without compromising significant features or the overall character and integrity of the historic property.

So how do you determine, based on your audit, what accommodations are "readily achievable"? According to the ADA, it is done on a case-by-case basis and there are several factors to consider:

1. "The nature and cost of the action;
2. The overall financial resources of the site or sites involved; the number of persons employed at the site; the effect on expenses and resources; legitimate safety requirements necessary for safe operation, including crime prevention measures; or any other impact of the action on the operation of the site;
3. The geographic separateness, and the administrative or fiscal relationship of the site or sites in question to any parent corporation or entity;
4. If applicable, the overall financial resources of any parent corporation or entity; the overall size of the parent corporation or entity with respect to the number of its employees; the number, type, and location of its facilities; and
5. If applicable, the type of operation or operations of any parent corporation or entity, including the composition, structure, and functions of the workforce of the parent corporation or entity."[24]

There is no definitive answer as to which barriers can be removed because it depends on the cost and level of difficulty, which vary site by site. Meaning what is readily achievable at one site might be impossible at another.

The Department of Justice provides a list in its regulations of "21 examples of modifications that may be readily achievable."[25] These include:

1. "Installing ramps;
2. Making curb cuts in sidewalks and entrances;
3. Repositioning shelves;
4. Rearranging tables, chairs, vending machines, display racks, and other furniture;
5. Repositioning telephones;
6. Adding raised markings on elevator control buttons;
7. Installing flashing alarm lights;
8. Widening doors;
9. Installing offset hinges to widen doorways;
10. Eliminating a turnstile or providing an alternative accessible path;
11. Installing accessible door hardware;
12. Installing grab bars in toilet stalls;
13. Rearranging toilet partitions to increase maneuvering space;
14. Insulating lavatory pipes under sinks to prevent burns;
15. Installing a raised toilet seat;
16. Installing a full-length bathroom mirror;
17. Repositioning the paper towel dispenser in a bathroom;
18. Creating designated accessible parking spaces;
19. Installing an accessible paper cup dispenser at an existing inaccessible water fountain;
20. Removing high pile, low density carpeting; or
21. Installing vehicle hand controls."[26]

This list, of course, is only intended to be illustrative and by no means all encompassing.

Once you have identified which barriers can be easily removed or modified, how do you prioritize the work? Your first step should be to consult with user-experts in your community. This could come in the form of focus groups with members of your community who have disabilities, asking members of your advisory committee (if you have one) what they think, or even consulting with local organizations that represent different disability groups, such as the Alzheimer's Association. Talking with the people who these changes are going to have the most impact on will help you identify what they see to be the most significant barriers and help you remove them more quickly.

The Department of Justice suggests first removing barriers that limit visitors' ability to get into the building. Parking is often an easy first place to begin because organizations and sites can designate more or closer spaces "because it enables many people with disabilities to 'get in the door.'"[27] Next, they suggest prioritizing access to where goods and services are made available to the public, such as the front desk or ticket counter. Following this is a focus on the restrooms and then everything else. While major structural changes can wait, accommodations that are "readily achievable" should be made as quickly as possible. This is where conducting an audit, talking to your community, and putting together a work plan can help you figure out which steps to take first.

NOTES

1. ADA National Network, "An Overview of the Americans with Disabilities Act," accessed September 16, 2022, https://adata.org/factsheet/ADA-overview.
2. Thomas C. Jester and Sharon C. Park, *Making Historic Properties Accessible* (Washington, DC: US National Park Service, Heritage Preservation Services, 1993), https://www.nps.gov/tps/how-to-preserve/briefs/32-accessibility.htm.
3. Jester and Park, *Making Historic Properties Accessible.*
4. Susan Lacke, "Historic Shouldn't Mean Inaccessible: Preservation and the ADA," Accessibility.com, October 19, 2020, https://www.accessibility.com/blog/historic-shouldnt-mean-inaccessible-preservation-and-the-ada.
5. Amanda Briney, "An Overview of Historic Preservation," *ThoughtCo.*, January 23, 2020, https://www.thoughtco.com/historic-preservation-and-urban-planning-1435784.
6. Mount Vernon, "Ann Pamela Cunningham," accessed October 10, 2022, https://www.mountvernon.org/library/digitalhistory/digital-encyclopedia/article/ann-pamela-cunningham.
7. American Historical Association, "Historians in Historic Preservation," accessed October 10, 2022, https://www.historians.org/jobs-and-professional-development/career-resources/careers-for-students-of-history/historians-in-historic-preservation.
8. National Trust for Historic Preservation, "Saving Americas Historical Sites," accessed October 10, 2022, https://savingplaces.org/saving-americas-historic-sites#.Y0SgZezMJAc.
9. National Park Service, "Historic American Buildings Survey," accessed October 10, 2022, https://www.nps.gov/hdp/habs/.
10. The Living New Deal, "Historic Sites Act," accessed October 10, 2022, https://livingnewdeal.org/glossary/historic-sites-act-1935/.
11. National Park Service, "Americas First National Historic Site," accessed October 10, 2022, https://www.nps.gov/sama/index.htm.
12. National Park Service, "Historic American Buildings Survey."
13. National Park Service, "National Historic Preservation Act," accessed October 10, 2022, https://www.nps.gov/subjects/historicpreservation/national-historic-preservation-act.htm.
14. National Park Service, "National Historic Preservation Act."
15. US Access Board, "ADA Accessibility Guidelines," n.d., https://www.access-board.gov/adaag-1991-2002.html#4.1.7.
16. US Access Board, "ADA Accessibility Guidelines."

17. Lacke, "Historic Shouldn't Mean Inaccessible."
18. Lacke, "Historic Shouldn't Mean Inaccessible."
19. "ADA Title III Technical Assistance Manual," accessed September 20, 2022, https://www.ada.gov/reachingout/title3l4.html.
20. "ADA Title III Technical Assistance Manual."
21. "ADA Title III Technical Assistance Manual."
22. The standards offers guidelines designed to help building owners protect irreplaceable cultural resources by promoting responsible preservation practices. National Park Service, "The Secretary of the Interior's Standards for the Treatment of Historic Properties," accessed May 14, 2023, https://www.nps.gov/orgs/1739/secretary-standards-treatment-historic-properties.htm.
23. To be eligible, the rehabilitation work be done must follow the standards outlined in the Standards for the Treatment of Historic Properties and a building must be on the National Register of Historic Places or be certified as contributing to the significance of a "registered historic district," among other things. For a full list of requirements, see https://www.nps.gov/subjects/taxincentives/index.htm.
24. "ADA Title III Technical Assistance Manual."
25. "ADA Title III Technical Assistance Manual."
26. "ADA Title III Technical Assistance Manual."
27. ADA National Network, "Accessible Parking," accessed September 20, 2022, https://adata.org/factsheet/parking.

3

Making the Past Accessible

Now that you hopefully have a better sense of the laws and their impact on your site, you understand that historic preservation and accessibility can coexist. Now it is time for the work to begin.

REVIEW, AUDIT, AND PLAN

With a foundation of what "readily achievable" means, you can now start down the path to being more accessible by evaluating your site. As a reminder, there are three steps to this process: conduct a review of the historical significance of the property, carry out a self-assessment accessibility audit, and then create a transition plan to address the barriers you have identified. After completing these three steps you will be ready to begin making your historic site or museum accessible.

STEP 1: SITE REVIEW

As historic sites and museums, the last thing we want to do is destroy our reason for being—using the power of place to teach lessons of the past and make connections to today. If we destroy the historic significance of a site or building, we destroy a piece of history, making it inaccessible to everyone. While we cannot make historic sites physically accessible to all who would like to visit, we can retain much of the historic integrity while also opening up accessibility at the site. The first step in your site assessment, which you may have already completed, is to determine which features of your site are historically significant. What parts are unique or important to the story you are trying to tell? Do you have any unusual architectural features? Did some major event occur in one of the rooms? Were there formerly structures (and therefore possible archaeological evidence) in the space between existing buildings? Your local SHPO, certified local government, or other preservation organizations can assist with the process of determining important elements inside and outside.

Much of the information can likely be found in the National Register, state/local landmark, or other similar applications if your site has any of these designations. Again, these decisions should not be made in a vacuum and should be in line with the Secretary of the Interior's Standards for the Treatment of Historic Properties (as discussed in chapter 2). After you complete this step, you will move on to self-assessment through an accessibility audit.

STEP 2: ACCESSIBILITY AUDIT

An accessibility audit, also called a self-evaluation, allows you to ensure that your museum or site is in compliance with federal accessibility laws, including the ADA. An audit can examine barrier removal, communications, and even a full range of programs and will give you a baseline to work from.[1] Title II organizations (state- and locally funded government organizations) are required by law to conduct an audit to evaluate the accessibility of their sites. Museums and historic sites that are privately operated organizations and fall under Title III of the ADA are not required by law to conduct a building accessibility survey. However, it is highly recommended that you complete one in order to ensure that your site's facilities, services, and programs are in compliance with federal accessibility laws.

You can either complete the audit yourself or, if funds allow, you can hire a consultant. If you plan to conduct the audit in house, there are a number of free and fee-based resources available to help you with your audit. If you are looking for additional sources on ADA requirements, the ADA National Network has guides, videos, fact sheets, and more to aid you in your understanding of the ADA.[2] The Institute for Human Centered Design's ADA Action Guide is another great resource where you can find the ADA Standard for Accessible Design Checklist, a do-it-yourself audit form, and even transition and action plan templates.[3] (See appendix A for additional resources for completing your audit.)

The ADA Standard for Accessibility Design is a useful tool, available for free online and in multiple fillable formats to suit your needs. In addition to physical accessibility, this particular checklist also looks at services, programs, and activities at your site or museum. The ADA Standard for Accessible Design Checklist is organized around the four areas in the ADA Title III regulations that the Justice Department recommends starting with:

- Priority 1—Accessible approach and entrance: Can visitors easily get into your building?
- Priority 2—Access to goods and services: Once they are in, can visitors easily purchase tickets, food, or other services? Can they easily get into all of the spaces where these things are being offered?
- Priority 3—Access to restrooms: Are there accessible restrooms? Can all of the elements in the restroom be easily reached (paper towels, soap, etc.)?

- Priority 4—Access to other items such as water fountains, fire alarms, and public telephones: Are these additional items available to people with different types of disabilities?

Once you find a checklist you like, grab your measuring tape, level, clipboard, and pencil and get started. This is a great opportunity to bring in partners, community groups, or members of your advisory council if you have one. Along with any staff or volunteers with disabilities, utilize these individuals and groups to help you identify barriers and offer suggestions for solutions. As with any time you are asking people with disabilities for input, ensure that they are being compensated for their time.[4] Their experience living with a disability will provide a more holistic picture of what the barriers at your site truly are.

Once you are ready to begin, whether on your own or with partners, examine each area listed on the checklist. There will likely be some areas that do not apply to your site; if this is the case, simply continue on to the next item. As you complete your audit, keep in mind any state or local accessibility regulations you also need to meet. In conjunction with the ADA, these laws are the *bare minimum* you should be doing in terms of access—think of it this way, they are the floor, not the ceiling when it comes to accessibility. By exceeding the requirements, whenever possible, you are opening up your historic site or museum to more people. Once you complete your audit, you are ready for the next step, the transition plan.

STEP 3: TRANSITION PLAN

Armed with your audit and site review, you can now proceed to the third stage in the process and create your transition or action plan. Your work to make your site more accessible will only benefit from creating a plan to remove or at least side-step barriers. A transition plan, as noted in chapter 2, will "articulate how your organization will address the myriad of access barriers identified during the audit with concrete solutions and realistic timeframes."[5] Again, while Title III organizations are encouraged to create a transition plan, Title II organizations are legally required by the ADA to do so, just as with the audit. This is another point where your organization can reach out to community members and staff (paid and unpaid) to help develop a plan to improve accessibility; their lived experiences are vital to the work and may be able to offer unique or different perspectives on barriers.

Some barriers identified during your audit may be simple fixes; for example, there is no sign where one is needed. Simple: add a sign. Other barriers may take a bit more time and creativity to try to address, or you may determine, in concert with your site review, that you simply cannot overcome them without destroying the historic integrity of that particular area of your site. However, for most barriers, you will be able to find a creative solution to the problem,

Sample ADA Transition Plan

This is an excerpt from one municipality's Transition Plan. The ADA coordinator added columns for cost estimates and sources of funds. Title II only requires listing physical obstacles, the methods used to make the facilities accessible, the schedule and the responsible official. To create your own use the Transition Plan form.

Facility ___City Hall_____ Date ___January 3, 20XX_____

Contact Person ___ADA Coordinator_____ Department ___Mayor's Office_____

Email ___adacoordinator@nameofmunicipality.gov___ Phone ___800-ADA-XXXX_____

Area	Access Issue	Solution	Target Date	Person Responsible	Cost Estimate	Source of Funds
South Entrance ramp	1:9 slope, cracks, square handrails.	New ramp.	6/15	Facilities Manager	$9,500	Capital budget
North Entrance	No sign indicating direction to accessible entrance.	Install sign.	2/4	Facilities Manager	$40	Maintenance and repairs

New England ADA Center, a project of the Institute for Human Centered Design
www.NewEnglandADA.org • ADAinfo@NewEnglandADA.org

Sample Transition Plan
Page 1

Figure 3.1. Sample Transition Plan. This transition plan is from the ADA Title II Action Guide for State and Local Governments, a website developed by the New England ADA Center, a project of the Institute for Human Centered Design. *New England ADA Center.*

Area	Access Issue	Solution	Target Date	Person Responsible	Cost Estimate	Source of Funds
First floor						
Single user toilet room	No tactile sign.	Install sign.	2/4	Facilities Manager	$40	Maintenance and repairs
City clerk	Counter at 44".	Lower section to 36" max. high, 36" min. length. Short term: provide clipboard at counter.	6/1	Facilities Manager	$450	Maintenance and repairs
City Council room	Inadequate maneuvering clearance at entrance door.	Install automatic door opener.	6/1	Facilities Manager	$1,100	Capital budget
City Council room	No assistive listening system.	Install FM system and sign.	10/1	Audio Visual Employee	$2,200	A/V equipment fund

New England ADA Center, a project of the Institute for Human Centered Design
www.NewEnglandADA.org • ADAinfo@NewEnglandADA.org

Sample Transition Plan
Page 2

whether it is through programmatic access, tactile or 3-D models, or something else entirely. Be sure to plan time annually to revisit your plan to assess whether or not any additional accessibility improvements can be made.

The ADA Action Guide has templates you can use to create your transition plan (as seen in figure 3.2), which they define as structural changes, action plan templates (nonstructural), and programmatic accessibility. To keep it simple, you could use either the transition plan or the action plan document. Working through possible solutions to the barriers found in your audit will help you translate those solutions into a concrete plan that will result in a more accessible historical site. As you are thinking through things, keep in mind that there may be multiple solutions to a single problem. Let's take steps up onto a front porch as an example. You might be able to start with a temporary fix such as a portable ramp while you work toward a more permanent solution (a more stable wooden ramp) or a much more permanent solution (a concrete ramp). You may find, however, that you do not need to invest time and money into the costliest solution. You may find that one of the other available solutions will work just as well at your site.

To determine where to start with the items on your transition plan, you can complete a cost/benefit analysis, looking at the resources and amount of time each task will require, to determine where to get started. As with the previous example of the ramp, you may find that some projects may have more than one phase. The projects that can be completed easily and quickly should be the ones you start with (the low-hanging fruit, if you will). Next look at short-term projects, those that will take a bit more time and resources. Finally, plan for those long-term projects, the ones that will take significantly more time or resources to complete. Accessibility is a process, so you do not have to try and do everything all at once. The key thing is to develop a transition plan that is attainable with realistic time-lines and then actually start on the work. The biggest hurdles you are going to face will come with those larger projects that take more time and resources—but do not give up! While increasing budget and staff time for accessibility projects can be a bit of a battle to start, it is important to remember that this is a marathon, not a sprint. Change will happen slowly, but it will happen.

In addition to looking at structural changes, you can also consider program-matic accessibility in place of physical accessibility. Many historic sites with their limited budgets will be unable to drastically change the site or building to allow it to be more accessible—it is just not feasible from a financial or staffing perspec-tive, as many of these modifications require specialized trades and can be very costly. When this is the case, provide access in a different way through alternative services, experiences, and information. Part II of this book offers several examples of programmatic access that will hopefully serve as an inspiration for your site.

PUTTING OUT THE VIRTUAL WELCOME MAT

Making the changes outlined in your transition plan may take some time to implement. One thing that you can do right now, which does not cost anything other than time, is to create a virtually welcoming space by including information on your website about what is, and is not, currently accessible. Setting visitor expectations ahead of time will ensure that visitors, staff, and volunteers all have a more pleasant experience. This is especially important when thinking about physical accessibility. Imagine a visitor travels to your rural location, an hour outside of town, only to find out upon arrival that their wheelchair is too large to fit through the doorway and, as a result, they cannot see anything and there are no alternatives for them to view or experience your site. They are going to be upset that they have wasted time and possibly money to get out to your location (and will now have to spend another hour to return, frustrated and disappointed, home). They are going to be annoyed that the information that the site is inaccessible is not clearly communicated on your website. Just as importantly, they are not going to feel welcome. Then, of course, there is always the chance that they will take out their frustrations on your staff and volunteers who are just trying to do their jobs. All of this can be avoided by simply communicating what visitors can expect to be able to experience at your site.

Accessibility information can be found in a lot of different places on various museum and historic site websites. Some list the information under the "Visit Us" section, whereas others include it under an "FAQ" page, and still others have separate pages entirely. Wherever you decide to include it, make sure that it is clearly labeled and easy to find. Be sure to detail which parts of your site are accessible

Figure 3.2.   *Illustration 34904964 Courtesy ©*
Mateusz Å»ogaÅ,a | Dreamstime.com

and which parts are inaccessible. Again, the point is to set visitor expectations by letting them know ahead of time what they can expect to be able to do while at your site. Also, it is important to keep in mind that everyone is different and so more information is better than not enough, provided it is clearly organized.

What to include:

Getting to the site

- Where is the accessible parking in relation to the main entrance and/or accessible entrance?
- If there is a separate accessible entrance, how do people access it? Where is it in relation to the main entrance?
- Is there a bus or train stop nearby? If so, how long of a walk is it to your site? Are there sidewalks along the route? How accessible are the sidewalks?

On site

- What does physical access look like? How many steps are there up to the front door? Up to the upper floor(s)? What are the paths made out of?
- What accessibility supports do you have on site? (wheelchairs to check out, sensory backpacks, Braille labels, etc.)
- What do you offer in place of physically being able to access spaces? (videos, photos and information in a binder, 3-D models, etc.)
- Are there places where it is okay to eat and drink? This will help people plan around needing breaks for food, medication, etc.
- Are there certain areas that are always loud and busy? Conversely, are there areas that are generally quieter?

Tours

- Are your tours guided or self-guided? If self-guided, is there an audio or digital version of the tour for people who are blind or have low vision?
- How long does a typical tour last? Knowing this information can help reduce anxiety and help plan transportation in case someone is not driving to the site.
- How much time do you need in advance of someone needing an ASL interpreter?

Having access to this information ahead of time will allow them to make the decision about whether or not they want to visit your site. Regardless of whether they do decide to come, they will know that your site is welcoming to people with disabilities and may consider a visit in the future when more opportunities and supports are available.

ADDITIONAL CONSIDERATIONS

Does your site have times that fluctuate with how busy you are? For example, on Tuesday and Thursday mornings you host area school children, making the site loud and chaotic. If someone has sensory sensitivities or cognitive disabilities, this could be a challenging time for them to visit. If you know what days and times are typically quieter, list those on your site so visitors who need to can plan around busy times.

Who can visitors contact if they still have questions? If you don't currently, create a dedicated access email (such as access@mymuseum.org) and make sure it is clear whom visitors should contact if they have questions about your site's accessibility or access features. Ideally, more than one person on staff will be responsible for responding to inquiries about accessibility, as access should be a part of everyone's job.

If you have developed any additional resources that could be useful, even if they were not originally intended to be an access resource, include those as well. These might be things like a map of your site that shows entrances, elevators, restrooms, etc. or a general history of the historic site. Anything that you think might help a person plan or use before they arrive at your site of significance can be included.

As you are putting your accessibility information together (and on the rest of your website as well), ensure that images on your site contain alternative text (more commonly called alt text) or image descriptions so that people who are blind or have low vision can access the images. Alt text "is a textual substitute for non-text content in web pages" and allows screen readers to read the alt text in place of images.[6] There should be a place within your website platform to insert an alt text description. If an image is purely decorative, you do not need to include an alt text label for it.

As you develop additional resources (see part II of this book), you can include those in the accessibility section of your organization's website. But even if you only list that your site is inaccessible to people with mobility devices and that you are working on making changes, that is a great start. It, at the very least, communicates to people that you are thinking about people with disabilities and how to make them feel welcome, even if you are not quite there yet.

NOTES

1. New England ADA Center ADA Title II Action Guide for State and Local Governments, "Resources," accessed February 26, 2020, https://www.adaactionguide.org/resources#.
2. ADA National Network, "National Product Search," accessed October 15, 2022 https://adata.org/national-product-search?keys=&type=All&tid=All.

3. New England ADA Center ADA Title II Action Guide for State and Local Governments, "Home," accessed October 15, 2022, https://www.adaactionguide.org/index.php/.
4. Compensation can take many forms besides just cash. If you cannot afford to pay everyone, at least provide a meal for them during the audit. Other ideas include memberships, items from your gift shop, gift cards, or free registration to programs.
5. Heather Pressman and Danielle Schulz, *The Art of Access: A Practical Guide for Museum Accessibility.*
6. WebAim, "Alternative Text," accessed October 24, 2022, https://webaim.org/techniques/alttext/.

Part II

Getting Creative, Strengthening Sustainability, and Promoting Relevancy

In this section, explore some of the programmatic and physical accessibility solutions enacted by a diverse selection of historic sites ranging from gardens to aircraft carriers to historic houses and more. These case studies offer creative ways visitors can engage with the museum while retaining the historic integrity of the places in question. The case studies cover a variety of accessibility areas including sensory, cognitive, physical, and others.

4

Small Museums, Big Decisions

BALANCING ACCESSIBILITY AND AUTHENTICITY AT THE
JACOBUS VANDERVEER HOUSE

Sean Blinn

Small museums are rewarding and dynamic places to work, but their size can often create a different set of challenges than their larger peers face. Budgets and staff size are limited. Immediate crises demand attention; strategic planning and big thinking can find themselves shunted to the side.[1] Staff often perform multiple roles, and the museum may not have the expertise and access to professional development that a larger museum might when it comes to accessibility.

These challenges are increased when the small museum is also a historic building. Accessibility in public facilities (or even basic construction codes) in the United States was not legally required when many buildings now considered historic were first built.[2] Buildings were often constructed using only materials available near at hand and to suit the owner's taste and budget. Accessibility was often an afterthought, included only when needed, left out when not. Accessible accommodations were generally not, nor still are, a standard part of home design. More often, these were done on an ad hoc basis and often not preserved.[3] Historic buildings must often be retrofitted to make them accessible. Moreover, historic sites often confront varying demands to present as authentic an experience as possible. It can be a challenge even in ideal situations, but visitors to small museums have the same accessibility requirements as visitors to larger ones, whether the museum was built 250 years ago or just opened. Thinking from the visitor's perspective instead of the institution's perspective can be a helpful first step in understanding the ethical and

Figure 4.1. The Jacobus Vanderveer House, Bedminster, New Jersey, in winter. *Courtesy Sean Blinn*

moral necessity of designing for equal access, even before addressing the bare minimum legal requirements specified by the Americans with Disabilities Act.

Accessibility projects can be, but are not always, complex. Regardless of the complexity, these projects should not be considered a burden. They improve the lives of museum visitors and make it easier to reach a wider range (and yes, number) of people. Rather than being seen as a challenge that is never quite resolved, accessibility projects can be thought of as a source of continual improvement for the visitor experience, and not just for those with accessibility needs. Accessibility can affect almost every element of museum operations, and everyone benefits from it.

The case study of the Jacobus Vanderveer House shows how accessibility can be considered as central to the historic house museum experience as historic preservation, education, and the desire to present as authentic an experience as possible. It also shows how significant improvements to accessibility can be affordable on even a small budget.

JACOBUS VANDERVEER HOUSE BACKGROUND

The Jacobus Vanderveer House (JVH) is a historic house museum in Bedminster, New Jersey, named after its first owner. The building was constructed circa 1772 as a 1.5-story private residence on a colonial-era farmstead, with a floor level about eighteen inches above ground level. It was expanded in the early

1810s with a two-story addition. The building footprint has remained largely the same since then. For seven months during the American Revolution, the house was the residence and headquarters of General Henry Knox, commander of the Continental Army's artillery division. Nearby, the Army established what is now known as the Pluckemin Cantonment, considered by many scholars to be the first institution in the United States to offer formal military education.[4] Over subsequent years, the building was used as a private residence, a rental property, and a boardinghouse, while slowly falling into disrepair. It was a small part of a significant municipal open space acquisition in 1989, after which the Friends of the Jacobus Vanderveer House organized to list the building on the National and New Jersey Registers of Historic Places, raise funds for preservation, and designate it for use as a museum, due to its importance in the Revolutionary War and as the sole surviving structure associated with the Pluckemin Cantonment.

About half of the original township land acquisition is now used for active recreation (mostly athletic fields) and a fenced-in dog park, with the remainder preserved as a wildlife sanctuary. A small number of footpaths provide park access for pedestrians; there is a single vehicle entrance to the park. The JVH sits at the far corner of the property at the end of a nearly half-mile driveway. A line of trees and undergrowth near the museum forms a physical and visual barrier separating the JVH from the rest of the park, further reducing its visibility. The museum's main parking area is a gravel lot shared with the dog park and some of the athletic fields, about four hundred feet from the JVH's entrance. Accessible parking is in a paved area adjacent to the museum.

The museum opened to the public in 2009, interpreting both the Knox and Vanderveer stories, and fits comfortably within the American Association for State and Local History's definition of a small museum.[5] Before opening the JVH as a museum, the Friends organization hired consultants to create a Historic Structures Report, Historic Landscape Report, Historic Furnishings Plan, and conduct extensive archaeological research on the site. These reports guided historic preservation efforts, the development of the museum collection, and interpretive strategies.

HISTORIC PRESERVATION

The home needed a considerable amount of work before it could be opened to the public as a museum. The original kitchen had been replaced around 1875, and the kitchen extant at the point when restoration began was deemed neither historic nor meriting preservation. Over the years, extensive modifications were made to other parts of the building, both interior and exterior, either to increase the building's value as a rental property or to match changing styles of the many eras the building lived through. Some of these choices continue to affect accessibility. The first major addition replaced the original staircase leading to

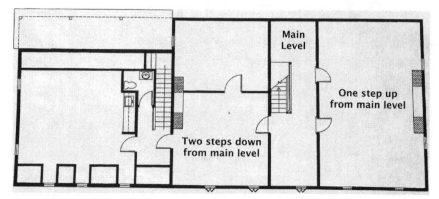

Figure 4.2. The plan of the second floor of the Jacobus Vanderveer House. Stairs from the first floor lead to the section marked "Main Level." The large room to the right requires visitors to take one step up from the main level. The sections of the house to the left require visitors to take two steps down from the main level. *Courtesy Jacobus Vanderveer House*

the second floor with a new one (straight instead of winding, wider, and with a gentler slope) in a new location. Two small first-floor rooms were merged together to create a single hallway. This alteration also raised a small part of the second story by about eighteen inches. Because of this, the second floor of the building now exists on three different levels, as shown in figure 4.2. The smallest part is at the top of the staircase, with one step up to a large room in the new wing, and two steps down to the original part of the building's second floor. This section of the house was considered historically and architecturally significant, so the difficult choice was to retain it as is.

The ADA, with its passage in 1990, was of course a factor in preservation and restoration plans.[6] For example, there was little evidence about the floor plan and level of the original kitchen other than its basic footprint, so when it was rebuilt in 2007, a deliberate choice was made to make it nearly level with the rest of the main floor and connected to the rest of the building by an interior ramp instead of steps, as the original may have been in the 1770s.

UNDERSTANDING THE VISITOR PROFILE

As with many aspects of museum operations, providing for accessibility means understanding its visitors. While this often focuses on demographic data—which is certainly important—it also requires understanding such factors as how people arrive at the museum, whether they travel in large groups, small gatherings, with tours, or individually. Knowing visitors' needs is essential for meeting them.

The Jacobus Vanderveer House's visitor demographics skew older, like many historic house museums in the Mid-Atlantic region. Excluding school groups, a heritage tourism assessment conducted in 2013 showed that only

6 percent of visitors were age thirty-five or younger, with the single largest category (38 percent) reporting their age between forty-five and fifty-four.[7] Attempts at attracting a young professional audience have been unsuccessful, which is also consistent with the experience of many of the JVH's peer organizations in central and northern New Jersey. Visitors often arrive in groups, especially during events tied to major holidays such as Christmas and the Fourth of July, or in connection with countywide history events. Remember that a museum that is not accessible to one member of a group (for example, family or friends) may lose the entire group. Equal access is essential for audience development, not just for those who directly use accessibility adaptations.[8]

Journey mapping, by which a museum examines the entirety of a visitor's time spent in the building, has grown in the last several years. Health and safety concerns during the COVID-19 pandemic led to many museums constructing journey maps that began even before visitors left their homes, starting with getting directions and purchasing tickets ahead of time, not just when they entered the museum.[9] As much as the pandemic dented the general public's appetite for spontaneity and forced people to think about the safety of travel to, from, and within museums, this has always been common, and often necessary, for people with disabilities, especially if they rely on public transportation to get around.

The Jacobus Vanderveer House had started to address this even before the pandemic. Despite the museum's location near the intersection of two interstate highways and alongside a major state highway, getting to the building can be a challenge. The museum's location at the far end of the park made signage important both on nearby roads and within the park itself. Its street address is not recognized by many GPS devices and online mapping services, sometimes directing potential visitors several miles away. An easy (and free) solution was to add the JVH as a place name in Google Maps. The museum website now directs users to enter that place name in Google Maps to receive turn-by-turn directions through the park and straight to the building's front door. A map like this can even be embedded into your website. This is an adaptation not initially thought of as an accessibility feature, but shows how something designed for one group of visitors can benefit others.

With only one road into the park, physically getting to the museum can be a challenge for some. Most of the JVH's visitors arrive by private vehicles, usually cars, with some arriving by tour bus. The line of trees separating the museum from the rest of the park makes it difficult for visitors to the park to see the museum. There is some foot traffic, but most people visiting the museum do not just happen upon it spontaneously. Unfortunately, there is no public transit within walking/rolling distance of the JVH. Museums that are accessible by bus or train should list the best routes on their websites—after all, there is no cost other than the staff time required to add it to the site. Museums like the JVH, however, should mention the *lack* of public transit on their websites to set visitor expectations.

In addition to providing parking and transit information on your museum's website, previsit materials can be useful for people planning their visit as well.

A previsit guide with a written description of travel to the museum, accompanied by photos of the spaces being written about, can help people prepare for their experience. Previsit guides, sometimes called social narratives, can be provided in print or on a website to assist visitors on the autism spectrum (and their caregivers) and others.[10] As with many accessibility supports, what benefits people with disabilities can also provide benefits to a wider audience. For example, as discussed, directions to the JVH can be a challenge, however, the photos and at least some of the text of the museum's previsit guide will be reused on the website to aid drivers attempting to find the site. (At the time of this writing, that is one of many accessibility tasks waiting to be completed—and yes, there is always one more!).

Several years ago, a change to park signage meant that the JVH's accessible parking spots found themselves located after a new "no parking" sign that directed visitors to proceed no further. A phone call to town hall quickly resolved the issue (showing the importance of maintaining good relations with local government!) but demonstrates that a museum's thinking about accessibility should extend well beyond its walls.[11]

THE MUSEUM EXPERIENCE

Interpretation is a series of choices, guided by professionals and scholars using the best practices available, working with a genuine, honest attempt to engage and educate visitors about the past. But as Linda Norris writes, it is an *interpretation* of the past rather than an exact recreation of it: "In houses without specific documentation, we make guesses at what kinds of furnishings would be right, but can we ever really know?"[12] The JVH is fortunate to have records of furnishings and possessions that existed in the house at specific points in history. But these legal records lack detail about materials, styles, and placement. Specific choices of objects to collect and display are left to interpretation. In a building with any length of history, this may involve not just choices but sacrifices.

The Jacobus Vanderveer House is no exception. During the building's two hundred fifty years, styles and uses have come and gone. A choice to restore the entire house to a single period might be more authentic for that one period but would require ignoring other points in time, sacrificing the ability to tell those parts of the story. Restoring different parts of the house to reflect multiple eras tells a more complete story but can create a presentation that does not reflect any single point in time at which the house existed.

Early on, the JVH chose to pursue the latter route, recognizing that at no single point in time did the building look the way it does today. The interior was guided by a "period room approach,"[13] while the exterior was restored to a uniform circa 1810 appearance. The museum's first floor, containing the bulk of the permanent exhibitions, is characterized by five main furnished rooms displaying the 1770s through the 1850s in the Mid-Atlantic and Boston styles.[14] Early in the planning for a museum, scholars performed paint analyses to ensure the walls, when restored, were painted in colors appearing roughly as they did when the house was first built; restoration projects followed this plan. Examination of estate records has shown some of the objects the Vanderveer family owned.[15] But the exact styles of objects on display are interpretations, based on contemporary choices between different options.

While historic sites aim for authenticity, they need to give significant weight to accessibility and visitor safety. In the case of JVH, the second floor is not fully physically accessible. While there are some small exhibitions in that space, interpretation is largely focused on the first floor. In order to safely get visitors to the upstairs exhibits, the historically authentic original stairs were not restored. Restoring that winding, narrow staircase (described previously) might have been more historically accurate, but at the cost of a significant loss of accessibility, not to mention visitor safety.

Thinking about authenticity can help you think about the visitor experience and accessibility. It is impossible to know for certain where the furniture was originally located in the JVH at any single point in time. Photography did not yet exist in the 1700s, and even if it had, a photograph would only represent

Figure 4.3. A section of the wall of the Jacobus Vanderveer House, with the interior of the wall left exposed to show construction details. *Courtesy Sean Blinn*

a snapshot of a single moment in the lifetime of a house owned by the same family for several decades. No doubt people in the past moved furniture around as much as people do now, moving chairs to a new location when needed, or pushing a table out of the way for a social event. Accessibility thus becomes a primary factor in where objects are placed.

In other areas of the house, a small amount of historic authenticity was sacrificed to interpretation and accessibility. In one part of the house, wooden support beams from the 1770s, hidden when the house was built, were deliberately left exposed as a result of the historic preservation work in the early 2000s. A large wall cutaway, with an approximately thirty-five-square-foot glass cover, shown in figure 4.3, was added to show a section of the underlying construction details. The merger of two rooms to create a hallway, mentioned earlier, was kept rather than converted back into two separate rooms. Taken together these choices resulted in better ventilation, easier traffic flow inside the museum, and in case of emergency, faster evacuation. It also made the house more accessible by opening spaces up and allowing mobility device users to navigate more easily.

Much of the resulting visitor experience would not have been possible had the house been restored to its original circa 1772 state. Underlying construction details were rarely on display behind glass displays in private residences in that era, much like any contemporary home. But these choices, while ahistorical, create a more educational experience. Museum professionals often make these sorts of interpretive choices, sacrificing a small and perhaps unnoticeable amount of authenticity for a better experience. Museum staff should be comfortable making similar choices to create a more welcoming space for visitors with diverse abilities. Many visitors rarely notice these adaptations and often welcome them when they are pointed out. Sadly, even today, there is resistance to sacrificing a sense of absolute historic accuracy to make museums accessible, but placing it in the context of interpretation can help gain agreement to centering accessibility in museum planning.

TECHNOLOGY AND ACCESSIBILITY

Technology can be a great equalizer, helping small museums produce content just as compelling as larger ones. Ease of distribution means the audience can potentially be as wide. Video is a good example. Creating it can seem intimidating, but any museum can produce high-quality, accessible videos. Even a low-end smartphone camera will almost certainly support HD video, and a newer DSLR camera may do even better. Add a tripod or other device for stability, some wireless headphones with a microphone, and high-quality video is within the price range of any museum. If paid narrators are beyond the museum's budget, the museum's best docents can narrate—after all, that's their job! The core of any museum experience is the content, not special effects, and if it's interesting, people will come back for more. Don't forget that when a museum shares its videos on social media, its fans and followers may share them with their own friends and family, too, for free.

Like many museums, the JVH created a set of short video tours when it was closed during the COVID-19 pandemic. Two narrators toured each room in the museum while a third person filmed. Recording took just over an hour, with only a small amount of time needed later to edit and upload the content to the internet. Videos ranged from two to six minutes each, making them a good length for anyone looking for a quick break or diversion. In total, the videos ran just over half an hour, approximately the length of some guided tours of the museum.

Although intended primarily to fill a need caused by pandemic closures, these videos also make the museum available to people who cannot otherwise visit, whether due to distance, accessibility, or ongoing health concerns. They may not match the experience of physically being inside the museum, with the opportunity to explore and ask questions, but they show what can be done at essentially zero cost and within the skill set of almost any museum.

Before the pandemic, the JVH had received grant funding to create larger-scale videos, both to introduce visitors to the museum and to build a virtual reconstruction of the lost military site. These videos were designed to be sensory friendly. The narration for each was recorded in a calm, level voice. Likewise, despite artillery being the subject of one video, there are no loud booms or bright flashes of light. While some might say these choices lack the drama that would come from alternating whispered tones with shouting and explosions, it was an easy choice because it opened the experience to a wider range of visitors.

Music and sound effects can help set a mood, convey emotion, and punctuate certain points (but please don't think it's a deal-breaker to exclude it—your content is always the most important element of a video). The JVH has used music in some but not all of its videos. As with spoken narration, the soundtracks are free of rapid volume changes. In one, the soundtrack was composed expressly for the video; in another, the JVH used public domain music in the background in a way that did not distract from the content. The latter option is especially beneficial for small museums because there are many sources of free public domain music on the internet.[16]

Closed captions, even those automatically generated by a video hosting platform, such as Vimeo or YouTube, make museum videos more accessible for people who are d/Deaf or have hearing loss, or who simply prefer to read along with the narration. While such captions aren't perfect, they can be used as a starting point and edited later for clarity and accuracy. Just as a museum would not entrust its object labels, wall text, and other interpretive and navigational media to an algorithm, the same care should be given to video captions.[17] The only cost to create captions is that of the time it takes to upload and edit the generated text. Remember to include captions in longer sections when there is music playing, but unaccompanied by any narration. Captions can say simply "[Music Plays]," or better, describe the emotion it is intended to convey, such as "[Triumphant Music Plays]." Use brackets to denote that this is a description and not words being spoken. Omitting captions when music is the only sound may make viewers mistakenly think there is narration but no captions, and they may stop watching as a result.

SMALL MUSEUM WEB AND SOCIAL MEDIA PRESENCE

Like many small museums, the JVH has a limited budget for promotion and advertising and relies on its website and social media. Just as museums should not be considered a purely visual experience, the same care can be taken with their online presence; Sina Bahram of Prime Access Consulting once called this the art of "how to make it suck less for blind people."[18] Having spent a considerable amount of time making the in-person museum experience accessible, do not make the museum's online presence—how many visitors learn about it in the first place—inaccessible to those same potential visitors.

While there is not space to go into all the details of website and social media accessibility in this chapter, there are resources that discuss how to make them both more accessible. The museum's online presence should be as accessible as possible because it can be a significant source of visitor traffic and is often the starting point in a visitor's journey. If it isn't, would-be visitors may be turned away before they even look up your opening hours and directions.[19]

Create a visual description (often called alternative text, or alt text) for images on the web or social media. The exact settings vary, but content creators can write a description that will be read by screen readers and other assistive technologies used by people who are blind or have low vision. This is especially important on platforms that are widely but inaccurately thought of as exclusively a visual experience, such as Instagram.[20]

Technology projects aren't limited to websites and social media. Mobile apps are now commonplace and many museums have created them. The JVH never built an app or even seriously considered one. Even with grant funding covering the financial aspects, apps can take a considerable amount of staff time and expertise to develop and maintain. Any museum considering this route should first ask itself what visitor benefits and experiences will be enabled that could not be delivered using other means. Also, consider the opportunity cost of building an app and what projects would have to be sacrificed to build and maintain it over time. For a small museum like the JVH, the benefits have never outweighed the costs. If there are benefits, by all means proceed, making sure to include accessibility from the start. Adding features to a technology project in a late stage of development is considerably more expensive and time-consuming than building it right from the beginning.

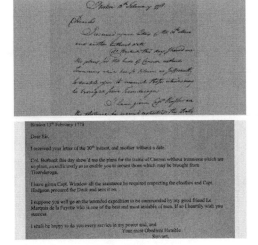

Figure 4.4. A letter written by Henry Knox, on display at the Jacobus Vanderveer House. Top: A replica of the letter (in part) showing 18th-century handwriting. Bottom: A contemporary transcription in a much more legible font. *Courtesy Sean Blinn*

ADDITIONAL CONSIDERATIONS

While there are any number of other things you can do to make your historic site accessible, there isn't enough time to cover them all in this one chapter (that's why you're reading this book!). However, here are a few quick things for you to consider.

VISUAL

One example includes reproductions of letters written by Henry Knox (the museum had the originals on display on loan for a period, courtesy of Morristown National Historical Park). Eighteenth-century handwriting is a challenge for modern visitors to read, even in good lighting and for people who do not normally need visual adaptations. A simple solution was to create transcriptions of the letters and post them adjacent to the eighteenth-century text, as shown in figure 4.4.[21] The existing versions use a serif font, Times New Roman, but the better practice is to use a sans serif font such as Arial for increased readability (as I said, there's always an additional project to improve accessibility, and yes, sometimes it really is this easy!). These transcriptions are available as free handouts, having the potential to extend the museum's educational experience after the actual visit is over.

SENSORY

Be aware of the sensory needs your visitors may bring to the museum. They come in all varieties and not all of them are visible. In many cases, sensory adaptations that benefit one group of visitors are likely to benefit everyone.

Because of the JVH's connection to the Revolutionary War artillery division, reenactors are frequently invited to fire cannons on the museum's front lawn (minus cannonballs, to the great relief of the neighbors). This is usually a crowd pleaser; cannons are exciting, with a flash of light and a loud noise. They often draw in street traffic from curious passersby driving by the museum or using the adjoining park (the trees may block the view, but cannon fire gets people's attention).

As exciting as this is to many visitors, it is most definitely not sensory friendly and has the potential to upset some visitors, especially if they are not expecting the noise. A secondary concern is that because cannon firings take place outside, visitors inside the building may not know when they happen until it is too late to see the full demonstration. Simple, low- to no-cost adaptations resolve both issues. The JVH creates a printed schedule of events for the day (good practice in any situation), and docents walk through the museum a few minutes before the cannons fire, giving notice. Visitors who want to see the cannons can move outside, and anyone who wants to avoid them can move to a quieter location. This costs nothing. As with many other adaptations, it shows how something that benefits a group with accessibility concerns (sensory, in this case) makes for a better experience for all.

TACTILE

Much has been written about touch tours and the importance of touch, especially for visitors who are blind or have low vision, but also for visitors whose learning style involves a tactile approach. With this in mind, during the warm summer months, the JVH runs an outdoor event at which visitors can use a quill pen to sign a replica of the Declaration of Independence. This has proven popular, especially with children, who learn about a core period interpreted by the JVH and get a brief encounter with what the museum sometimes calls 1770s-era texting. It is a tactile experience for young visitors and, as an extra benefit, an opportunity for parents to take (and hopefully share) a fun picture of their children.

FINANCIAL ACCESS

Financial accessibility should factor into a museum's event planning. As much as ticket sales are often a significant source of revenue, even a modest ticket price can be a barrier to participation. Before the pandemic, the Jacobus Vanderveer House was fortunate enough to obtain grants that fund school group events and field trips, including transportation, and was able to return to donation-only admission. For many schools, this enabled their only field trip of the year. Balance your museum's need for ticket revenue with the goal of overcoming financial barriers. Even if free admission times are limited to only specific days, hours, or events, they can make the museum accessible to people who might otherwise never visit. The JVH's previous $10 admission fee often deterred casual passersby in the park from visiting.

MATERIAL CHOICES

Something as seemingly simple as the choice of materials in a historic preservation project can be significant. The Jacobus Vanderveer House's accessible ramp, installed in 2007, is made of concrete and stone, firmly situated in place, and in excellent condition. However, some of the stone accents around the ramp edges were made of soft rock such as shale, which is common in the area, readily available, relatively inexpensive, often used in the past, and thus historically appropriate. Unfortunately, it has a tendency to crack because of wide seasonal temperature swings and frequent rains. While the ramp itself is structurally sound, small fragments of shale occasionally flake onto it, potentially making it harder to navigate for visitors who use a wheelchair, cane, or other assistive devices. As much as the issue is solved just by sweeping on a regular basis, using different materials might have prevented it in the first place. As in many other cases, a small and almost unnoticeable sacrifice of authenticity can improve the museum experience for everyone.

Likewise, historic structures are old by definition and may develop maintenance issues that require increased attention and budget to manage, especially in a building not originally designed for a large amount of traffic. The JVH's floors are almost all original construction; in the main section of the house, they are celebrating their two-hundred-fiftieth birthday at the time of this writing. Every so often the museum inspects them to make sure they are structurally sound. It pays to be mindful of these issues as early as possible because what most visitors might never notice could pose a hazard, especially to anyone with accessibility requirements.

EMPLOYMENT

Small museums have small staffs, with each person often filling several roles. Each hire is significant and should be treated with care, starting with the application process. The job listing's language affects who applies. An excellent resource to help improve employment advertising is the Gender Decoder, which is based on research showing that hidden bias affects applicants' perception of the job and whether they would be a "fit" with the museum.[22] Even when unintended, unconscious bias can prevent potential employees from even applying.[23] The tool is free as of the time of this writing and takes just a few seconds to use. Don't forget that organizational culture can perpetuate existing patterns of bias. Maximizing accessibility means turning the lens of justice inward and looking at ourselves.

CONCLUSION

Anyone who has ever worked to increase accessibility in a historic site knows the feeling that there is always more to do. These pressures can seem even greater at a small institution with resource and staffing constraints, perhaps never designed with accessibility in mind. Combine the two and it can feel overwhelming. But it is better to do something than nothing.

Accessibility can be addressed at any point in the museum's life, from the time before it even opens to the public, to the creation of new exhibitions, expansion, and renovation. Be bold! One of the strengths of small museums is their ability to be flexible and creative. Build on that. The sooner you start the easier and more affordable it will be.

Might there be objection from some quarters? Sadly, discrimination against people with disabilities is still widespread and there may be reactions ranging from skepticism to overt hostility to accessibility projects. But remember that every adaptation was done for a first time, including those that are nearly universal nowadays. Accessibility is good business sense and helps with audience development. It is a requirement, not an option, for a museum in the twenty-first century. Always remember that compliance with the ADA is the *minimum* of what you should do.

The Jacobus Vanderveer House has been working through accessibility since before it even opened as a museum, and there is still more to do. But always having something more to do means there is always an opportunity to improve the visitor experience. Be confident in your ability to pick workable, manageable projects, and start with those. Then do more. And something more after that. Small museums and the staff who work there are visionary, creative, innovative, and not afraid to try something new. There's no time like the present to start.

TOP TEN THINGS TO REMEMBER

1. Making a museum accessible is an opportunity to make visitors' lives easier. It isn't a burden or annoying checklist item; it is an operational, business, and moral imperative.
2. Think from your visitors' perspective, not from the museum's. Understand who visits and, at least as important, who *doesn't*. Use accessibility measures that will help them.
3. Accessibility affects everything about a museum, so consider it in everything.
4. Don't allow a fixation on authenticity to deter the pursuit of accessibility. Museums *interpret* the past and have already accepted such adaptations as artificial lights and running water. Museums make

sacrifices all the time for safety and interpretation. Use that to address any objections.

5. Do what small museums do best: be nimble and quick to adapt.
6. Low cost does not mean low impact. Accessibility doesn't have to be expensive. Social media is affordable. Video tours can be produced at little cost. Even the lowest-cost adaptations can make a big difference for visitors who need them.
7. Develop a complete journey map, stretching from when your visitors leave their homes to their arrival at the museum, through their return home. Visitors with accessibility needs already go through these steps. Make it easy for them and they are more likely to visit.
8. Consider financial accessibility, and offer times for free admission.
9. Eliminate bias in job ads. Accessibility means ensuring that *everyone* has equal access to being hired and can bring additional perspectives to the table.
10. Have the confidence to know that you can do this—because you can!

NOTES

1. This is by no means unique to small museums, of course!
2. According to the National Register of Historic Places, to be considered historic a building needs to be at least fifty years old. National Park Service, "How to List a Property," accessed September 10, 2022, https://www.nps.gov/subjects/national register/how-to-list-a-property.htm.
3. The Franklin Delano Roosevelt Library and Museum in Hyde Park, New York, presents an interesting case of preserving and interpreting historic accessibility features. After contracting polio (or Guillain-Barré syndrome, as some now believe), Roosevelt was a wheelchair user for the remainder of his life, and his home, adjacent to his presidential library, preserves the adaptations made so he could maneuver through the building on his own. It represents a rare look into the history of such adaptations in a historic house.
4. See Carl Prince, *Middlebrook: The American Eagle's Nest* (Somerville, NJ: Somerset Press, 1958); Clifford Sekel Jr., "The Continental Army in Winter Encampment at Pluckemin, New Jersey. December, 1778–June, 1779" (master's thesis, Wagner College, 1972); and especially John Seidel, "The Archaeology of the American Revolution: A Reappraisal & Case Study at the Continental Army Cantonment of 1778-1779, Pluckemin, New Jersey" (PhD dissertation, University of Pennsylvania, 1987) for background on the Pluckemin Cantonment of 1778-1779.
5. American Association for State and Local History, "Small Museums," accessed March 29, 2022, https://aaslh.org/communities/smallmuseums/. A 2007 definition described a small museum as one with an annual budget under $250,000, a small staff size, and with volunteers performing significant functions.

6. Initial archaeology began at the site in 1998, with additional studies taking place through 2006. The Historic Structures Report described earlier was completed in 2001, the first of the reports created before restoration began in 2007—all well after the ADA's enactment.

7. Heritage Consulting, Inc., Heritage Tourism Assessment and Interpretive Plan for the Jacobus Vanderveer House Audience Research, Philadelphia, August 2013, 58.

8. Heather Pressman and Danielle Schulz, *The Art of Access: A Practical Guide for Museum Accessibility* (Lanham, MD: Rowman & Littlefield, 2021), 14.

9. Barco, "Please Don't Touch: The Rise of Coronaproof Museum Technology," *Blooloop* (blog), accessed March 19, 2022, https://blooloop.com/museum/opinion/post-covid-museum-technology/.

10. For more information on how to create a social narrative, please see chapter 5 of *The Art of Access*.

11. See Sean Blinn, *Advocating for Your Organization with Local Government* (Nashville, TN: American Association for State and Local History, 2020).

12. Linda Norris, "Authenticity Is a Lie," *The Uncatalogued Museum* (blog), July 11, 2016, https://uncatalogedmuseum.blogspot.com/2016/07/authenticity-is-lie.html.

13. Laura C. Keim, "Why Do Furnishings Matter?" in *Reimagining Historic House Museums: New Approaches and Proven Solutions*, ed. Kenneth C. Turino and Max Van Balgooy (Lanham, MD: Rowman & Littlefield, 2019), 214.

14. The JVH uses the Mid-Atlantic style to interpret the Vanderveer story. Boston native Henry Knox's story is interpreted using styles from that region.

15. Henry S. Vanderveer, estate inventory dated 1813. [Copy in the possession of the Jacobus Vanderveer House.] Wills and estate records can be good sources of information about what a family owned.

16. Museums may find music available at any price point, but pay close attention to copyright and licensing agreements for *any* music you use because the terms and conditions may be unique to that specific piece. Music may be licensed for some purposes but not others (for example, for nonprofit organizations), and music licensed for personal use may not be licensed for institutional use. Likewise, what is in the public domain in one country may not be in another, which may affect who is able to view the museum's videos, and music hosted on a website in one country may not be in the public domain in another. If you have *any* questions about copyright law and how it affects music you want to use, consult an intellectual property attorney licensed to practice in your jurisdiction.

17. The New York City Mayor's Office has an excellent summary of captioning on various video platforms at https://www1.nyc.gov/assets/mopd/downloads/pdf/MOPD-Audio-Description-and-Caption-Guide.pdf.

18. Sina Bahram, "I Know Why the Caged Bird Sings: Freeing Museums From Behind the Glass," filmed November 2015 in Minneapolis, MN MCN Ignite video, 6:26. https://www.youtube.com/watch?v=h44hDbfUIo0.

19. A good starting point to learn about website accessibility is the World Wide Web Consortium's Web Accessibility Initiative. The W3C WAI develops standards used by websites around the world and provides resources, training, and information at https://www.w3.org/WAI/. The Web Accessibility Evaluation Tool (WAVE) located at https://wave.webaim.org/ allows users to enter a URL to get a report on specific areas where improvements are needed to make websites more accessible.

Social media accessibility can be slightly more challenging, if only because each platform's accessibility features are specific to that platform and tend to change more quickly than web standards.

20. The Cooper-Hewitt has excellent guidelines for image description: https://www.cooperhewitt.org/cooper-hewitt-guidelines-for-image-description/.

21. With cursive writing taught less and less, this adaptation may become essential anytime handwriting is on display, even contemporary samples!

22. The Gender Decoder is available at http://gender-decoder.katmatfield.com.

23. Gender Decoder, "About This Tool," accessed March 22, 2022, http://gender-decoder.katmatfield.com/about.

5

Accidentally Accessible

WHEN HISTORIC PRESERVATION LEADS TO INCLUSIVE INNOVATIONS

Sarah Kirk

Accessibility is one of those words that represent a vast collection of meanings. To some, it is a wheelchair ramp into a building, while it is dyslexia-friendly fonts to someone else. In many cases, accessibility accommodations can lead to a better experience for everyone. Diversity, equity, accessibility, and inclusion (DEAI) have become guiding terms for museum programming, exhibits, and educational offerings. Ensuring museums achieve the DEAI standards set by leading institutions, such as the American Alliance of Museums (AAM), is essential. Since AAM approved its DEAI Policy and Framework in 2014, institutions have become increasingly aware of the importance of creating more equitable visitor experiences.[1] Museums are for everyone and, therefore, must ensure everyone can enjoy them in a similar way.

Museums, especially historic buildings, battlefields, and agricultural sites, are notoriously difficult to navigate for people with any form of mobility aid or disability. Many of these structures were built before the Architectural Barriers Act of 1968 required governmental buildings to become accessible.[2] It was not until the Americans with Disabilities Act (ADA) went into effect in 1992 that many buildings became available to people with mobility disabilities.[3] As discussed in chapter 2, historic structures should comply with the ADA as much as possible and barriers should be removed, if "readily achievable." While this ensures the integrity of historic structures remains intact, it also means that individuals with mobility-related disabilities have unpredictable experiences at historic places because each site has different levels of access and available accommodations.

The Peter Wentz Farmstead in Worcester, Pennsylvania, is one example of a museum that is not fully accessible due to its historic nature. In part because of the lessons learned from the exhibit described in this chapter, the staff is mindful of this and is creative when producing exhibits and programs. These innovative and equitable experiences create a welcoming environment not only for visitors with mobility disabilities but for everyone.

THE PETER WENTZ FARMSTEAD

The Peter Wentz Farmstead is a well-preserved farmhouse built in 1758 and officially added to the National Register of Historic Places in 1973. The museum educates visitors on the Pennsylvania German Wentz family, eighteenth-century farming, and its use in 1777 as General George Washington's temporary headquarters. The site is county owned and managed by four museum staff and three farm staff members. The Peter Wentz Society is the nonprofit that assists with governing, fundraising, and volunteering at the site.

The farmstead was owned by the Wentz family until after the American Revolutionary War, when it was sold to Devault Bieber and again in 1794 to Reverend Melchior Shultz. The house remained in the Shultz family until 1969, when the property was sold to Montgomery County, Pennsylvania, and turned into a museum. It was preserved during the patriotic cultural movement of the

Figure 5.1. A south view of the Peter Wentz Farmstead house. *Photograph by Sarah Kirk. Courtesy of Montgomery County, Pennsylvania*

1970s for the 1976 bicentennial and furnished to reflect how it appeared when Washington was headquartered there in October 1777. Celebrating the fact that Washington had slept in their home, the Shultz family kept aspects of the house unchanged, including the largest bedroom, which was believed to be where he stayed during his encampment. This bedroom has original floors, wall built-ins, doorknobs, and even some original paint from the time when Washington stayed in the house. The home's most well-known feature is the decorative paint discovered on the walls during an analysis conducted during the site's preservation in the 1970s. The first layer found, assumed to be from the mid-eighteenth century, included walls with polka dots, stripes, diagonal lines, and other unique designs. The wall decorations were recreated, with some areas of original paint still viewable by the public under protective plexiglass.

The house's first floor is wheelchair accessible, and chairs are placed throughout the space, allowing visitors to sit. The second floor, which includes a loft, three bedchambers, and a textile room, can only be accessed by using two sets of stairwells. Both stairwells are referred to as "pocket stairs." They are steep, wooden winder steps that gradually become wider to one side, allowing the steps to curve without building a landing. These steps are difficult for most people to navigate, and any visitor with a mobility aid is not able to tour the second floor. Generally, programs are hosted on the first level of the house or in the visitor center, allowing for equitable experience and level of engagement.

EXPANDING THE NARRATIVE

As many conversations seem to begin at small museums, one day the staff sat at the lunch table, discussing upcoming projects. One such project was to expand the site's interpretation to include Jack, an enslaved man on the farm during the mid-eighteenth century. Jack sought his freedom twice during his enslavement at Peter Wentz Farmstead, and two runaway advertisements were published describing him as well as his clothing. It was suggested that if funding could be found, it could support an exhibit featuring his outfit recreated based on one of the runaway advertisements. The staff was enthusiastic about finally highlighting Jack during tours in a more tactile and in-depth way but could not help but wonder, "now what?" As the staff researched, designed, and made the displays, what were first perceived as obstacles regarding the historical integrity of the building led to accessible opportunities, ultimately enhancing the overall visitor experience.

In addition to wanting to interpret Jack, the staff was also debating how to better utilize the loft space, located above the summer kitchen, at the rear of the house. Before the exhibit about Jack, the space was occupied by large copper kettles used for apple pressing, spinning wheels, and a hands-on feather mattress area for visitors to experience what an eighteenth-century mattress could have felt like. All other rooms in the historic home were used deliberately, while the loft space felt thrown together, with a mishmash of items without a common thread or storyline. The hope was to create a hands-on learning area here where, in addition to the mattress, visitors could also handle recreated items commonly found at an eighteenth-century German Pennsylvania farmstead. The "Jack" exhibit was not initially intended for this space, but as the project progressed and as the importance of place-based learning began impacting the work, it was a natural coupling.

ACCESSING JACK

The house tour at the Peter Wentz Farmstead consists of dates, names, and events associated with the family from their period of ownership and its use during the American War for Independence. To ensure Jack's name was not lost among the wide breadth of information, the staff chose to recreate his clothing to physically represent him in the space. The goal of this addition was to offer a different type of learning, relieving visitors of relying on their imagination and forcing them to hang on to every word of the tour guide. The museum does not have any personal objects attributed to Jack in its collection, therefore, reproduction clothing was used as a substitute.

Both Jack's runaway advertisements were studied. The 1770 advertisement was selected to be displayed as it was closer to 1777 the year generally interpreted at the site. The educator and curator compiled all the known primary sources linking Jack to the farmstead and wrote a compelling narrative for staff and board as to why recreating his clothing would enhance the overall interpretation of the site. In addition to the inclusive interpretation, the clothing could be handled by visitors, creating a tactile and hands-on experience. The project was estimated to cost around $2,000.[4]

> RUN away, on Christmas day last, from the subscriber, living in Worcester township, Philadelphia county, a Negroe man, named JACK, about 34 or 35 years of age, about 5 feet 5 or 6 inches high, and his left leg much thicker than the right; had on, a new white linsey jacket, an under ditto, without sleeves, buckskin breeches, light blue yarn stockings, new shoes, with large brass buckles, and a good wool hat. He says he has liberty from me to look for another master. Whoever takes up said Negroe, and brings him to me, or secures him in any of his Majesty's goals, so that I may get him again, shall have the above reward, and reasonable charges, paid by PETER *WENTZ*. N.B. All Masters of Vessels are forbid to carry him off, at their peril.[5]

This is the text of the 1770 runaway advertisement published regarding Jack's pursuit of freedom. In addition to the physical information gained in the post, it also mentions Jack told Peter Wentz that he had "liberty from me to look for another master." It is not understood what Jack exactly meant with that line, but it inspired the name of the exhibit, *Jack: The Pursuit of Liberty from Enslavement*. It was decided the exhibit would be composed of the recreated historically accurate clothing from Jack's 1770 runaway advertisement, facsimiles of both his runaway advertisements, a mattress, and other daily life objects that might be used by an enslaved person. This included a horn cup, wooden plate, bowl, spoon, chamber pot, and a few well-worn hand towels. Displaying these objects as if Jack had just left would make the space feel alive. To further enhance the visitor experience, the staff encouraged kinesthetic discovery by enlarging and printing the 1770 runaway advertisement so that visitors could match the article of clothing to the items listed: linsey jacket, waistcoat of the same material, buckskin breeches, yarn stockings, shoes with brass buckles, and a wool hat.

The detail put into Jack's clothing was thorough. Not many visitors understand what a "linsey" jacket or waistcoat is, but once they feel the fabric and discuss the material with the tour guide, they discover it is made of linen and wool thread. The linsey materials were handmade by a weaver using historically accurate materials. The buckskin breeches were purchased from Colonial Williamsburg and made as a facsimile to a pair in the collection at Old Sturbridge Village, which was thought to have been owned by an enslaved man in the eighteenth century. The blue yarn stockings were also handmade, with one leg larger than the other, as indicated in the runaway advertisement. Every detail of the clothing made the experience of bringing Jack into the space more authentic.

Jack's time of enslavement at the Peter Wentz Farmstead was unique to him, but the overall realities of eighteenth-century Pennsylvania enslavement had to be addressed to explain Jack's situation. A common misconception is that enslavement was a Southern institution and never occurred above the Mason-Dixon Line. This dividing line is roughly about sixty miles south of the Pennsylvania farmstead. Many visitors were shocked to learn that enslaved individuals were at the Peter Wentz Farmstead. This common reaction was a motivating factor in making the exhibition about Jack permanent.

A PLACE FOR THE EXHIBIT

Choosing the location of Jack's exhibit was important, not only for the logistics of the project but also using the physical location of the space as a learning tool. Place-based education can occur naturally at living history sites or site-specific museums, and this method of educating was important to the success of the exhibit. The Center of Place-Based Education at Antioch University describes place-based learning as "anytime, anywhere learning [that] leverages the power of place to personalize the learning."[6] Early on during the planning process of the exhibit, it was decided that place-based education would be a core element of this project.

With place-based education at the center of the project, the location of the exhibit was important. Assuming the Wentzs followed typical eighteenth-century enslaver behavior, Jack would have not slept in the house, but that building is the only one included on the tour, and the sawmill where he likely would have slept was torn down in the nineteenth century. Given this, the staff had to analyze the spaces in the house in relation to Jack's station and status. The first floor of the house museum was already occupied by a parlor, a kitchen, a period equivalent to a family room, a bedchamber, and a detached summer kitchen, none of which would have been spaces that Jack occupied. The second floor had three bedchambers, a textile room, and loft. The site does have an outside barn, but it is not interpreted during a tour. So given Jack's status, the only logical and likely location for the exhibit was the loft on the second floor. Although the most plausible space of the exhibit on the tour, the loft is an accessibility nightmare. The historic preservation requirements and inaccessible locations of the space inspired the staff to be creative when designing this exhibit.

As a county-owned historic site, the museum must adhere to Title II-level ADA standards. This means that all programs and opportunities must be accessible to all visitors.[7] The building did not have to be ADA compliant because of its age, but all other aspects of the site must at least meet the standards in

Figure 5.2. Jack's clothing is displayed on a thin mattress tick, covered in a natural linen blanket. The clothing from left to right: shoes with large brass buckles, light blue yarn stockings, buckskin breeches, wool hat, light linsey jacket. The light linsey under jacket is to the right of the mattress, on a chair. *Photograph by Sarah Kirk. Courtesy of Montgomery County, Pennsylvania*

Title II. With these standards in mind, the staff knew that placing the exhibit in the loft made historical sense and was a suitable location for tours, but they also had to develop a plan to ensure all visitors could access it.

In addition to the ADA standards being met, staff navigated the challenges of creating an exhibit in a historically protected space. Due to the age and preservation of the building, no alterations were allowed to the structure. This included placing nails in walls or ceiling beams. As visually appealing as this space is, with its exposed, angled beams, cedar shingles, and plaster on the lower part of the walls, it is not an ideal environment for an artifact-based exhibit. There are randomly placed old nails in the beams, but none are situated in such a way to use or support panels. In addition to the low beams of the A-framed roof, the space is not temperature or environmentally regulated, making it impossible to safely display historical objects. In addition to artifacts, extreme temperature and humidity fluctuations also can damage panels. With this knowledge, the staff researched creative methods of displaying interpretive information. Ultimately, it was decided that the panels would be displayed on black metal easels. The sleek lines of the easel and panels were visually appealing and meant the panels could easily be moved or replaced if damaged by the heat. The panels could also be height adjusted to meet the requirements of various spaces and programs. All the objects in the exhibit were reproductions, most being Jack's recreated clothing and historically reproduced bedding. These objects could easily be transported just like the easels. The largest object was a bed tick that could be rolled up, moved, or stored as needed. With the simple solution of easels, the entire exhibit gained the ability to be mobile. Although place-based education was an important element of this exhibit, flexibility was needed to ensure educational equity. Allowing the exhibit to be mobile did remove the place-based aspect, but it allowed more people to be educated about Jack, which was the main objective of the exhibit.

Having the exhibit travel was an example of the curb cut theory. The "curb cut effect" demonstrates how if you design something for people with disabilities, it can benefit everyone. This theory uses the example of a wheelchair-accessible curb cut and how that accommodation benefits individuals with mobility aids and is also utilized by people pushing baby strollers, shopping carts, etc.[8] The easels initially were chosen to mitigate the multilayer preservation limitations of working in the space but instead allowed the project to become accessible too.

A DIVERSE STORY LED TO A DEAI EXHIBIT

The "Jack" exhibit project is a story of intentional diversity leading to equity, accessibility, and inclusion. Writing an exhibit focused on someone who did not dwell within the walls of the main house led to unexpected obstacles that are not encountered in the visitor center, which houses more traditional panel-based exhibit spaces. The visitor center meets ADA standards and the space can easily be manipulated to meet the needs of an exhibit, such as hanging panels or painting the walls. The "Jack" exhibit could have been displayed in the visitor center but in a far less impactful way. Ensuring his story was told as a part of the tour guaranteed the whole story of the site was included, rather than only part of the story. The loft functioned as a realistic sleeping space for Jack and also resolved the issue of the space being used without intention. With that said, the location of the exhibit should be routinely evaluated, and the findings should dictate if the exhibit is brought permanently into a more accessible location. Moving forward, the museum can look to expand on what is available for visitors including things such as virtual or 3-D tours (such as those described in chapter 9), large-print and Braille versions of exhibit text, and so on. Accessibility is fluid and barriers should be regularly evaluated.

When *Jack: The Pursuit of Liberty from Enslavement* opened, the curator offered a lecture hosted in the visitor center about the project. This event proved the optionally mobile exhibit could work in other locations, even if it lost aspects of the place-based immersion the loft offers. The participants from this program spoke highly of the exhibit and verbally confirmed they learned new information on the topic of Northern enslavement. A formal evaluation is needed to measure the level of learning experience in the loft versus the exhibit being displayed in the visitor center. This evaluation should assess the impact of place-based learning versus the benefits of consistent accessibility.

The historic preservation limitations of the loft space not only led to an equitable educational opportunity, but it also reflected how inexpensive accessibility projects can be. By thinking outside the box and utilizing easels instead of mounting the panels to the wall, staff created an exhibit experience that could be utilized in the loft, the visitor center, and even at offsite programs. This exhibit forced the staff to pivot from its typical process and exemplified how accessibility can be simple and inexpensive.

GOING BEYOND JACK

The "Jack" exhibit was created to tell a more diverse story of the farmstead by highlighting one individual. In addition to enslaved people at the farm, like all Pennsylvanians during this period, the Wentz family would have encountered people from a variety of cultures and ethnicities. To continue telling the eighteenth-century Wentz story without acknowledging this would have conveyed only a partial truth. The farm and sawmill would not have functioned without enslaved labor, so adding Jack's exhibit was a natural progression to telling a more factual story. The decision to tell this history was simple, but educating this topic in an authentic and accessible way was a multilayered challenge for the museum's small staff. One example of the challenges was gaining the trust of some supervisors in the county. Understandably, they wanted to ensure the exhibit was impactful while also being aware of the sensitivity needed when addressing this topic. The farmstead is governed by the county's Parks and Recreation Department, so all exhibits directly impact the credibility of the department. To gain their trust, the educator and curator put together a time-line and primary source presentation and outlined the methods used to ensure integrity in all aspects.

As the staff and volunteers researched using the primary documents associated with eighteenth-century enslavement in Pennsylvania, it became apparent that interpreting this topic is an all-encompassing responsibility. The all-white staff knew they needed outside consultants to guide them through this process. The staff had never been educated on enslavement with such complexity before other than offering information on Jack during the tour and wanted to ensure they approached the topic in a way that would make visitors feel respected. While being white does not hinder someone's ability to educate on enslavement, it should, however, impact how the topic is approached. Caucasians do not feel the burden of systematic racial injustice, which originated in America during the precolonial period. To discuss this topic with integrity and cultural consciousness, consultants from the black community were needed.

To create this community connection, a half-day conference and associated program were hosted, titled "Creating Conversations: Interpreting Slavery." Speakers included Brenda Parker, former coordinator of African American interpretation at George Washington's Mount Vernon; Cheyney McKnight, founder and owner of Not Your Momma's History; and Joseph McGill, founder of the Slave Dwelling Project. They discussed the various levels of accountability associated with responsibly interpreting enslavement at museums. They described levels of emotional responses from visitors when learning about enslavement, and how to navigate those feelings professionally and empathetically, and the physical and emotional toll on black interpreters discussing enslavement and the need to offer in-house and professional support to employees and volunteers due to the subject matter. Speakers also discussed the importance of just starting these conversations and stressed these moments do not have to be formal.

After the conference, the curator and educator hosted a training session for the interpretation volunteers and staff who guide tours and assist with school programs to utilize their newly gained knowledge as these individuals would be the ones directly talking to the public about Jack's time at the farmstead and enslavement in Pennsylvania. In addition to using primary sources to educate the volunteers on enslavement at the site, the staff also explained the current language to use when discussing enslavement. It addressed any concerns the volunteers had about discussing this topic with the public.

CONCLUSION

Since *Jack: The Pursuit of Liberty from Enslavement* opened in 2019, the site has been awarded the distinction as a National Underground Railroad Network to Freedom site through the National Park Service. The distinction was given due to the primary sources linking enslavement to the property and Jack's pursuit of freedom. The site has continued researching enslavement, including enslaved people traveling with General George Washington during his encampment at the site. The curator and educator who researched, designed, and created the exhibit have since transitioned to other museums, but the lessons learned from working collaboratively on this project have influenced their careers. Both now lead with accessibility at the forefront of projects, knowing these accommodations will create an overall better outcome for all visitors.

NOTES

1. American Alliance of Museums, "Diversity, Equity, Accessibility and Inclusion," November 30, 2017, https://www.aam-us.org/programs/diversity-equity-accessibility-and-inclusion/#:~:text=Diversity%20and%20Inclusion%20Policy%20Statement,people%20and%20museums%20we%20represent.
2. US Access Board, "Architectural Barriers Act," accessed July 25, 2022, https://www.access-board.gov/law/aba.html#:~:text=The%20ABA%20stands%20as%20the,August%2012%2C%201968%20be%20accessible.
3. While the ADA was passed in 1990, entities were given time to make changes. Titles I, II, and III went into effect in 1992. US Department of Justice, "Laws, Regulations, & Standards," accessed July 25, 2022, https://www.ada.gov/2010_regs.htm.
4. The museum approached its local Quester groups for potential funding. The Questers are groups of at least six individuals who meet to discuss topics related to history, historic sites, and antiques. They are from local chapters and are associated with the state chapter. The Questers fund projects that generally involve educational programming enhancements or recreating historical objects used at a site. The grant proposal was well received by the Quester groups, who agreed that Jack's story would enhance the site's interpretation and understood the value of having his clothing recreated in the space. The museum received the requested funds.
5. "Runaway from Prescriber," *Pennsylvania Gazette*, January 11, 1770.
6. V. T. Ark, E. Liebtag, and N. McClennen, *The Power of Place: Authentic Learning through Place-Based Education* (ASCD, 2020).
7. John P. S. Salmen, *Everyone's Welcome: The Americans with Disabilities Act and Museums* (Washington, DC: American Alliance of Museums, 2013).
8. According to a study in Sarasota, Florida, nine out of ten pedestrians walked along the curb, following the curb cut, instead of stepping over the curb.

6

In Pursuit of an Equitable Experience

THE MOLLY BROWN HOUSE MUSEUM ACCESS LOUNGE

Heather Pressman

The Molly Brown House Museum, located in Denver, Colorado, is known for its most famous resident, Margaret "Molly" Brown.[1] Margaret is best known for surviving the *Titanic* disaster, however, she was also a fierce advocate for women's suffrage, children's and workers' rights, and devoted her life to many causes. Her home, restored to its 1910 appearance, allows visitors to immerse themselves in a different time while learning about Margaret's life and connections to modern-day topics.

ABOUT THE MUSEUM

Historic Denver, Inc., which owns and operates the Molly Brown House Museum, was formed to save the home from likely demolition as urban renewal ravaged downtowns across the country, including in Denver in the 1960s Founded by a group of grassroots volunteers and preservation enthusiasts in December 1970, the museum was opened a few short months later in March 1971. Historic Denver continues to operate the museum to this day, using the museum as a premier example of historic preservation. Historic preservation is a guiding principle in the work that the organization does, whether at the museum on tours and programs or in the community working to save the built environment. Thanks to experienced staff and board members, the museum is fortunate to benefit from the guidance of preservation professionals with any and all work on the museum, including helping inform any physical changes that are made to the building, especially as it relates to removing barriers.

Constructed in 1889, the Queen Anne Richardsonian Romanesque Victorian home was designed by Denver architect William Lang and built for Isaac and Mary Large. The Browns purchased the home in 1894, shortly after coming into their wealth. Margaret owned the home until her death in 1932 when it, as well as its contents, were sold at auction. After Margaret's death, the home had a number of lives: it was a single-family home, a Jane Addams halfway house for girls, apartments and rooms for rent for "single men" (code for a safe space for gay men), and finally became a museum.

Since its inception more than fifty years ago, the museum was only physically accessible to individuals who could climb the sandstone stairs to the front door. In 2014, the museum launched a capital campaign that raised funds to restore the iconic front porch, exterior masonry, windows, wood flooring, and more. The capital campaign also included the installation of a Limited Use/Limited Application (LULA) lift on the rear porch that would allow visitors to access the ground level, up to the main floor of the home, as well as into the basement education center. This multiyear restoration and capital project was completed in 2019. With the installation of the lift, visitors with mobility devices could now reach spaces that had previously been inaccessible to them. Installing an elevator that reached all four floors of the house museum was not an option as it would have required the removal of one of the historic bedrooms and a bathroom. The lift on the other hand only required minor modification to the enclosed back porch, however, the board of trustees decided to go forward with this fairly small structural alteration in order to make the museum accessible to a whole segment of visitors who previously had been unable to visit.

The decision to modify the back porch was not taken lightly and was discussed in earnest by Historic Denver's board of trustees, which is primarily made up of preservation professionals. The board of trustees worked to find a sensitive solution to meet the need for an accessible lift while preserving the historic character of the home. The area of the home that was chosen for the location of the lift complied with creating barrier-free access while minimally impacting any character-defining exterior or interior features, per the Secretary of the Interior's Standards for the Treatment of Historic Properties.[2]

Prior to the installation of the lift, visitors who used mobility devices simply could not visit the home. Individuals who could manage a few stairs could visit the first floor, but in order to reach the upper floors, they would be required to climb up and down two flights of stairs, including descending a very narrow and steep servants' staircase. On tours where someone could not climb all those stairs, they were offered the option to listen to the tour via an audio amplification device. The docent would wear a transmitting microphone and guests would listen to the tour via a headphone receiver set as the docent took the remainder of the group through the upper floors of the museum. While they were listening to the tour, visitors would be taken into the home's kitchen to wait. They were given a seat on a somewhat wobbly but historic-looking chair

Figure 6.1. The Molly Brown House Museum is located in Denver, Colorado, and was home to one of the *Titanic*'s most famous survivors, the "Unsinkable" Margaret Brown. The four story Queen Anne Victorian was built in 1889 and opened as a museum in 1971. *Courtesy Molly Brown House Museum*

and a binder with pictures and information in it to look at while they waited in the dimly lit kitchen. Unfortunately, due to the nature of the materials used in the construction of the house, the audio devices rarely functioned in the way they were intended, with the sound cutting in and out. Also, if someone on the upstairs tour asked a question of the docent, visitors using the audio devices could only hear what the response was and not the question. Once the tour finished on the upper floors, the docent would lead the visitors downstairs to the kitchen, where those who did not ascend to the upper floors could rejoin the tour and learn about the kitchen space as one group. Staff at the museum began to brainstorm ways to improve this experience, especially once the lift was operational.

CREATING THE ACCESS LOUNGE

The idea was born to create an "access lounge," a comfortable place where visitors could wait for their tour to return from the upper floors and have a reliable way to get the same information they would have gotten from the docent. The museum was fortunate to receive a grant from Denver Arts and Venues to outfit the access lounge. This space was designed to be comfortable and engaging. The decision was made to place the lounge in one corner of the enclosed back porch that extends the length of the back of the house. The lounge space itself is approximately six feet by eight feet. Already hanging on the back porch were vinyl banners (approximately three feet by five feet long) of the floor plans of the upper floors. These were rehung so that they were in the access lounge area to give visitors a sense of what the upstairs space looks like. Because there are no fragile artifacts on display in that portion of the house, it was able to be brightly lit, making it easy to view the floor plan images.

With the grant funds, the museum purchased a bench and a set of two sturdy wooden chairs. Following recommendations from *Smithsonian Guidelines for Accessible Exhibition Design*, these were purchased with backs and armrests as they are "essential for people who have mobility impairments: arms and backs offer people support points when lowering themselves into as well as when rising out of seats."[3] These were placed in the access lounge to offer visitors a place for them to comfortably wait until the rest of their tour rejoined them on the first floor of the home.

To solve the problem of unreliable transmission of the tour via audio devices, the museum purchased an iPad Pro (due to its large screen size) and a locking iPad stand. Working with a volunteer who had film and video editing experience, the staff recorded a tour of the spaces on the upper floors. The volunteer edited, captioned, and even added music and title card transitions to the video. He then created an interactive slide so that people could choose which video they watched and in what order they watched them. In addition to the video, several binders containing a large-print version of the tour, as well as photos of the rooms and information about the various family members who occupied them, were available to browse while waiting to rejoin their group. The goal was that anything that a visitor would see or hear about on the second and third floors had some sort of equivalent in the access lounge.

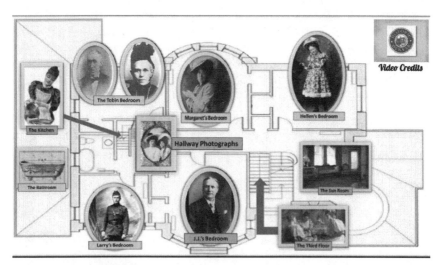

Figure 6.2. An interactive slide allows visitors to choose which video they want to watch. *Courtesy Molly Brown House Museum*

CREATING AN EQUITABLE EXPERIENCE

Around the time the access lounge was coming together, the museum received the donation of a large bookcase, approximately five feet tall by six feet wide. According to the donor, the bookcase had been in the house when the Browns lived there, however, there was no documentation or other evidence to prove this was the case. Regardless of its provenance, the bookcase fit perfectly into the nook where the access lounge was going to be. Initially, the shelves were used to hold the binders with printed tours and photographs of the family. The plan had been to incorporate some touchable items as well.[4] While the space was being utilized and the experience was certainly nicer than in the past, the space still felt a little flat and often the binders were strewn about the shelves, leaving the space looking messy.

When the museum decided to convert one of the historic bedrooms into a rotating exhibit space, locking plexiglass cases were added to the bookshelf in the access lounge so that a smaller yet equitable version of the exhibit could be created for individuals who were unable to ascend to the upper floors. Using the remaining grant funds, and splitting the cost with the exhibits budget, custom-fit plexiglass boxes were purchased to safely secure objects. Exhibit panels were recreated on a smaller scale (but still in a large-print font) and laminated

Figure 6.3. The access lounge at the Molly Brown House Museum. *Courtesy Heather Pressman*

with a heavy-duty lamination to ensure that they would remain durable for the duration of the exhibit. Later, a vinyl oriental "rug" was added to the space to make it more welcoming.

The COVID-19 pandemic forced the museum to rethink how it could safely provide tours of the home when reopening after its initial four-month closure. The decision was made to create a self-guided tour. From June 2020 through the fall months of 2021, this was the only way to take a tour of the museum (the museum now offers a combination of guided and self-guided tours). While the access lounge was initially designed with people with disabilities in mind, we found that visitors of all kinds enjoyed having a space to sit while they wait for other members of their party to rejoin them, whether they are on a guided or self-guided tour. This is a great example of how designing for individuals on the periphery benefits everyone, as the Institute for Human Centered Design has stated.

A variety of tactile materials have been introduced to make the access lounge a more engaging space. There is now a basket filled with touchable items, like those found on the second and third floors of the home. For example, a push button light switch, damask fabric like that which covers the walls in one of the bedrooms, and pieces of a plaster ceiling rosette. In addition, there are also interactive elements including a talk-back board (a place for visitors to make comments and leave feedback), as well as puzzle cubes with six different historic images on them.

BEYOND THE ACCESS LOUNGE

A silver lining of the pandemic is that the creation of a self-guided tour option makes visiting the museum more available to individuals with sensory sensitivities. Prior to the pandemic, guided tours of up to twenty people were taken through the home's rooms, some barely big enough for the group to fit safely with the artifacts. Groups would often remain in these spaces for upward of five minutes. Being in confined spaces with many other people all while being expected to hold still can be nightmarish for people with sensory sensitivities. This is where the self-guided tour adds the flexibility for guests to make the tour work for their specific needs, something that was previously not an option in a large guided tour.

In 2022, the museum received a grant to support its sensory work. This grant was broken into three parts: an assessment of the museum's spaces, processes, and programs; sensory training for staff and volunteers; and sensory support materials. An autism expert and advocate visited the museum several times and created a slate of recommendations based on what she saw during a self-guided tour experience and during one of the museum's on-site education programs, as well as the information available on the website and through an interview with staff.

Staff and volunteer training was provided by the same autism expert alongside a self-advocate from the autism community. No matter what role someone has, they are likely to interact with someone with sensory sensitivities through the course of their work.[5] The training covered what sensory processing is, what the world is like for people with sensory processing disorders, and things that museums and other spaces can do to support this portion of their audience. The final portion of the presentation was to talk about some of the support materials that were purchased on behalf of the museum. As a part of the recommendations that this expert made, she included using everyday items that could be purchased for a fairly low cost and incorporated into the existing touch baskets throughout the museum. The idea is to have materials available that mimic the items on display that cannot be touched. For example, have velvet fabric scrunchies available for people to touch and feel, to mimic the feeling of a velvet dress or couch on display. Another example was to have faux decorative feathers as a tactile experience versus touching the plumes on the hats displayed. This is a simple, low-cost way to turn "do not touch" into "please touch."

One final item that was recommended as a part of this grant was to purchase a set of "ghost chairs." These clear, acrylic chairs blend seamlessly into the rooms but offer places for visitors to stop and rest if they need it. Again, while these were purchased with a specific audience in mind, many different visitors use them and school-aged kids are fascinated by them. While these chairs do not have arms on them, they are a lot sturdier than the folding stools otherwise available to guests as they move around the museum. Having seating that is available throughout the house ensures that visitors can enjoy the

Figure 6.4. A "ghost" chair in the library of the Molly Brown House Museum. *Courtesy Heather Pressman*

house whether they are able to remain standing throughout the whole guided or self-guided tour or whether they need to rest. These chairs help ensure the experience is equitable.

WHAT'S NEXT?

Access work is an ongoing and iterative process. While some days providing access at a historical site can seem insurmountable, especially given the demands put on the staff's time, there are solutions that can invite all audiences to enjoy our spaces more fully. Some of those solutions are capital projects like adding a lift to circumvent stairs, while others are simple, creative solutions to provide engaging experiences within the historic site. When we are unable to provide a physical change, we can use materials, technology, and comfortable environments, as explored earlier, to lay out the welcome mat for all our audiences.

NOTES

1. While known as the Molly Brown House Museum, Margaret Brown was never actually called Molly in her lifetime. It was a nickname that was given to her after her death and was made famous by the 1960 *Unsinkable Molly Brown* musical by Meredith Willson and Richard Morris because it was thought easier to sing. The musical was later turned into a film starring Debbie Reynolds in 1964. While historically inaccurate, the musical and film are largely responsible for generating interest in saving the home and creating Historic Denver in 1970.
2. National Park Service, "The Secretary of the Interior's Standards for the Treatment of Historic Properties," accessed May 14, 2023, https://www.nps.gov/orgs/1739 /secretary-standards-treatment-historic-properties.htm.
3. Smithsonian Accessibility Program, "Smithsonian Guidelines for Accessible Exhibition Design," accessed October 18, 2022, https://www.sifacilities.si.edu /sites/default/files/Files/Accessibility/accessible-exhibition-design1.pdf.
4. Work on the access lounge began in earnest just as the COVID-19 pandemic started. As a result, some of its features were delayed due to the uncertainty surrounding how the virus was spread.
5. Current estimates are that one in thirty-six children have been diagnosed with autism. (https://www.cdc.gov/ncbddd/autism/data.html) and that one in twenty people have a sensory processing disorder (Star Institute, "Understanding Sensory Processing Disorder," accessed October 20, 2022, https://www.spdstar.org/basic /understanding-sensory-processing-disorder).

7

Subway Sleuths

NOT YOUR TYPICAL MUSEUM PROGRAM

Sara Thomson

The New York Transit Museum is the home of the national award-winning Subway Sleuths program.[1] This semester-long afterschool program takes advantage of being in the museum's unique space. The Transit Museum is located in Brooklyn, New York, in a decommissioned subway station. The Court Street Station was opened in 1936 as part of the New York City–owned Independent Subway System. The station operated as a terminal for the HH Shuttle from nearby Hoyt-Schermerhorn Station with the hope that it would connect with the planned 2nd Avenue Subway in the future. However, those plans fell through, and few subway riders utilized the shuttle. Due to lack of use and no plans for the future, the Court Street Station was decommissioned from service in 1946.

The station would live on though. The station and the tunnel connecting it to Hoyt-Schermerhorn Station was maintained for training transit workers and even used for filming, including the 1974 movie *The Taking of Pelham One Two Three*. On July 4, 1976, in honor of the United States's Bicentennial Celebration, New York City transit workers opened an exhibit on transit. The exhibit was so popular that it never closed and eventually became the New York Transit Museum. Parked along both sides of the subway island platform are vintage elevated train cars and subway train cars. In the museum's collection, the oldest wooden elevated car was built in 1904, and the oldest subway car is from 1916. The station's signal tower continues to track subway trains operating in the area in real time, just as it did in 1936. The museum also features turnstiles ranging from the years 1904 to 1993 as well as an exhibit on surface transportation such as trolleys and buses.

The Transit Museum recognized years ago that visitors on the autism spectrum made up a considerable and passionate percentage of their audience. A common specialized interest of people with autism is related to transit. While it is difficult to prove why this is, theories include the ability to categorize models and to study the systemization of transit including routes, maps, and schedules. Simon Baron-Cohen, professor of developmental psychopathology and director of the Autism Research Centre at the University of Cambridge in England, asserted, "Trains are a specific example of a system, in this case a mechanical system," and "People with autism have a preference for predictable, systematic information. Joining a program for young train enthusiasts thus plays to their strengths—in understanding systems—but embedding this in a social format."[2]

The museum desired to encourage and foster this specialized interest and began developing the Subway Sleuths program. In 2011 they collaborated with autism specialists to grow the program into a robust structure of activities using a strength-based approach. Each goal-oriented session provides opportunities for group collaboration and different forms of social engagement. Among the philosophies and strategies that the specialists brought to the program were those of Paula Kluth and Patrick Schwarz that can be found in their book *"Just Give Him the Whale!": 20 Ways to Use Fascinations, Areas of Expertise, and Strengths to Support Students with Autism*. They assert in their book, "Students are often told not to carry on about their fascinations and to avoid long monologues related to their passions. We disagree with this advice, as many students with autism have too few opportunities to shine. . . . If possible, look for natural opportunities for learners to show their smarts."[3] In Subway Sleuths students are always encouraged to show their "train smarts."

Subway Sleuths takes place twice per year during a spring semester and a fall semester. Each semester is made of three groups: two groups of second and third graders who meet after school on weekdays, and one group of fourth and fifth graders who meet on Saturday mornings. Each group meets once per week for a total of ten sessions. Regular attendance is important as each session builds on the previous session. Students receive the most benefit when everyone attends regularly because their relationships grow and projects develop.

Each group is facilitated by a team of a special education teacher, a speech-language pathologist, and a Transit Museum educator. There is no set curriculum; the facilitation team plans each semester according to the interests and goals of their specific group. After each session, they reflect and then finalize the plans for the next session. There are tried-and-true activities, which will be described later.

To begin each semester, a call for applications is announced and advertised. In addition to general information about the Subway Sleuths program, the announcement includes more specific information such as when sessions will take place and the cost of the program. An application is most often submitted by a child's family, but at times they are assisted by a teacher or case manager.

The application requests information on the child's diagnosis including details on language skills and social challenges. With this information, the team can begin understanding what supports the child may need. The other major question on the application asks what the level of interest in trains is and how it is demonstrated. It is important to confirm the applicant's train interest because that is what is being used to motivate the children to fully participate and make connections with each other. Also, if a child does not have an interest, then they may be bored because the activities revolve around transit.

The application period is approximately four weeks, and as applications are submitted, the program manager will review them. The program manager may feel they need more information about an applicant and can contact the family to supplement the application. After reviewing all applications, the program manager will invite potential candidates to a screening session. Typically, two screening sessions are scheduled for each group, with up to five candidates invited for each screening session. The thirty-minute screening sessions are facilitated by the team and observed by an autism consultant who was involved in the development of the program.

There are strategies and resources built into the screening sessions and the program as a whole to support the candidates. First, a social narrative is emailed to the children's families that describes in first person and with photos and images what to expect during the screening. The social narrative introduces the facilitators, different spaces in the museum, and the plan or schedule. The facilitators will also show a simple visual schedule throughout the session to remind everyone of the plan. The facilitators carry other items in case they are needed, such as noise-reducing headphones and fidgets. The team has reviewed the applications and discussed who may need more language support or who may need reassurance if they get anxious.

A screening session typically consists of three different activities, loose and structured, so the candidates have multiple opportunities and entry points for demonstrating their interest in both transit and the program. To begin, a part of the team will retrieve the screening group from the museum lobby and walk them in a line to another space in the museum while their caregivers wait in the lobby. The first activity is conducted in an enclosed gallery space that has been set up with chairs around a table with a New York City subway map and art supplies on it. One or two facilitators will already be seated at the table and will invite the children to join with minimal prompting. The team first observes how much the candidates are initially drawn into viewing the map and the conversation. There are markers and stickers on the table if the group wants to trace subway routes or mark favorite stations. The facilitators will follow the lead of the children and what they are drawn to and then initiate more prompting if and when needed.

Next, the group travels through the museum together downstairs to the subway platform and vintage train cars. This is a time when the candidates may definitively express their train interest, when they are immersed in the museum collection and concrete objects of their specialized interest. They may convey their excitement or state knowledge they have of certain train cars. They may ask to visit certain train cars. However, the group all enters one train car together to play a game named Hold the Pole. During this game, everyone sits in the train car near one or two of the poles that standing subway passengers would hold on to during their trip. A facilitator will start by instructing everyone to hold the pole if they ride the 7 Train or if they like pizza, for example. Everyone for whom the statement is true will hold the pole. The students then see a visual representation of who are making connections. The facilitators model language for noticing these things and encourage the students to make their own observations. During the game, students are also invited to lead a round if they would like.

Finally, the group returns to the gallery space for one last activity, which is simply named Trains and Tracks. The candidates are provided with toy wooden train tracks and wooden train cars that look just like New York City subway cars. This is a loosely structured time when the facilitators again try to sit back and follow the lead of the children. The facilitators keep the group informed of how much time they have left until it is time to clean up. After putting Trains and Tracks away, the facilitators walk the candidates back to their caregivers in the lobby and say goodbye.

Figure 7.1. Subway Sleuth students and facilitators grab the subway car pole during a round of the game Hold the Pole. *Photo courtesy of the New York Transit Museum*

After screening all of the candidates, the program manager, facilitators, and consultant discuss the acceptance of students. Because the Transit Museum has live, electrified train tracks, safety is an important consideration. Students must be able to travel with the group in an independent, safe way, and it is explicit that the program does not provide one-to-one support for this. (The only time additional staff was added to a group to provide more direct support was when a student who is blind was accepted into the program.) Next, the team considers again the interest levels of the candidates in transit in general, in the museum collection, and in the activities. They will also ponder how the interests relate to each other and who has similar interests to help ascertain if they can construct a comprehensive curriculum for all the students for the semester. Finally, the team considers the language and social profiles of the applicants. It helps when students have similar profiles to form a more cohesive group, but it is not required. The facilitators and consultant contemplate if they will be able to provide a beneficial and enriched program for all students if they have varied profiles. They want to be sure they can provide a supportive environment for their students and propose how they will manage that. The team never wants the demands of the activities or the program to become too frustrating for an individual.

After the families are informed of their children's acceptance into the Subway Sleuths program, they are required to complete the registration form. The registration form gathers more detailed information about the children such as interests (transit-related or otherwise), dislikes, and challenges. The team uses this information to assist in planning their sessions, such as determining what activities might be interesting for the whole group and how to better support the students. For example, if the team learns a student becomes easily frustrated during art-making activities, then they will have a plan in place for adaptations and options. Also important for the program manager, the registration form collects information on emergency contacts, allergies, and which other individuals have permission to pick up the student from the museum. By signing the form, families grant photo releases and for the children to possibly attend an offsite field trip during the program. Families can also request a scholarship application if they require financial assistance with the full cost of the program.

Before the first session, the team has a planning meeting. Again using the information collected on the registration forms and using their experience from the screening, they might decide on a theme for the semester, such as an ongoing art-making project of creating a miniature subway station or a series of map activities. The team also considers what the objectives are for a particular group based on what areas the participants have the opportunity to grow in.

In the Subway Sleuths program, activities fall into three categories: experience sharing, coordinating actions/collaboration, and problem solving/group project. During experience sharing, facilitators endeavor to create shared moments of connections between the students. Students demonstrate this by verbally or nonverbally acknowledging a shared experience or attempting to connect to others. They may make a comment or ask a question to add on to a shared thought. The development of episodic memory is also encouraged. Students may respond to a statement of past experience or recall past information when viewing a photo from a previous session.

During coordinating actions/collaboration, facilitators are observing the students regulating themselves to others and showing interest in being a part of the group. The students may check in with or reference each other. They engage in working together toward a common goal. This can range anywhere from staying in line when walking through the museum, to building Train and Tracks in a circle when the facilitators challenge them, to completing a semester-long project of creating a whole subway station model together.

The problem-solving category includes more than just identifying a problem and its solution, although that certainly is useful to observe. More specifically in Subway Sleuths, the team examines how the students take on roles and use flexibility within those roles and within a collaboration. Students may suggest roles for themselves or for others when planning an activity, or they may accept a role suggested by another. They may demonstrate a willingness or flexibility in changing roles or taking on a less preferred role as well as incorporating others' ideas into their thinking or plan. One specific example of taking on roles and having flexibility within your plan is when the group designs a subway car together, and one student accepts the role of adding the wheels while another takes on the role of designing the doors.

At the beginning of the first session, the facilitators introduce the official Subway Sleuths visual schedule to the students. The schedule is on a large poster board, so it is always visible. It is divided into four sections and each section is numbered like the colored bullets of the subway lines. There is also a "subway car" made out of a small box that is moved from section to section to indicate where the group is in the schedule. This "subway car" marker is a physical reinforcement for providing more concrete information. Also, the Sleuths can take on the role of moving it. The facilitators will additionally establish some Sleuth language or fun transit-related language that the Sleuths can enjoy and better relate to. For example, the facilitators may say "go local" instead of just saying "walk," or they may remind the group to "stay on track" if they start going off topic.

One of the first things a group does together during the first session is create their Subway Sleuth badges. Facilitators prepare round paper circles with a special Sleuth design and each participant's name for both the students and facilitators. Everyone can color and add stickers to their badge. Originally, the papers were then turned into metal pins with a plastic coating, but after considering the difficulties of having to wear the pins and the sounds of the metal hitting anything, a new process began. Now, the pins are printed on cardstock and then laminated after being decorated. Next, they are attached to lanyards so everyone can easily wear their badges.

Whether the badges were made into pins or into lanyards, it is important to include the students in the production process. They may have helped the facilitator operate the pin-punching machine or helped punch holes for their lanyards. Either way, the goal is for the Sleuths to take ownership and value their badges. When everyone has their new badges, everyone is invited to do a group high-five and cheer "Go Sleuths"; this is a great example of constructing a shared moment of connection. The facilitators make a big deal of declaring the students are now official Sleuths; they want their students to be proud and confident.

The badges are then used throughout the semester. First, they are a simple reminder of that connection with the rest of the group and that this is something to be excited about and proud of. Facilitators may ask one Sleuth to hand out the badges to everyone; this would be an important role for a student to take on. In other groups, facilitators may hand out all the badges but to the wrong students, so then the students must find the student to whom the badge belongs to. At the end of the session, groups may "rewind" or take turns stating what their favorite part of the session was. As they rewind, they each return their badge to complete that day's session.

As mentioned earlier, the facilitators plan the semester's activities with their specific group in mind. They may try some of their favorite activities at first to see what works. As the semester moves forward, they may incorporate an activity into the schedule each week for a predictable structure, such as always ending with Trains and Tracks. To keep a game interesting and to continue further growth, the facilitators may slightly tweak the game each week. For example, with Trains and Tracks, the students may start by setting up their tracks however they want, and then the next week they may try to achieve a challenge together such as building the tracks as long as they can or in a circle. After completing the challenge, the Sleuths can request their favorite toy subway car to try out on the tracks.

A popular Sleuth game is Trading Spaces. The students and the facilitators sit on a subway car with bench seats, half of the group on each side and facing each other. Without speaking, one person tries to get the attention of someone sitting on the opposite seat and smiles to let them know they would like to trade spaces, or switch seats. If the second person wants to trade they can nod in agreement, and then the two people switch seats. If the second person does not want to trade seats, then they can shake their head no, and the first person will move on and try to switch with someone else. Sleuths may combine fun additions into the game, such as giving each other high-fives when they are trading spaces or clapping to assist a Sleuth who is blind. Trading Spaces accomplishes objectives of practicing nonverbal communication, respecting others' choices, and practicing flexibility when your plan does not work out and you need to choose a new plan.

Another game that relies on nonverbal communication is Architect and Builder. Working as partners, the Sleuths have to construct a structure out

Figure 7.2. During the game Trading Spaces, the Sleuths try to gain each other's attention and get ready to trade seats on the subway car. *Photo courtesy of the New York Transit Museum*

of building blocks without speaking. The first student is the Architect and cannot touch the blocks but points to them and uses gestures to indicate to the second student, or Builder, how to build the structure. In addition to practicing communicating nonverbally, the Architect must exhibit patience as the Builder tries to understand the Architect's plan, and the Builder must accept the plan of the Architect. The Sleuths realize the importance of collaboration to reach a common goal.

Sleuths also navigate asking questions and listening to each other's clues when they play Find the Mystery Sleuth. One or two Sleuths hide in the museum (often in a train car) with a facilitator while the rest of the group waits for them to be ready. Each group has a walkie-talkie so they can talk to each other. The bigger, waiting group asks questions to determine where the small group might be hiding. The hiding group must respond with helpful information without giving the answer away and may even think of clues. The bigger group recounts all of the clues they have, and once they feel they have enough information, they work together to find the hiding mystery Sleuth.

Like the classic Red Light/Green Light game, the game of Exprocal supports the children's body awareness and listening skills. One Sleuth is the "dispatcher" who will call out the directions and stands apart. The rest of the Sleuths line up about forty feet away from the dispatcher. When the dispatcher calls out "local," the Sleuths can walk slowly toward the dispatcher, and when the dispatcher calls "express," they walk quickly. (The word Exprocal is a combination of "express" and "local.") The Sleuths must freeze where they are if the dispatcher calls for a "full stop." The first Sleuth to reach the dispatcher wins and gets to be the next dispatcher. There are also variants that can adjust this game. For example, different-colored tape is applied to the floor, and each Sleuth follows one color like it is their own train track. There is still a dispatcher calling out the directions, but in this version, there is no winner or loser, which can be helpful for group management. After some time playing, the facilitators will instead ask for a new dispatcher. In the past, some groups have also invented new directions to add to the game.

Based on the family game of Hedbanz, the Sleuths play a headband game with a transit focus. Working in partners or small groups, one player wears a paper headband that the facilitators have attached with a photo of a certain subway car or bus. The player then asks yes or no questions to the others to try to narrow down what is pictured on their headband. If needed, the player can ask for a hint.

Subway Sleuths has its own version of Go Fish that is called Go Sleuth. Facilitators made picture cards with pairs of matching subway train routes, such as the 7 Train or the N Train. Sleuths engage by having to ask each other by name for a matching card, and it is a lot of fun asking, "Jon, do you have any 7 Trains?" It is a life skill to remember someone's name, call them by name to get their attention, and make a request. Students may also cope with disappointment and frustration if another requests a card they have or wanted. A fun and silly addition to this game is facilitators also make matching playing cards with each of the students' photos on them. Groups enjoy playing this game while sitting on the floor of a vintage train car in the museum.

Another favorite activity is Mystery Box. The facilitators choose an object from the touch collection that is able to be safely handled and places it inside a box before the session begins. Each Sleuth takes a turn reaching inside the box to feel and handle the object without looking. They describe what the object feels like to each other, and using everyone's information, they try to guess what the object is. The Sleuths practice using descriptive language and asking questions and listening to others' information to solve together what the mystery object is. Objects that have been used are a train operator's brake handle, a transit worker's lantern, and a subway car's contact shoe.

During one semester, Mystery Box served as a great example of how a student can reach their potential and demonstrate their abilities in the Subway Sleuths program. One student during this semester was quieter than their fellow Sleuths. According to the information gathered from the family and from the schoolteacher, the student presented as having fewer language skills than other Sleuths. However, whenever the mystery object was revealed, this student would share their knowledge about the mystery object, speaking with

Figure 7.3. After they discovered the object in the Mystery Box was a subway car handhold, a facilitator holds it up for a Sleuth student to try out. *Photo courtesy of the New York Transit Museum*

fluency and confidence. This example illustrated a further point from Kluth and Schwartz: "Another reason to encourage the student's interests as part of his or her conversation toolbox is that many learners demonstrate better communication skills when they are speaking about fascinations."[4] By being in the authentic space of a subway station with real objects, the student was motivated and better able to demonstrate their true abilities. The goal then of this example is to embolden the student in these positive situations so that they build confidence to participate in other conversations.

At a midpoint in the semester, families receive a Subway Sleuths newsletter. This newsletter describes some highlights from the semester thus far, such as creating the Sleuth badges in the first session, and some of the popular activities. It also may include the special Sleuth language used during sessions or some things to look forward to in future sessions. Of course, there are plenty of photos to accompany the text. The team enjoys sharing these newsletters with families, and the families appreciate learning more about what their children are doing in the museum, especially when a child may not be forthcoming with details.

The newsletters also function as communication between staff and caregivers. One challenge every semester is managing the caregivers' expectations around communication about their children's progress. They sometimes request a report on "how their child is doing," which is not something the team is able to provide. While the team does record notes on sessions and students, this is for internal use for tracking how the semester is advancing for the whole group and for reflection to better plan future sessions. It is important to remind families that this is an afterschool museum program and not a therapeutic program.

At the last session, families are invited to join at the end for a Subway Sleuths celebration. When appropriate, the special educator and speech-language pathologist will speak to the caregivers about the highlights and some objectives of the semester while the Sleuths and their siblings will play games. Sometimes the caregivers are then also invited to try playing a game with the museum educator. It is wonderful to see when the Sleuths explain the game to their families. Next, the Sleuths and their families join together for a slideshow of photos from the semester. The Sleuths display their episodic memory by recalling what happened in the photos and how they felt about it. Finally, the Sleuths are presented with their award certificates. The facilitators carefully consider an "award" for each Sleuth that incorporates qualities of the Sleuth with a transit theme. A student who loved art making might be given the "Creative Conductor Award," a student who always cheered on their peers might receive the "Enthusiastic Engineer Award," and a student who shared a lot of transit information could obtain the "Detail Dispatcher Award."

After the extremely positive experience that participants and their families have with the Subway Sleuths program, many families then ask what's next. They continue looking for more opportunities as their children grow older. These requests provided one reason for developing a new program for teenagers who identify as neurodivergent and again have a passion for transit. The program Transit Quest was launched in 2018 and functions similarly to a summer camp. Transit Quest is always one of the last weeks in August, before New York City public schools open for the new school year. In addition to all of the objectives of Subway Sleuths, Transit Quest accomplishes another goal with its intentional timing; participants who may have spent less time socializing with peers during the summer school break can ease back into it before school starts in September.

The weeklong program begins in the mornings, and every day includes special VIP experiences. Among these experiences are unique ways we can use our collection and historical spaces. On Mondays, when the museum is closed to the public, we arrange a ride on a few of our vintage subway cars from our station home to our closest neighboring subway station that is still operating in the transit system. On another day we take a field trip together to the decommissioned subway station outside City Hall, a station affectionately known as Old City Hall Station. The subway was opened on October 27, 1904, at this station, which features vaulted tile ceilings and arches, chandeliers, and leaded skylights. The station was closed to the public in 1945. Trains no longer stop there although trains do still use its tracks to turn around. People can only visit this elegant and historic station on special tours with the New York Transit Museum, and it is a difficult ticket to acquire. Therefore, for many Transit Quest participants, visiting this station is a once-in-a-lifetime opportunity.

The New York Transit Museum's subway station home provides many opportunities for authentic experiences and programs. The museum with its turnstiles and subway cars hosts the Ready to Ride program, an introduction to or a refresher of travel training for groups with intellectual and developmental disabilities to engage in the steps, safety, and social etiquette of riding the subway in New York City. The museum provides school classes, families, and individual visitors with hands-on learning experiences. For the Subway Sleuth children, the museum is a comforting space where they are empowered to share their knowledge and affirm their specialized interest in transit with like-minded peers. The Subway Sleuths are reminded that once they are a Sleuth they are always a Sleuth and are invited back to reunions. They are reminded that the New York Transit Museum is their home.

NOTES

1. The Subway Sleuths program received a National Arts and Humanities Youth Program Award in 2016.
2. Maia Szalavitz, "Making Connections," *Popular Mechanics*, November 18, 2015, https://www.popularmechanics.com/culture/a18227/subway-sleuths-mta -autism-program/.
3. Paula Kluth and Patrick Schwarz, *"Just Give Him the Whale!": 20 Ways to Use Fascinations, Areas of Expertise, and Strengths to Support Students with Autism* (Baltimore: Paul H. Brookes Publishing Co., 2008), 85.
4. Kluth and Schwarz, *"Just Give Him the Whale!"* 95.

8

Accessibility Evolving at The Henry Ford

Caroline Braden

Specialized accessibility programs designed for particular audiences are one way that historic sites and museums can help people of varying ages and abilities feel welcome, included, and engaged with the diverse offerings of a site. The Henry Ford in Dearborn, Michigan, a site with both indoor and outdoor venues, has offered specialized accessibility programs since 2015. Starting with touch tours for people who are blind or have low vision, offerings have expanded to include programs for people who are on the autism spectrum, d/Deaf, and who are living with dementia (and their care partners).[1] This chapter will cover how programs started and developed for each of these audiences, as well as how they evolved during the COVID-19 pandemic. Hopefully, the information contained here will inspire others interested in developing and offering programs for any of these audiences at their own institutions.

BACKGROUND ON THE HENRY FORD AND ITS EARLY ACCESSIBILITY EFFORTS

The Henry Ford is a large history-focused institution located on over one hundred acres and composed of four main venues. First, there is an indoor museum, the Henry Ford Museum of American Innovation, which has exhibits on everything from cars to airplanes to agricultural equipment. Second, as an additional part of the museum, there is a movie theater called the Giant Screen Experience. Third, there is an outdoor venue called Greenfield Village, which has about eighty historic structures, including Thomas Edison's Menlo Park Laboratory, the Wright Brothers' Cycle Shop, and Henry Ford's boyhood home.

Finally, there is the Ford Rouge Factory Tour, a modern, working factory at which visitors can watch Ford trucks being manufactured.

Prior to 2015—the year in which an accessibility-focused staff position was first created at The Henry Ford—the institution did not have any specialized accessibility programs. There were, however, some accessibility offerings, such as wheelchairs and motorized scooters, ramps into select historic buildings in Greenfield Village, and training for some staff on interacting with people with autism. These few offerings were at least a start and, when combined with The Henry Ford's diverse array of venues and content, provided much that could be built upon and incorporated into more audience-specific accessibility programming.

GAINING IDEAS AND INSIGHTS FROM THE COMMUNITY AND LARGER FIELD

When determining accessibility programs to have, it has always been (and will continue to be) important to understand what the intended community is interested in and what will benefit them. Over the years, this has involved talking with people with disabilities, as well as with disability service organizations, to help with program development, staff training, sharing information, and more.

Additionally, when deciding upon the types of programs to have and the format of these programs, it has been immensely beneficial to keep up to date with programs and other accessibility offerings from museums across the country. This has involved doing online research, corresponding with contacts in the accessibility field, and traveling to see accessibility programs. During the pandemic, this involved observing more programs virtually, especially in the spring of 2020, when museums were just starting to transition their on-site programs to virtual. Whether in person or virtually, observing the ways in which other institutions have implemented their programs, as well as what they have included in them and how they have engaged their audiences, has been immeasurably useful in providing ideas for accessibility programs at The Henry Ford.

PROGRAMS AT THE HENRY FORD FOR PEOPLE WHO ARE BLIND OR HAVE LOW VISION

The first accessibility program developed at The Henry Ford was a touch tour for people who are blind or have low vision. This program resulted from a request in the summer of 2015 from two individuals who are blind. They were planning a visit to the Henry Ford Museum of American Innovation and contacted The Henry Ford, wondering if it would be possible for them to go on a touch tour. A few of The Henry Ford's presenters (who are similar to docents or tour guides) had given such tours before, but only rarely and not in many years. Using an outdated list of stops from previous touch tours, in concert with several conversations with conservation staff, presenters were able to provide

Figure 8.1. An attendee to a touch tour at The Henry Ford touches a car on display in the Driving America exhibit inside Henry Ford Museum of American Innovation while a presenter staff member describes the car to her. *Courtesy Caroline Braden*

these two individuals with a touch tour. The insights gained from that tour, as well as the feedback from the two visitors, were very helpful and led to the creation of a more standardized touch tour for the museum.

The touch tour, which was available upon request by 2016, is an hour and a half long and includes opportunities to touch various artifacts and hand-held models of artifacts. Objects on the tour include some that could already be touched by any visitor, such as a large locomotive called the Allegheny. Visitors are also able to wear gloves to touch other artifacts chosen by curators, such as specific cars in the *Driving America* exhibit. Additionally, small boxes of hand-held models (some of which were 3-D printed, others of which were purchased in the museum store) were created for use by presenters during the tours.[2]

To initially help develop this tour, The Henry Ford worked with many individuals within the community who are blind or have low vision. Not only did they provide feedback as to what would interest and benefit them, they also attended many practice touch tours given by presenters and helped share information about the new tour with others who would be interested.

In addition to these individuals, The Henry Ford worked with an organization called the Michigan Department of Education–Low Incidence Outreach (MDE-LIO) on a specialized training for the presenters giving these tours. MDE-LIO provides resources to students who are blind or have low vision across Michigan. For the training, staff were joined by a teacher of students who are blind or have low vision, as well as a woman who is blind. The training included information on working with individuals from this community, practice providing detailed verbal descriptions, and experience using the technique of sighted guide (in which people walk in pairs, with one person being blindfolded and putting their hand on the upper arm of the other person to be guided around the space). This training was repeated multiple times over the years so as to make sure enough presenters were trained on how to give this type of tour if a request should come in.

While the Henry Ford Museum of American Innovation was the only venue for which a standardized touch tour was developed, over the years, staff have also helped coordinate touch tours and experiences for Greenfield Village and the Ford Rouge Factory Tour. For Greenfield Village, these tours have involved groups visiting buildings with tactile objects, such as the Weaving Shop (where they could touch woven cloths), Printing Office (where they could feel raised letters used for a printing press), and Cohen Millinery (where they could touch and try on decorated hats). At the Ford Rouge Factory Tour, these experiences have involved touching objects such as sedum (a plant used on the living roof of the truck plant), as well as having presenters provide verbal descriptions of the visuals in the factory.

Feedback on the touch tours has been positive, with one person who helped develop the tours saying:

> In the 1990s and early 2000s, when I was busy raising my five children, we spent time having experiences at The Henry Ford, inside and outside. For me those times involved hearing the kids delight with what they saw and I was pretty much left out of that because I am blind. All this changed when The Henry Ford hired [Accessibility Manager] Caroline Braden to find ways of making displays and experiences something that could be enjoyed by and engaged in by the blind. Caroline organized various tours where I brought others who were blind. We worked with presenters who described displays to us as well as enabled us to touch and interpret other displays which were usually off limits. I appreciate that it became understood that in order to engage in a display we need information which others received by sight. I remember learning about the Ford assembly line by participating in building a car and we were able to do this with our own timing, which provided for more opportunity for tactile observation. One of my favorite memories was in the stable where we brushed and felt how tall those horses were. I had no idea of their grandeur until that day. At the same time, we were always encouraged to give suggestions and feedback. This is when it became obvious to all that each blind person is an individual and uses their other senses to gain information.

With the uncertainty surrounding the COVID-19 pandemic and how the virus was transmitted, The Henry Ford temporarily stopped offering tours and tactile experiences and thus stopped offering touch tours. If The Henry Ford was going to continue serving this audience without a touch tour (at least temporarily), it was going to need to go in a new direction. Fortunately, in the spring and summer of 2020, The Henry Ford's accessibility manager observed a type of virtual program being offered by other institutions (such as the Guggenheim Museum and the Tenement Museum) that seemed like something that The Henry Ford might be able to offer. This program—called a virtual verbal description program—involves providing very detailed descriptions of visuals that are shared on the computer screen, as well as relevant background and context about what is in the images. This type of program also includes time for conversation and questions.

The Henry Ford offered its first virtual verbal description program in the fall of 2020 and has continued to host programs at least four times per year. Rather than using museum presenters for these, curators have instead presented on topics within their areas of expertise while providing verbal descriptions of visuals. Topics for these programs have varied greatly, ranging from Greenfield Village buildings to furniture to Studio Glass to the Magic Skyway ride at the 1964-1965 New York World's Fair (a collaboration between Ford Motor Company and Walt Disney). By having a different theme for each program, The Henry Ford has been able to cover a vast array of topics through these programs—many more than could have been covered with the touch tours.

To initially help develop this type of program and choose the topics, The Henry Ford's accessibility manager corresponded with several community members that the institution had worked with in the past who are blind. Initial information about the program was shared with them and with various organizations serving people who are blind or have low vision. Since then, the institution's list of attendees has grown exponentially, as attendees have shared information about the programs with their contacts. The Henry Ford now typically receives more than forty registrants to each program, up from twelve for the first program. Additionally, attendees to these programs have been coming from across the country and Canada—something that was not easily possible with on-site touch tours but is much more possible with virtual programming.

The Henry Ford's first virtual verbal description programs were an hour long. They have since expanded to an hour and a half or two hours, as it takes quite a bit of time to provide descriptions and to ensure that there is plenty of time to answer the attendees' questions. The attendees do not seem to mind staying for a longer program. In fact, they seem to really enjoy these programs and will stay for however long is necessary as they are so appreciative of the fact that these programs are specifically designed with them in mind.

The feedback received after these programs supports this. For example, after the program about furniture, one attendee emailed saying, "I just wanted to say thank you to all involved for an absolutely fabulous experience. The narration, the provided detail, the descriptions and the answers to the questions raised were absolutely spot on. I am an avid antique music box collector, and this was just really really superb and very well done. Thank you so much." Another attendee's mother emailed after that program saying, "Thank you for continuing to provide the virtual verbal programs. My 21-year-old daughter would otherwise never see these exhibits."

The virtual verbal description programs have been so successful that The Henry Ford plans on continuing to offer them on a regular basis, despite resuming in-person touch tours. In this case, the virtual verbal description programs really were a silver lining of the pandemic for The Henry Ford.

PROGRAMS AT THE HENRY FORD FOR PEOPLE WHO ARE ON THE AUTISM SPECTRUM

In 2016, The Henry Ford expanded its accessibility offerings to include sensory-friendly programs for people who are on the autism spectrum or have sensory processing disorders.[3] These programs were inspired both by work that The Henry Ford had already started to do, including staff training with the Autism Alliance of Michigan, as well as by other museums' sensory-friendly programs. In researching and observing other museums' programs, The Henry Ford's staff noticed several similarities. For example, many organizations offered early access times to visit, as well as previsit supports such as social narratives (which include pictures and text to walk people through a visit) and sensory maps (which show areas with loud sounds, bright lights, and other potential sensory triggers). Many institutions also had designated quiet spaces and provided additional supports such as noise-canceling headphones and fidgets.[4]

It was in late 2015 that The Henry Ford's accessibility manager observed a sensory-friendly event with many of these offerings at the Michigan Science Center. Observing that event and gaining ideas from it helped lead to The Henry Ford's first sensory-friendly event in 2016. This first event and each of the institution's sensory-friendly events since have included the following: a social narrative, sensory map, access to noise-canceling headphones, and a designated quiet space. The Henry Ford has also offered exclusive access times to some of its exhibits and special events, such as Hallowe'en in Greenfield Village, as well as periodic sensory-friendly movies (with the lights turned up and the sound turned down) at the Giant Screen Experience. To help with staff support and awareness, The Henry Ford has hosted several trainings since 2016 on interacting with individuals who are on the autism spectrum or have other sensory processing disorders, which have been provided by the Autism Alliance of Michigan and other similar organizations.

Over the years, The Henry Ford has received much positive feedback on its sensory-friendly events, with one family emailing after a sensory-friendly Hallowe'en event to say:

> I can't adequately express just what a weight was lifted being in a place where the kids could just be themselves! No getting embarrassed by melt downs. Everyone knew what you were going through. I could literally cry it was that life giving! There are so few places you can go with kids where they can just be their loud, silly selves. I've never had that kind of joy in an outing with the kids.

I felt like, for the first time, I could fully participate in the fun without having to worry about the "social norms" we have to typically navigate so carefully around. I can't imagine anything else being so impactful for families with special needs. Thank you so much for this.

To help with the planning of its sensory-friendly events and offerings, The Henry Ford created an autism advisory group in 2017, which has continued in various capacities since then. This group is composed of parents and teachers of individuals with autism, as well as several people with autism. The purpose of this group is to provide feedback on and ideas for The Henry Ford's sensory-friendly programming. The group members have also sometimes walked around exhibits or events with staff to share insights on potential sensory triggers. While the group as a whole has been helpful, it also has been very beneficial to have the individual contacts within the group to reach out to with questions related to the continued development and expansion of sensory-friendly offerings.

From 2016 to 2019, these offerings included sensory-friendly events about four times per year. Then, in the fall of 2020, The Henry Ford received a grant from the Institute of Museum and Library Services to help expand its sensory-friendly programming. The grant had three main parts. One was expanding the number and variety of sensory-friendly events and offerings, which increased from four per year to at least fifteen per year. The second was developing a new program for teens and young adults with autism. The third was expanding staff training for interacting with individuals with autism (specifically, by creating a new e-learning staff training module). With the grant coming during the pandemic, The Henry Ford had to get creative about ways to continue having the offerings and events that staff said they would when the grant was written in 2019.

One way that The Henry Ford did this was by starting to have virtual sensory-friendly programs. These programs have continued since their start in 2020. Each virtual program has a theme, such as trains, baking, animation, racing, makers, or baseball. Staff include a variety of components in these programs, such as a movement activity, story, craft, music, and social time. Staff also create and send visual schedules (with text, images, and time estimates for each activity) to help prepare attendees for what to expect during the programs. Sometimes staff have also created take-home kits with materials that attendees could pick up in advance at the Henry Ford Museum of American Innovation, such as a kit of puppet-making materials that was created for a program held in connection with a traveling exhibit on Jim Henson.

The Henry Ford has had quite a bit of success including guest speakers in these programs, particularly individuals who are on the autism spectrum themselves and can share something related to the theme of the program. For example, during a baking-themed program, a teenager who is on the spectrum and has a baking business joined for a baking demonstration. During an animation-themed program, three people who are on the spectrum and passionate about animation shared their work. For instance, one talked about her blog ("The Autistic Animator's Desk"), another demonstrated how to draw a character, and the third narrated a video that he had created about his 2-D animation process. For a racing-themed program, a NASCAR driver on the spectrum talked about his journey to NASCAR, and for a baseball-themed program, an individual who has started an organization for people with autism to learn to play baseball inspired attendees with the story of his organization.

Overall, the virtual programs have given people who have similar interests an opportunity to connect, and there has been a regular group of attendees for each one. Many of the regular attendees have tended to be in their teens and twenties—an audience that The Henry Ford had intended to engage separately with an on-site program when writing the proposal for the grant but that they did not start offering until more than a year after the grant was received. The virtual programs have also allowed for more direct interaction with the attendees—something that was often missing with the large-scale on-site events.

Attendees are very appreciative of the virtual programs, with one family responding to a survey sent after the animation-themed program with the following comments:

> They LOVED absolutely everything about this program!! They were fully engaged, happy, excited! At the end, they walked out of the office with stars in their eyes and with such a look of excitement! Both girls want to work in art/animation/comics and to be able to listen to a real live animator was thrilling!! . . . We would ABSOLUTELY attend more of these amazing virtual sensory programs. . . . Thank you for seeing our kids for who they are and for going to them where they are and for INCLUDING them in the Wonderful Henry Ford programming. I'm so grateful you are giving our kids a "place" to be themselves while not discounting all the amazing things they may be capable of contributing to our world. *tears*

After developing a template that was found to be successful, staff discovered that they could keep using that template for all of the virtual programs for this audience. This template also proved to be effective for the institution's first on-site program for teens and young adults with autism—an audience that staff had talked about engaging for several years and finally did so for the first time in November 2021. As with the virtual programs, staff incorporates a variety of different components (such as a story, craft, scavenger hunt, and movie) into these on-site programs. Staff also create visual schedules like the ones for the virtual programs to walk attendees through what to expect.

As with the virtual programs, attendees (and their families) are very appreciative that the programs for teens and young adults are offered—in this case because there is quite a lack of programming available for this particular age-group. As one parent put it after a program during which the NASCAR driver mentioned earlier joined to share his experiences, "There are not many activities designed for young adult autistics. Thank you so much for filling this void and providing such a high quality, inspiring, and enjoyable event." Similarly, after the same program, another family mentioned, "This is the first time that autism has been shown in a positive way with adult content. She left feeling empowered and hopeful."

In addition to the virtual and teen/young adult programs, The Henry Ford has many other sensory-friendly events for all ages on site throughout the year. For example, there is a sensory-friendly movie each month (with the theme of the movie being connected with the virtual and on-site sensory-friendly program themes for each month). Sensory-friendly days are also offered in connection with exhibits and special events (such as Hallowe'en and Holiday Nights in Greenfield Village). While there is more demand for on-site events than virtual ones—and a need to use more staff time and resources to plan and hold those—there is still interest by this audience in virtual programs. As with the virtual verbal description programs, The Henry Ford plans to continue offering some virtual sensory-friendly programs, depending on demand, because having a combination of virtual and in-person programming allows for as many opportunities for engagement as possible.

PROGRAMS AT THE HENRY FORD FOR PEOPLE WHO ARE D/DEAF

In addition to the other audiences already discussed in this chapter, The Henry Ford has also had several events over the years for people who are d/Deaf and use American Sign Language (ASL). The first of these events—a Deaf Community Day—took place at the Henry Ford Museum of American Innovation in late 2016. The idea for this community event was born out of a realization that the institution was starting to offer quite a few accessibility programs and offerings for other audiences, but not yet for the d/Deaf community. In working with a local teacher of students who are d/Deaf, staff planned a day that included ASL interpreters stationed with museum presenters at various key artifacts around the museum. The attendees at the event received a map showing these locations and could visit each to experience a short presentation that was interpreted in ASL. The next year, staff tried something similar for Greenfield Village, with ASL interpreters stationed in several of the buildings throughout Greenfield Village. While these events were extremely popular with the d/Deaf community, and the feedback received was positive, unfortunately, due to staff time and resources being put toward other accessibility programs, they were not repeated on a regular basis.

After a couple of years of not having specialized programming for d/Deaf audiences, The Henry Ford was contacted by the Sign Language Studies Program Coordinator from Madonna University (a local university), who wondered if it would be possible to collaborate on an event involving their students who were learning to be interpreters. This collaborative event was held at the Henry Ford Museum of American Innovation in 2019. During the event, student interpreters from Madonna University were paired with certified sign language interpreters at various sites throughout the museum. The d/Deaf community was invited to attend and, once again, the feedback was positive.

In 2020 and again in 2021, The Henry Ford intended to hold a similar type of event with Madonna University in Greenfield Village. Unfortunately, both times, the event was canceled due to the pandemic. In 2021, however, the planned on-site event was converted into a virtual program. For this program, students from Madonna interpreted presentations that were given virtually by curators from The Henry Ford (with the interpreters and curators each joining via their own computers). The recordings of these programs were then captioned and shared with individuals from the d/Deaf Community.

Presenting virtual programs was a great opportunity to try out a specialized program for the local d/Deaf and hard of hearing communities. If resources allow, The Henry Ford plans on doing more programs for this audience in the future, either virtually or in person.

PROGRAMS AT THE HENRY FORD FOR PEOPLE WHO ARE LIVING WITH DEMENTIA AND THEIR CARE PARTNERS

Since 2017, The Henry Ford has been collaborating with the Alzheimer's Association Michigan Chapter to provide programming for people who are living with dementia and their care partners. This program, which is called the Bruce H. and Rosalie N. Rosen Community Connect Program, "provides people living with Alzheimer's disease and other forms of dementia and their care partners a broad range of free (unless otherwise noted) social and cultural opportunities throughout Metro Detroit."[5] The Alzheimer's Association handles the registration and marketing, while The Henry Ford provides the content.

The Henry Ford started collaborating with the Alzheimer's Association after they contacted the institution expressing interest in bringing a group to visit. After several pilot programs in 2017, the institution started having a program on site once per month in 2018, each with a different theme. Themes have ranged from Summertime Travel to Road Food (such as diners and fast-food restaurants) to the Space Race to Baseball to Gardens of Greenfield Village. The programs, which are two hours in length when on site, include stops throughout the Henry Ford Museum of American Innovation, Greenfield Village, or the Ford Rouge Factory Tour. Several of the programs have included a snack or food component related to the theme, such as pie and other samples of diner food for the Road Food–themed program.

Collaborating with the Alzheimer's Association has also made it possible to tap into their already-existing contacts with the Detroit Symphony Orchestra (DSO) and, as a result, to have collaborative programs involving all three organizations. For example, a musician from the DSO once played one of the violins from Henry Ford's collection (these violins are not played very often, so that was a special treat). One participant said that this event was one of the best hours of his life. Another program focused on Henry Ford's interest in and revival of old-fashioned dancing. During this program, a string quartet from the DSO played songs that Henry Ford and others would have danced to, and participants did some dancing. These collaborative programs have always been popular and well attended.

Once the pandemic started, The Henry Ford stopped offering in-person programs for people with dementia. After a few months of observing other museums' virtual programs, The Henry Ford started to offer these programs virtually. Offered until May 2022, the virtual programs were an hour long, half as long as the in-person programs. They typically included a presentation from a curator and questions aimed at fostering conversation and sparking memories.

As with the in-person programs, the goal was to have topics that participants could relate to from their lives. For example, topics included the following: amusement parks, clothing, the evolution of luggage design, the invention of the chocolate chip cookie, holidays, and the evolution of wristwatches. It was particularly fun and brought a sense of connection when participants were encouraged to bring and share something from their homes that connected with the theme of the program. For example, during an ice cream–themed program, people were encouraged to enjoy ice cream from their homes while listening to the presentation. That was one of the most fun and memorable virtual programs!

In 2020 and 2021, The Henry Ford, Alzheimer's Association, and DSO continued their three-way collaboration through virtual programming. For

Figure 8.2. Attendees to a virtual Community Connect program hold up ice cream that they brought to tie in with the program's theme for the day. *Courtesy Caroline Braden*

example, in 2021, a program was held in connection with a temporary exhibit at The Henry Ford called *The Jim Henson Exhibition: Imagination Unlimited*. For this program, the DSO musicians played and recorded three songs while in the exhibit. The recordings were shared during the program and the musicians joined the program live to answer questions about the music and their instruments. A curator from The Henry Ford also shared information about the exhibit. Collaborative virtual programs like this were just as unique and well received as the ones that had been held in person.

Overall, for this audience, the virtual programs allowed people to attend from a wider geographical range, in addition to people who may not have previously felt like spending the time and energy to come on site to a program. The virtual programs were less time-consuming and complicated to plan and implement and did not have the complexity of on-site setup. They also allowed for presentations of artifacts that would have been more difficult to show in person (such as large pieces of luggage for the luggage-themed program). Participants' microphones were generally left unmuted during the virtual programs, which helped with spontaneous conversation, and there were not too many issues with background noise or having to mute people (although that was always an option).

While there were many positives to the virtual programs, there were also some negatives. For example, when programs are in person, both the husband and wife or the care partner and the person they are taking care of are part of the same shared experience. With the virtual programs, however, oftentimes the spouse or care partner would turn on the computer screen and leave it on for the person with dementia to just sit and watch, while the person without dementia did other things, so it was not as much of a shared experience. There was also a general decrease in the total number of participants in the virtual programs throughout 2021 as new opportunities for in-person engagement became available and people were not as available or interested in attending virtual programs.

From July 2020 until May 2022, The Henry Ford held only virtual programs for this audience. That almost changed several times in 2021, as the Alzheimer's Association was ready to go back to in-person programs. However, so few people registered for the in-person programs that three programs in a row had to be canceled. It seemed like participants were not ready yet to be back in person. Additionally, with participants growing older over the two years, some were no longer comfortable driving and others had changed their living situations. Also, with some people now attending virtually from farther away that meant that they would have quite a long distance to travel for an in-person program.

When in-person programs did start again, the groups that came in the first couple of months were quite small. Over time, the sizes of the groups have grown. There have been numerous comments about how appreciative people are to be back visiting in person and there has been more interaction between the care partner and the person living with dementia than for the virtual programs.

For people who are living with dementia and their care partners, there are benefits to both virtual and in-person programs. Thus, The Henry Ford will likely have a combination of both moving forward. For example, there may be more virtual programs during the snowier months when it is more difficult to travel to on-site programs and more on-site programs during the warmer months. If not for the pandemic, The Henry Ford likely would not have started virtual programs for this—or any—accessibility audiences, so having that now does provide opportunities for more flexibility in the future.

FINAL THOUGHTS

Though most of the accessibility programming at The Henry Ford began prior to the COVID-19 pandemic, the pandemic led to significant evolutions, impacting the types of programs offered by the institution, the format of those, and how audiences are served through them. It is likely that at least some of the virtual programs that started during the pandemic are here to stay. They make it possible to reach a broader audience from a wider geographical area, enable audiences to have different ways of engaging with the institution, provide time and space for connection with and between participants, and allow for access by people who may not be comfortable or able to visit in person. However, some accessibility programs have worked better virtually than others. For example, while virtual verbal description programs have been very successful for The Henry Ford, virtual programs for people with dementia (which worked well early in the pandemic) fell off in numbers as other in-person engagement opportunities presented themselves. Additionally, several of the in-person programs mentioned (such as the sensory-friendly programming) have experienced their own evolutions in ways that will impact them moving forward.

The evolution of all of The Henry Ford's accessibility programs—and the insights gained from them—will continue to inform how the institution serves its audiences in the future, enabling staff to use what has been learned during the pandemic to provide programming that helps people of all ages and abilities feel welcome, included, and engaged.

NOTES

1. Deaf with a capital "D" means people who identify as culturally Deaf and are actively involved in the Deaf community, usually having a shared sign language. Lowercase "d" deaf refers to the physical condition of having hearing loss. People who identify as deaf do not necessarily have a strong connection to the Deaf community or use sign language. For more information, see AI-Media, "The Difference Between d/Deaf and Hard-of-Hearing," accessed September 7, 2022, https://www.ai-media.tv/ai -media-blog/the-difference-between-d-deaf-and-hard-of-hearing-2/.

2. There are a variety of low-cost, creative ways to create tactile objects for touch tours/experiences. For example, clear glue or puff paint can be used for simple, do-it-yourself raised-line graphics. It is also possible to use a Swell Form Graphics Machine to create more intricate tactile maps, diagrams, and raised images. Replicas or reproductions are another possibility, as are sensory items like feathers or velvet, which can be used to mimic the textures of objects.
3. At The Henry Ford, the term "sensory-friendly" is used to refer to events for people who are on the autism spectrum or have sensory processing disorders. There are many other terms used to refer to the same types of events, including low sensory, sensory inclusive, sensory sensitive, etc.
4. For more information on autism, see Centers for Disease Control and Prevention, "What Is Autism Spectrum Disorder?" last modified March 31, 2022, https://www .cdc.gov/ncbddd/autism/facts.html. For more about how museums are supporting visitors who are on the autism spectrum, see Aditi Shrikant, "How Museums Are Becoming More Sensory-Friendly for Those with Autism," *Smithsonian Magazine*, January 5, 2018, https://www.smithsonianmag.com/innovation/how-museums -are-becoming-more-sensory-friendly-for-those-with-autism-180967740/.
5. For more information about the Alzheimer's Association Michigan Chapter's social engagement programs, see Alzheimer's Association, "Michigan Chapter Social Engagement Programs," accessed September 7, 2022, https://www.alz.org/gmc/ helping_you/social_engagement.

9

Making Vanishing Structures Accessible

PROVIDING VIRTUAL TOURS OF ENDANGERED HISTORIC SITES
IN LOUISIANA

Megan S. Reed

It all started with a question: Can we create 3-D replicas of historic sites that address accessibility concerns? The question of how to create virtual tours has been circulating for many years, but for most cultural institutions, it never became a top priority. That changed in 2020 when the COVID-19 pandemic was identified in the United States. Cultural institutions and stewards of historic sites including the National Park Service were forced to rethink public accessibility to their sites while following legal compliance to ensure reasonable access for those with disabilities. This shifted the question to: Could the National Park Service create a virtual 3-D space that would give visitors an online experience similar to being physically present at the site while addressing accessibility needs for all audience members, including those with disabilities?

There are many applications for 3-D technology, being that it is easily accessible, widens exposure, and provides entertainment to the public.[1] However, as with any technology, there are some concerns and challenges with its use. The world of 3-D technology is not only constantly evolving, but accessibility guidelines continue to be researched and developed for the use of these online products.[2] This presented a challenge for the National Park Service when trying to create an online virtual tour as not all digital spaces can easily conform to digital accessibility regulations.

Since 2019, staff at the National Center for Preservation Technology and Training (NCPTT), a unit of the National Park Service, began researching 3-D technology as a potential tool to record historical sites, develop preservation methods, and increase audience exposure to underrepresented historical sites. As part of this study, NCPTT tested the Matterport platform (described in detail shortly) to create a more interactive and engaging tour that still conforms to current federal Section 508 accessibility regulations. This chapter discusses the ways NCPTT addressed different accessibility concerns of historic sites located in Louisiana (where NCPTT is based) when creating virtual tours and dives into the different ways 3-D tour platforms, including Matterport, can be leveraged to address these concerns to tell the different stories of sites that are in danger of being lost.

IDENTIFYING ACCESSIBILITY CONCERNS

When trying to choose a virtual platform, NCPTT first had to identify the challenges that the historic sites face when addressing accessibility to their institution. NCPTT staff noted that some institutions had cut down public access to their sites due to limitations of staff or resources. Other sites are not able to be open to the public because they cannot meet certain accessibility standards, such as wheelchair access, and are not able to modify their buildings or landscapes. NCPTT staff also noted that sites in Louisiana such as the Cane River National Heritage Area and El Camino Real National Heritage Trail do not actually own all the historic properties they interpret, and some buildings are privately owned by individuals. Staff also noted historic parks and sites, such as Cane River Creole National Historical Park, are in rural areas not easily accessible to the public and do not have consistent access to cellular or internet connections. Staff also noted another common concern by cultural institutions is historic sites that are in danger of being destroyed by natural disasters such as hurricanes or tornados and/or lack of resources to maintain the buildings.

The second concern NCPTT staff had was making sure that the virtual tour platform met compliance regulations with Section 508 of the Rehabilitation Act of 1973. The National Park Service, like all federal agencies, must follow federal regulations when sharing electronic information with the public. This includes compliance with Section 508 of the Rehabilitation Act of 1973, which requires information to be independently accessible by those with disabilities, including, but not limited to, those with mobile, cognitive, audio, and visual disabilities.[3] Section 508 was updated in 1998 as advances in digital technology evolved since the 1970s and required that the act be amended to ensure that accessibility is provided to all individuals with disabilities.[4]

The National Park Service, as a unit of the Department of the Interior, strives to meet and exceed these standards when it comes to addressing digital technology and access.[5] Following the guidelines set by the Department of the Interior, the National Park Service outlined requirements for all audio and visual media to meet Section 508 by providing captions for all who have a hearing disability and verbal descriptions for all who have a visual disability.[6] While the use of 3-D technology addresses many accessibility concerns around physical access to a space such as rough ground, stairs, ladders, or narrow doorways, challenges arose when trying to ensure reasonable access to those with visual disabilities. At the time this chapter was written, the world of 3-D technology did not offer many accessibility options that conform to making online spaces welcoming to visitors who are blind or have low vision.[7]

CHOOSING A VIRTUAL TOUR PLATFORM

NCPTT staff considered many things when choosing a virtual tour platform: first, it had to address all the accessibility concerns mentioned earlier; second, staff wanted to test the flexibility of camera options, clarity of the images, ease of use for all users, and importing different content files. While non-3-D virtual tours also allow people to visit faraway sites from the comfort of their own homes with the use of an internet connection, 3-D technology allows visitors to virtually immerse themselves into the tour space as though they are present inside the property. Further, 3-D tours offer the option to engage in areas of the site that may not normally be open to the public. This technology provides additional access to people who otherwise would be unable to explore the site, whether due to physical or travel limitations.

Matterport was chosen after the staff explored different options for virtual platforms. The combination of Matterport's interpretive features and flexibility of camera choices allowed NCPTT staff to test and assess the boundaries

Figure 9.1. Screenshot of MatterTags and the SearchWindow in Matterport tour of Slave Cabin One. *Courtesy National Park Service*

Making Vanishing Structures Accessible

of the platform to confirm that it is an option that will meet all requirements for creating a 3-D virtual tour.

KEY MATTERPORT FEATURES TO ADDRESS ACCESSIBILITY

When looking at platforms for a 3-D tour, sites need to be sure to look at how flexible the platform is as well as the types of options available to both users and designers. NCPTT staff was drawn to Matterport due to its incredibly flexible features that allow for a vast array of interpretation strategies for historic sites. Matterport's "Tag" feature permits tour designers to add detailed information about the space as a virtual pin for users to access during the tour.[8] Each tag is enabled with a variety of different functions including the opportunity to embed multiple media formats, such as images, audio tracks, videos, PDFs, and website URLs for visitors to explore. The color of each tag can be customized using contrasting color options or icons that make it easier for those who are color blind or have low vison to be able to see pins within the space and identify

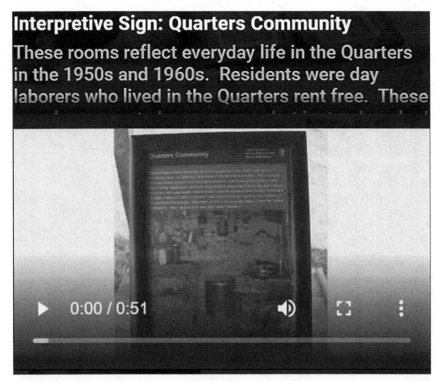

Figure 9.2.1. Screenshot of the images with alternative text descriptions, captions and audio description of Interpretative signs and photography at Slave Cabin One. *Courtesy National Park Service*

Inside the image:

Image: Photograph of the Cabins taken November 1904

Historic photograph of the cabins with a large tree in the center. A large group of people are standing in front the tree.

Figure 9.2.2. *Courtesy National Park Service*

different types of information. The tags allow historic sites to directly upload media files, such as historic photography, to the tours without the need to host the data in an external online location. NCPTT utilizes this feature to add historical background materials and ensure that all content had captions and audio descriptions made specifically for their tours.[9]

An extended feature of tags that the team found beneficial for users is the ability to create a hyperlink URL to another location within the space or to link to another virtual tour that is related to the site. This makes it possible for a person viewing the dining room to click on an embedded URL link within the tag and immediately enter another room, such as the bedroom, without having to move virtually through each of the in-between spaces. This feature offers more flexibility and navigation assistance to those who may have trouble orienting the space with either the hotkeys and/or the mouse while also assisting those who cannot visually comprehend or navigate a 2-D image on a computer screen easily. The Matterport system has internal program hotkeys using preprogrammed keyboard shortcuts and the arrow keys instead of using the mouse that allow the users to navigate the virtual space.[10] This gives users more flexibility to explore the space and conforms to the guidance set by the Web Content Accessibility Guidelines initiative to expand functionality to the keyboard.[11]

Matterport has a search button feature that includes a complete list of the embedded tags along with their corresponding information, such as label spaces, saved measurements, and interpretive notes.[12] Those with hearing or visual disabilities can use the search feature to locate tags that include audio or visual descriptions and access those tags within the search feature. This feature allows the information in the tags to be read by a screen reader. Tour designers can also reorder the tag list in the search function to sort the information for easier navigation.[13]

One of the features NCPTT was looking for in creating a tour was end-user functionality on both computers and mobile devices. Matterport spaces can be opened on a mobile device and users can access all the features while on the go or while visiting the site. There are a few aspects of virtual tours that can create challenges for both historic sites and visitor users. First, visitors must either have the URL link or must navigate to find the link on the site's website or search for it on Matterport's "Discover" page to access the space remotely. Second, not all historic sites or museums are located in areas that have clear, unlimited access to network services. If this applies to your site, be sure to keep this in mind as you are exploring platform options. Given the remote location of the Cane River Creole National Historical Park and many other National Park Service sites, NCPTT explored platforms that include offline tour options. Having a downloadable tour allows sites to present their tour spaces without the need for internet connectivity.[14] Historic sites can purchase and/or use a tablet to showcase their virtual tour while giving a physical tour on site, or visitors can download the tour prior to their visit. This opens accessibility to visitors who may not be able to follow along on an in-person tour due to a disability and allows more flexibility to explore the space at their leisure.[15]

FLEXIBLE CAMERA OPTIONS TO CAPTURE THE SPACE

The second key feature of Matterport is the availability of camera options to capture the space. Matterport relies on a mobile app called Capture to scan and upload the spaces to an online cloud account platform, leaving users plenty of camera options to use to capture the space from a smartphone camera or an external 360 camera. There are a wide variety of 3-D cameras available on the market and Matterport offers a list of compatible 360 cameras with their software including the Theta Rioch and the Insta360 cameras.[16]

NCPTT staff tested capturing a space using a smartphone camera and external 360 cameras. As part of this test, NCPTT decided to experiment with the Theta 360 camera and Matterport's own high-performance 360-degree cameras called the Matterport Pro2 and Pro3 to provide the best virtual tour options for historic sites.[17] The NCPTT team found that when using a smartphone to capture images, there was some image distortion. While this result is not ideal, using a smartphone to capture and create a 3-D virtual tour is still an option. The Pro2 camera contains a set of nine lenses to capture the floor, ceiling, and eye-level spaces at the same time. This combination of camera lenses and angles aids in reducing image distortion seen in captures made with smartphones. The Pro3 camera has a single high-performance lens that allows the user to capture exterior spaces such as gardens and monuments as well as interior spaces. While these cameras are a higher-budget option and the spaces created with the camera can only be uploaded to a professional or business account through Matterport, cultural institutions can still use this technology through services offered by NCPTT or through Matterport's online services.[18]

A final benefit of using the Matterport platform is the different account options for their account holders. Matterport offers cultural sites the option of either a free or a subscription account with a monthly or yearly fee. A free account offers one private digital space, not shareable with the public. A starter subscription account includes five digital spaces, whereas a professional account includes up to twenty-five spaces, both shareable with the public. Cost, of course, depends on the subscription level, and there are discounts for annual versus monthly subscriptions. Higher-level plans are also available for those who need them.[19] While most historic sites may never need to have twenty-five or more tour spaces, cultural institutions can have the option to start out with either the free or starter account and then grow to a professional account as they so choose.[20]

For organizations that wish to use a 3-D camera to create a tour but cannot afford to purchase one themselves, Matterport does offer the option to transfer spaces between account owners, providing a low-cost option for these museums or historic sites. This provides cultural institutions the option of paying a one-time service fee for having someone with a higher-level account create the virtual tour space using the images scanned with the higher-quality 3-D camera and then transferring the tour to the institution's account with maintaining the annual lower subscription cost afterward.[21]

CASE SUBJECTS

NCPTT decided to team up with their neighbor, the National Park Service's Cane River Creole National Historical Park and the owners of the Faerie Playhouse located in New Orleans, Louisiana, to test the suitability of Matterport for creating fully accessible virtual tours. NCPTT conducted its first test at Cane River Creole National Historical Park and focused on creating an interactive tour of one of the slave cabins located at Magnolia Plantation on the site to increase accessibility to that part of the park's story. At the Faerie Playhouse, NCPTT focused on creating an engaging interactive tour of the private home that is at risk of disappearing (more on this shortly). Both sites not only address all the accessibility concerns mentioned earlier in this chapter, but they also both represent uplifting the voices of minority groups whose histories are lesser known to the public.

CASE STUDY ONE: MAGNOLIA PLANTATION IN NATCHITOCHES

Cane River Creole National Historical Park is the home of two of the largest plantation sites still existing in the state of Louisiana. The park is also a part of the Cane River National Heritage Area and El Camino Real National Heritage Trail. Oakland and Magnolia Plantations are located along the Cane River in a rural area of northwestern Louisiana, south of the city of Natchitoches (famous for its meat pies and *Steel Magnolias*). These plantations provide visitors with the unique experience of exploring some of the original historic structures from the time when they were still part of a functioning cotton farm.[22]

Magnolia Plantation was founded by Jean Baptiste LeComte in 1753 as a tobacco farm and was then later converted to a prosperous cotton farm by his son Ambroise LeComte. Magnolia, like its neighboring plantations, relied heavily on an enslaved workforce to farm the land. During its functioning years as a farm, it was estimated that there were about 275 enslaved people living within seventy cabins at Magnolia Plantation. By the end of the Civil War, many of the formerly enslaved workers remained on the plantation to work as part of the newly formed

Figure 9.3. Overview of Magnolia Plantation. *Courtesy Megan S. Reed*

Chapter 9

sharecropping system in the South. Even after the rise of the Civil Rights Movement, sharecropping lasted well into the 1970s with families still living in the original two-room brick structures built during the time of slavery. Of the seventy original slave structures, only eight buildings still exist on the property today.[23]

Due to the park's rural location, the park warns its visitors that smartphone map and navigation apps are not able to accurately direct a visitor to the site. Additionally, in 2018 a section of Highway 119 that lies north of the park's entrance washed out and remains closed to all traffic, which causes confusion to travelers when visiting the area who are not aware of the closure. There is now only one entrance to access the park, located on the southern boundary. The park's eight extant slave and tenant farming houses are currently located on the opposite side of the park's gravel parking lot across a large open field; a single gravel path and a wooden bridge separate the two areas.

Only one house, located at the southern end of the row, is open to visitors. To protect the historic integrity of the building, the park has closed off parts of the house; visitors can only access areas around the front doors and the door connecting the two rooms. The narrow spaces make accessibility difficult for those with disabilities to explore the site on their own. It is these accessibility concerns that drew NCPTT to the cabin as a test subject for the Matterport virtual tours.

CASE STUDY TWO: THE FAERIE PLAYHOUSE IN NEW ORLEANS

The Faerie Playhouse is located in the northeast part of New Orleans, Louisiana, on Esplanade Avenue. The house was once the home of Stewart Butler, a famous activist for the LBGTQ+ community in the 1970s in New Orleans. His home became the site of many LBGTQ+ activist and civil rights movements during the late twentieth century and early twenty-first century. When he passed away in 2020, Stewart left his home to a nearby community church with the caveat that Stewart's caretaker could remain in the house for however long he wishes, and the church can take ownership when he leaves. The church is discussing alternative methods to use the building once it fully takes control of the property. Since Stewart's passing, his caretaker has maintained the home the same as when Stewart and his partner, Alfred Doolittle, were alive. The house is thus a time capsule of Stewart and Alfred's lives and the communities they were a part of with all their collections still intact. The LBGTQ+ community of New Orleans is advocating to keep the house as a community space in some form. Because the home is owned by a private entity, it is not open to the public. The house has narrow alleyways both in front and on the side, making wheelchair access ramps impossible to add and making it less likely the house would be open for public tours. The house and its collection are in danger of being demolished, sold, or altered from their current state. It is these accessibility concerns and a chance to take a snapshot of a home that holds so much meaning for the community that drew NCPTT to use the home as a test subject for a virtual tour.

CAPTURING THE SPACES

The NCPTT team decided to use the slave cabin at Magnolia Plantation as the first test pilot of the virtual tour program in the fall of 2021 and identify challenges and potential solutions. It is essential to test out a new program and take the time to develop a standard operating procedure (SOP) to check for bugs and obstacles prior to the start of any project. The Faerie Playhouse was documented in the summer of 2022 to test the new SOP based on the issues that arose at Magnolia Plantation. At both locations, the team used both the Matterport Pro2 and the Theta 360 cameras to compare and test the different methods to capture the spaces at both sites.

Before scanning either site, a site review was conducted to remove any items that might detract from the visitor experience during the tour. At the slave cabin, the team first tidied the site, removing the stanchions, notice signs, and any other equipment that was not related to the cabin or the exhibit display. After the space had been staged, the team walked around the site to determine how a visitor would explore the space and what key features needed to be highlighted in a virtual tour. The positions of the camera would later become the viewing locations for visitors to move around the digital space, so it was important to decide the positions and locations of the camera within the space. Because the cabin is a small space, it didn't require many setup placements to capture all the interpretive features of the building. After agreeing on the camera's location, the team set out to capture the interior space using the Matterport Pro 2 3-D camera.

Two team members began by opening the Matterport Capture app on both their iPhone and Android phones respectively. Once the NCPTT team verified that both users could use the app and connect to the Pro2 camera, they began capturing the interior of the historic site. Once the camera finished, the images were uploaded to the app and then the program began automatically aligning the data in the digital space. Capturing the interior space took a little over an hour as team members practiced understanding how the app worked and overcoming errors that occurred during its usage. For example, one challenge identified during the capturing process at Magnolia was that if two users were logged into the same account on their respective mobile devices, once capturing the site began on one device, it had to be finished using the same device. As a result, one team member completed the capturing process of the space while another team member set out to photograph all the interpretative signs and images displayed on the site to later be added during postprocessing. A second challenge identified was the distance between the controlling mobile device and the camera—in order to not be included in the scan, the team members had to hide from the camera but could not be too far away or the connection between the camera and the mobile phone would be severed.

To resolve these issues when scanning at the Faerie Playhouse, the team purchased an Apple iPad Pro tablet to use with the Capture app and cameras.

Figure 9.4.1. NCPTT's staff setting up the Matterport Pro2 Camera and the Theta 360 camera for digital capture. *Courtesy National Park Service*

This allows the team members to switch places in taking turns to capture the space by passing the individual tablet between the members. Further, the connection distance between the iPad and the camera was found to be greater than that between the camera and a cell phone. Unlike the slave cabin, the Faerie Playhouse has a much more complicated interior. The building is larger with many rooms, separated by narrow doorways. The space also includes hundreds of interpretative features that needed to be collected and the rooms had several reflective surfaces including mirrors and glass, requiring the team to work around to avoid being seen by the camera. As a result, it took more scan setups to capture the space using the Matterport Pro2 to not only highlight all of the interpretive features of the space but to ensure that there was enough overlap between the image setups for the program to correctly align in the digital space.

After the interior scans of the sites were completed, the team members set out to test capturing the exterior surroundings of the buildings. While it was possible to capture the outside space of a building, NCPTT does not recommend it unless certain conditions are met such as sufficient shade from clouds, trees, or other buildings to block the sun's infrared radiation that interferes with the Capture app's ability to align the images from the cameras correctly. Unfortunately, at the slave cabin, the environment surrounding the building was an open space, free of any trees or tall buildings that could have offered any shade or blockage of sunlight. Even after switching to both the Theta 360 camera and the team members' mobile devices, the team was unable to successfully

Figure 9.4.2. *Courtesy National Park Service*

capture the exterior space in 3-D for "walkable" tour locations. Instead, the team decided to take 2-D panoramic photography images of the outside using Matterport's 360 Photography option on the camera.

Unlike the slave cabin, the Faerie Playhouse is located on an urban street, surrounded by both tall buildings and trees that offer coverage from the sunlight. The team members noted the sun's position over the building and worked around the sun's path during the capture process. The team used the Theta 360 camera to capture portions of the exterior of the building where the shade cover was thinner. One challenge that arose when using the Theta was noticing how unstable the camera was within the environment. Because the Theta is set up with a monostand (a thin pole with three feet at the base) it was easily destabilized by wind and with any vibrations that occurred around the camera in the city. Another issue noted was that it took the Capture app longer to process the images with the Theta 360 than the Matterport Pro2. Due to these obstacles, the team would often have to redo the capture setups with the Theta 360 camera. Despite these setbacks, the team members were able to successfully capture the exterior of both the front of the Faerie Playhouse and the backyard. Once the team confirmed that they captured the spaces they uploaded the 3-D rendering to their Matterport cloud account.

MEETING SECTION 508 COMPLIANCY USING MATTERPORT FEATURES

After the uploads were complete, the team was able to review the features mentioned earlier in this chapter to make the virtual tour spaces Section 508 compliant. Prior to the August 2022 updates, Matterport could only link media files that were hosted on an external media platform. For this reason, the slave cabin tour only has media embedded from alternate platforms. The team was able to add YouTube videos; media from Flickr, Instagram, Facebook, and Twitter posts; and a 3-D model of the cabin. For the Faerie Playhouse, the team utilized all the available features to test how different media could be directly uploaded to a tour. The team was able to upload audio and video files, PDF documents, and images to the tags.

The team tested how to add captions and audio descriptions to all the images and interpretative signs displayed at the sites. The team used Flickr to host all the media files for interpreting the slave cabin and then embedded the media in the tour. One team member created an audio narration for all the interpretive signs at the cabin by reading the text aloud over a PowerPoint presentation of the image that was then exported as an MP4 video. The resulting video was uploaded to Flickr and then added as a tag feature to the tour. The team continued adding images of the photography and typing out the alternative text captions for each image in the tags. For the Faerie Playhouse, the team decided to maintain the same method to combine audio files with images in videos, but instead hosted the videos on YouTube. With the August 2022 updates, all the photography and documents were directly added to the tags with descriptive captions that could later be used by screen readers in the search feature.[24] To make content easier for users with screen readers to identify quickly, staff added heading labels and descriptive titles to each of the tags and reordered the tags to sort them by room location.[25] The team also included hyperlinks to connect the common areas of interest within the tour and to assist with navigating between the interior and exterior spaces.

The team also tested to see if captions could be added to the 2-D panoramic images the team took to capture the exterior of the slave cabin and its surrounding landscape as an alternative to the missing 3-D "walkable" tour space. Unfortunately, there was no way to add alternative text captions to the images. The team realized, however, that you can add the images as interpretative tags with alternative text captions instead. It is important when choosing a platform to check that the media files can include descriptive text.

The Matterport tag default color is a blue-green, but each tag has the option to be customized by the account owners. For the slave cabin, NCPTT staff color-coded the tags for each type of media: blue for images and interpretive signs, red for orientations, and yellow for the 3-D model. When choosing the colors, NCPTT staff ensured that there was sufficient contrast for someone with color blindness to be able to identify the differences in tag color and type. While with the Faerie Playhouse, staff decide to stick with one contrasting color, yellow, but used the icon options within the tags to differentiate between the different media files within the tour.

The final task was to create a walkthrough tour complete with audio narration to describe the space. A team member utilized Matterport's Highlight Reel feature to create a walkthrough video tour of the entire building.[26] They created stopping points in each room of the tour to allow time for narrative descriptions to be added later. Staff then added one of the 360 photographs of the outside at the end of the tour to add a description of the outside space at the historic site. NCPTT staff then screen recorded the walkthrough tour and added the verbal description narration to the video. A similar process was followed to create a walk-through video of the Faerie Playhouse, with the audio description combining visual descriptions along with historic information.[27]

CONCLUSIONS

The National Park Service's National Center for Preservation Technology and Training began this project to address not only the accessibility concerns brought up by cultural institutions but also to test if virtual tour platform features could be used to meet the federal Section 508 mandate for accessibility.[28] Regardless of the platform or specific camera, the case studies presented here offer valuable lessons in what accessibility features can and should be incorporated into your virtual 3-D tour.

Chapter 9

One lesson was understanding the basics of how the software worked to stitch together the images taken. There needs to be enough overlap between scanning locations for the program to stitch the captured images to create the 3-D space, this is true regardless of the camera type you use. Another is understanding which camera is best to use for the spaces. For interior spaces, mobile devices and 360 cameras are an option. However, if cultural institutes are trying to capture any exterior or outside features, they will need to consider how the sunlight will affect their digital space. Currently, only the Matterport Pro3 can successfully capture exterior spaces on their 3-D platform.

Matterport offers flexible options to fit any cultural institution's budget or needs. If the institution has a higher budget, they can hire a technician or buy their own Matterport camera to create their space with the high subscription package. A lower-cost option is for the institutions to buy their own compatible 360 camera available on the market such as the Insta360 Camera or the Ricoh Theta camera, like the one mentioned earlier, and combine it with the starter or professional subscription. A low-cost option for museums is to create the tour space with a smartphone or tablet and only pay for the annual subscription cost for their tour. If cultural institutions truly want a low-budget tour, an alternative option is to create their tour space with their mobile devices uploaded to the free account then use the highlight reel option to create a video animation of the space as an MP4 and post it on their website.

When testing began, it was uncertain whether the Matterport program features were sufficient to meet federal needs and regulations. With Matterport's newest updates and features in May 2022, cultural institutions including those within federal agencies can now have the option to leverage all that Matterport has to offer to create fully compliant 3-D virtual tours for all their visitors.

The research center at NCPTT is dedicated to exploring how we can push the boundaries of technology in ways that can benefit not just the National Park Service but all fields within Cultural Resources. NCPTT staff are excited to be able to offer Matterport 3-D technology as part of their technology suite to create 3-D virtual tours for historic sites. Both the Magnolia Plantation slave cabin and the Faerie Playhouse virtual tours are now available to the public. The tour of the slave cabin can be viewed on the Cane River Creole National Historical Park website. The Faerie Playhouse tour is currently available on LGBT+ Archives Project of Louisiana and on the NCPTT website. Both tours can also be viewed through the Matterport Discover gallery. NCPTT is continuing to explore innovative ways that 3-D virtual tours can be used to tell unique stories and highlight different aspects of history at historic sites.

NOTES

1. Jennifer Moore, Adam Rountrey, and Hannah Scates Kettler, "3D Data Creation to Curation: Building Community Standards for 3D Data Preservation," American

Library Association, 2022, 269, accessed July 14, 2022, https://www.ala.org/acrl/sites/ala.org.acrl/files/content/publications/booksanddigitalresources/digital/9780838939147_3D_OA.pdf.

2. Moore, Rountrey, and Kettler, "3D Data Creation to Curation," 271.
3. Section508. "Integrating Accessibility into Agency Diversity, Equity, Inclusion and Accessibility (DEIA) Implementation Plans," last modified December 20, 2021, accessed July 14, 2022, https://www.section508.gov/manage/deia-guidance/
4. US Access Board, "Section 508 (Federal Electronic and Information Technology)," n.d., accessed July 14, 2022, https://www.access-board.gov/law/ra.html#section-508-federal-electronic-and-information-technology.
5. US Department of the Interior, "Accessibility Statement," n.d., accessed July 14, 2022, https://www.doi.gov/accessibility.
6. Sylvia Burn, "Requirements to Create Accessible Audio and Visual Media," US Department of the Interior, September 7, 2017, accessed July 14, 2022, https://www.doi.gov/sites/doi.gov/files/uploads/ocio_directive_2017-003_requirement _to_create_accessible_audio_visual_media_-_signed_07sep17_2_2_0.pdf.
7. Moore, Rountrey, and Kettler, "3D Data Creation to Curation."
8. Matterport, "Add Tags to Your Space," last modified April 6, 2023, accessed July 14, 2022, https://support.matterport.com/s/article/Create-a-Mattertag-Post?language=en_US#reorder-new-tags.
9. Matterport, "Add Tags to Your Space."
10. Matterport, "Keyboard Shortcuts for 3D Showcase & Workshop," last modified April 7, 2022, accessed July 14, 2022, https://support.matterport.com/s/article/Keyboard-Shortcuts-for-3D-Showcase-Workshop?language=en_US.
11. Web Accessibility Initiative, "Web Content Accessibility Guidelines (WCAG) Overview," 2005, last modified June 30, 2022, https://www.w3.org/WAI/standards-guidelines/wcag/.
12. Paul Reynolds, "Matterport Space Search Now Available," Matterport, last modified July 19, 2022, accessed July 19, 2022, https://matterport.com/blog/matterport-space-search-now-available.
13. Matterport, "Add Tags to Your Space."
14. Matterport, "Introducing 3D Showcase for iOS," last modified July 19, 2022, accessed July 19, 2022, https://matterport.com/blog/introducing-3d-showcase-ios.
15. Matterport, "Introducing 3D Showcase for iOS."
16. Matterport, "Supported 360 Spherical Cameras," last modified April 13, 2023, https://support.matterport.com/s/article/Supported-360-Spherical-Cameras?language=en_US&categfilter=&parentCategoryLabel=.
17. Matterport, "Meet the World's Leading Spatial Data Platform," last modified 2022, accessed July 14, 2022, https://matterport.com/.
18. Matterport, "Meet the World's Leading Spatial Data Platform."
19. Matterport, "Meet the World's Leading Spatial Data Platform."
20. Matterport, "How to Transfer a Space Between Organizations," last modified March 17, 2023, accessed May 8, 2023, https://support.matterport.com/s/article/How-To-Transfer-a-Space-Between-Organizations?language=en_US.
21. Matterport, "How to Transfer a Space Between Organizations."

22. National Park Service, "Magnolia Plantation," last modified November 6, 2021, accessed July 14, 2022, https://www.nps.gov/cari/learn/historyculture/magnolia-plantation-history.htm.

23. National Park Service, "Magnolia Plantation."

24. Reynolds, "Matterport Space Search Now Available."

25. Matterport, "Add Tags to Your Space."

26. Matterport, "Highlighted Reel & Guided Tour in Workshop 3.0," last modified April 4, 2023, accessed July 14, 2022, https://support.matterport.com/s/article/Highlight-Reel-und-gefhrte-Tour-in-Workshop60272?language=en_US.

27. Matterport, "How Do I Create a Video of My Matterport Space," last modified January 20, 2023, accessed July 14, 2022, https://support.matterport.com/s/article/How-do-I-create-a-video-of-my-Matterport-Space?language=en_US.

28. US Access Board, "Section 508 (Federal Electronic and Information Technology)."

10

On Track for Access

Elizabeth J. Nosek

There are currently over 959 tourist railroads and railway museums in the United States.[1] Ranging from small local and regional museums to larger "national" complexes, these museums showcase every type of railcar imaginable including steam and diesel locomotives, city trolleys, hoppers, stock, and passenger cars. When you compare this number with the number of tourist railroads and railway museums found in other countries, such as ninety-seven in Canada, ninety in the United Kingdom, or twenty-seven found in Australia and New Zealand combined, the number of US tourist railroads and railway museums is staggering.[2]

However, these museums did not just appear overnight. The first American railroads were introduced in the 1820s. By the 1870s, one could cross the continental United States on board a train in two weeks or less, as opposed to the four to six months it could take by wagon, making rail travel an efficient and popular form of transportation. It wasn't until after World War I and the advent of automobiles and air travel that the industry began to decline. Clubs began to form in the 1930s, 1940s, and 1950s. Actual railroad museums came into existence in the postwar era. As Adam Burns wrote on the website *Railroad Museums*, "The railroad museum is not a new phenomenon although the number of [railroad] preservation organizations have grown considerably since the 1970s. The oldest is the Railway & Locomotive Historical Society, Inc. founded in 1921."[3] Today, this venerable organization continues to serve its membership with an archive housed at the California State Railroad Museum and ten chapters throughout the United States that preserve and interpret locomotives and publish and disseminate railroad history.[4]

Like all museums, these institutions have important stories to tell, many of which reflect our own stories. Not only are railroads arguably one of America's oldest industries, but they continue to play an essential role in today's economy. Within their story are numerous other tales that reveal the inventions and strategies that helped to build today's transportation industry. These tales also help us understand the role they played in building the world in which we live today, and which continues to impact our lives.

Railroad museum visitors from around the world flock to these specialized museums to stand in awe before what today appears to them to be mammoth machines. In fact, these museums are among the few places you can see this equipment up close.[5]

It is these rather large vehicles that tell so many of our stories. A good number of the guests who come to visit a railroad museum are unaware of the important role the industry has played in our lives—both past and present. It is the institution's role to help visitors see just how relevant these narratives are to their own lives. Like any museum, railroad museums use their collections of steam and diesel locomotives, cabooses, passenger and stock cars, menus, china, lanterns, telegraph equipment, uniforms, and more to make connections between railroads and an individual's own experience. Museums have long been the "go-to" institution for not only preserving these histories of human development but also helping visitors to make sense of them through exhibitions, publications, and other programming.

Museums serve as community anchors. According to the Merriam-Webster Dictionary, a museum is "an institution devoted to the procurement, care, study, and display of objects of lasting interest or value."[6] A broader definition for museums was adopted by the International Council of Museums in 2022: "A museum is a not-for-profit, permanent institution in the service of society that researches, collects, conserves, interprets and exhibits tangible and intangible heritage. Open to the public, accessible and inclusive, museums foster diversity and sustainability. They operate and communicate ethically, professionally and with the participation of communities, offering varied experiences for education, enjoyment, reflection and knowledge sharing."[7] It is not surprising to find that all museum visitors bring a wide range of expectations and abilities to any museum visit. Some of these can be more challenging for a railroad museum to address than others.

There are innumerable connections that we as museum staff can make with our visitors based on the impact railroads have had at every level of our lives. These range from overlying systems such as standard time and whole industries like telecommunications to individual products such as first aid kits. Whatever the subject, their stories are embedded into the very fabric of the objects exhibited for our visitors.

Like their counterparts, including maritime, transportation, and agricultural museums, railroad museums have struggled with how they can make their spaces, and thus their collections, more accessible to the public. Each of these museum types is unique, exhibiting a variety of large vehicles and equipment that can be particularly challenging to make accessible to all visitors without invasive and/or irreparable changes to the historic objects' fabric.[8]

In hopes of helping museum practitioners make the past more meaningful to a wider range of people, the remainder of this chapter will discuss efforts railroad museums are making to be more accessible, from both an accessibility standpoint and a visitor services perspective. A special focus will be given to specific actions being undertaken at the Colorado Railroad Museum in order to support visitors of differing abilities.

SETTING THE STANDARD FOR ACCESS

The Heritage Rail Alliance is an organization composed of railway museums and tourist railroads that conserves railroad history through the unique preservation efforts of education, research, and the free exchange of information among members and working industry professionals.[9] Their efforts to create a document recommending professional museum standards while at the same time identifying and integrating the unique characteristics of railroad museums began as early as 1997 with support funding from the Institute for Museum and Library Services.[10] The resulting document or "toolkit" provided a path forward for rail museums striving to elevate their level of professionalism in the museum field. The Heritage Rail Alliance's updated and revised *Recommended Practices for Railway Museums* was adopted on April 25, 2019, and addressed accessibility concerns in section 11 with the following:

"11. Accessibility
Museums must make facilities and operating equipment accessible to all, to the extent this can be done without compromising historical integrity, collections security, and visitor safety.

11.1 Museum buildings and facilities must be accessible as defined by state and/ or federal law; in the U.S., the Americans with Disabilities Act of 1990, and subsequent amendments (ADAAA, 2009) are the relevant documents to reference. Specific information is contained in standards set by the American National Standards Institute; such regulations generally exempt historic vehicles if the historic quality would be compromised. Historic buildings do not receive a blanket exemption, especially in the case of buildings receiving substantial remodeling or alteration. However, some U.S. states also have historic building codes, which offer alternative solutions to providing accessibility, among other items.

11.2 Museums must devote an appropriate portion of their resources to developing strategies that provide for intellectual and/or physical access to collections by all, regardless of ability or disability. Museums should consult with experts in the field of accessibility when altering or constructing new facilities in order to avoid the increased expense of refitting facilities found not to be in compliance.[11]

The railway museum community is a close-knit one that communicates through a variety of methods including listservs such as Railway Preservation News. This listserv has been hosting spirited discussions on ADA compliance for a number of years. In 2006, Drew Meek, an architect associated with the Great Plains Transportation Museum in Wichita, Kansas, pointed out that rail equipment that is still on its wheels is just that—equipment, not a facility, and therefore not required to meet ADA standards. He did point out that railroad museums should focus on making their sites and facilities ADA compliant, advising against placing the gift shop, video presentation room, etc. in an inaccessible display if it is practical to do otherwise.[12] That same year, architect and contributor to the Railway Preservation News listserv Randolph Ruiz posted, "I believe it violates the spirit, if not the letter of the law, to create exhibits that

Figure 10.1. Visitor Cody Smith boards train at the Colorado Railroad Museum. *Photo courtesy of Elizabeth Nosek*

are not accessible to all visitors. The exceptions for historic railcars exist to prevent requiring alterations that would damage their historic integrity." He goes on to suggest ramps, lifts, and platforms as alternative methods to accessing railcars, and where that is not possible providing "equivalent" exhibits that are accessible through video feeds or publications.[13]

While so much of the focus on accessibility at railroad museums is on ramps and wheelchairs, those museums operating trains might be able to provide additional accessibility to guests by simply adding an additional train ride onto the day's schedule.[14] This is especially true for smaller railcars such as the Colorado Railroad Museum's Galloping Goose (motorcars that were adapted to rails by the Rio Grande Southern Railroad). While the Colorado Railroad Museum saw that this created more opportunities for riding the train, they also found that adding nonhistoric railcars to the consist does this and more (a consist is a group of rail vehicles that are coupled together). Not only can these cars add more seats for the train, but they also enable a museum to modify them to be wheelchair accessible. The museum had already been utilizing open-air cars for people with mobility devices. The new cars were closed cars, which meant that museum trains were now able to be wheelchair accessible year-round.[15]

One of the many ways to ensure that an institution is committed to providing guests with the most accessibility possible is to integrate it into the institution's various planning documents. The Colorado Railroad Museum's Interpretive Master Plan, created in 2020, clearly identifies specific accessibility needs by incorporating a number of future goals into the plan:

- accessible walking paths
- accessible restrooms (with larger stalls)
- more places to sit and rest
- clear, thematic, wayfinding signage (design guidelines that take accessibility into account)
- well-groomed facility with buildings and grounds in good repair
- elevated platforms that allow visitors to easily see inside pieces of rolling stock (train cars, locomotives, etc.).
- a mobile-friendly website that allows guests to access information on personal devices[16]

Good planning goes a long way in setting positive standards for accessibility, whether it is through the efforts of a professional organization or an individual museum's strategic plan. Such goals provide a blueprint for future success.

BASIC NEEDS FOR ACCESS

Railroad museums are by the very nature of their collection often housed on multiple acres. For instance, the California State Railroad Museum sits on five acres, the National Railroad Museum in Wisconsin covers thirty-three acres, and the Steamtown National Historic Site in Pennsylvania occupies approximately sixty-two acres. Visitors at the Colorado Railroad Museum, which covers about fifteen acres, must not only traverse loose gravel and dirt but trackage composed of narrow- and standard-gauge rails, which often sit four or more inches above the ground. Add historic railcars that have steep, almost ladderlike stairs built in an era when accessibility was not on people's minds and the museum a challenge to traverse.

However, by incorporating paved and cement walking paths, more places to sit and rest, and a well-groomed facility with buildings and grounds in good repair into its Interpretive Master Plan, the museum has provided development staff with the necessary ammunition they need to pursue funding for these physical improvements. The result has been that since the Interpretive Master Plan's adoption in 2020, the museum has created easy-to-navigate grade crossings over tracks that run through visitor pathways, added benches in strategic areas so that guests needing a break are able to rest, and begun extending cement and paved walkways that make access easier for visitors utilizing wheelchairs, walkers, and canes. Furthermore, ground has been broken for a viewing platform that will allow visitors to look into the interiors of Chicago, Burlington & Quincy Business Car No. 96 and Colorado Midland Observation Car No. 111 while providing a roof that will protect the historic cars (and visitors) from the worst of weather.

The Interpretive Master Plan was only part of the solution; being selective about which grants and sponsorships to pursue was the other. The Colorado Railroad Museum looked for specific funding partners whose goals aligned with its accessibility efforts. These funders tend to be more public oriented and some also report to government agencies. Thus, recreation and community granting agencies as well as specific foundations tended to come to the front of the line for funding accessibility projects.[17]

Accessible restrooms have been another huge improvement to the site. The museum's original bathrooms were built in 1959 and are often referred to as the "narrow-gauge" restrooms (a play on their small size and width, similar to a narrow-gauge railroad). They do not accommodate wheelchairs and were difficult for those using walkers and/or canes or even strollers to easily access. While a changing station was installed, it was not easy to use due to lack of space. The museum did have more modern, wheelchair-accessible bathrooms available in its contemporary library building. However, these facilities were only accessible during library hours. By adding an additional exterior doorway, reconfiguring an existing interior doorway, and adding a cement walkway around the building, a second set of bathrooms were made available to visitors during museum hours.

Site-specific issues have inspired a more creative plan for additional bathrooms on the eastern side of the museum grounds, where utility easements pose major challenges to any new facilities. Plans for semipermanent facilities to be installed next to the museum's large picnic pavilion are under way. Not only will these bathrooms be accessible to people with mobility devices, but they will also be semiportable to allow for future flexibility.[18] This solution to a unique challenge will hopefully provide visitors with yet another amenity that makes their visit more accessible.

PHYSICAL ACCESS

While most railroad museums offer themed gallery spaces, efforts to make them more accessible are continuously under way. In 2019, Steamtown National Historic Site announced the completion of new permanent exhibits that were universally designed to enhance site orientation and visitor understanding. These were funded through the National Park Service's Targeted Accessibility Improvement Program. The museum worked with the National Park Service's Interpretive Center in Harper's Ferry and the National Center on Accessibility, as well as welcoming local residents to review ideas and project prototypes to make sure they were addressing visitors' needs. The results included a raised letter/Braille orientation map table that featured the core museum complex, a tactile scale model exhibit of the roundhouse area with a hand-operated turntable and adjoining interpretive panel, a vintage passenger coach mockup allowing visitors to immerse themselves in the experience, and a cutaway Spang, Chalfont & Company Locomotive No. 8 that includes a raised letter/Braille panel and a three-dimensional scale model of the locomotive.[19]

At the 2022 American Alliance of Museums Annual Conference, a session titled "Inclusive Design and Accountability: A Methodology of Museums of All Shapes and Sizes" took the issue of visual accessibility a couple of steps further than what curators usually consider in exhibit design.[20] The presenters explored graphic design elements such as color contrast, typography, and label layout. Traditionally designers utilize these elements to help elicit emotions and convey messages in support of an exhibit's underlying message. They can also be used to help make label copy more legible, clear, and visually appealing to both general visitors and those with visual impairments. The session also discussed how environmental design techniques can be used to make gallery spaces more navigable for all visitors. Using an exhibit at the Boise Art Museum as a case study, the panel shared effective strategies like using high-contrast colors with distinct edges, setting labels at an angle and placing them slightly lower than the norm, and lighting space around platforms so visitors can distinguish between the floor and platform in exhibit spaces.[21] Low lighting levels are one of the most common complaints received from visitors about the interpretive exhibits at the Colorado Railroad Museum. Gallery lighting levels are often defined by the preservation needs of the artifacts being exhibited, loan agreements, and available equipment. When implemented, the graphic design techniques presented at this session can help museum visitors feel more secure as they navigate through exhibit spaces.

Barriers to physical accessibility are another challenge some of the museum's visitors face. When the museum temporarily shut down during the COVID-19 pandemic in March 2020, no one was able to visit the site, let alone the galleries. The entire staff worked to find new ways to make programs and exhibits available to visitors, primarily through online videos. The resulting YouTube channel features a variety of programs: "Big Train Tours" highlights the museum's locomotives and railroad cars, "Small Wonders" explores smaller objects from the museum's permanent collection and changing exhibits, "Story Time & Craft" provides a monthly program for young families, "Throwback Thursdays" features behind-the-scenes tours of the work being done in the roundhouse and vintage imagery, and *Dining on the Rails* (a food blog) explores railroad dining menus and recipes from the collection. While begun for the pandemic, the museum quickly came to understand how these virtual programs made its exhibits, collections, and programs available to a much broader audience. Where before visitors needed to be able to physically access the gallery spaces and rail yards on the museum grounds, they could now connect with this information hundreds of miles away and at no cost. If they were able to access the physical museum grounds, the virtual programs allowed the museum to augment their experience with more detailed interpretive information on a mobile device.

In addition to typical visits, museumgoers enjoy visiting their favorite museums during special events when there are additional activities to enhance their experience. The Colorado Railroad Museum offers a range of these events including Dinosaur Express Train, Harvest Haunt Express, Day Out With Thomas™, and The Polar Express Train Ride™. While the additional activities and amenities such as train rides, performers, and special foods offer more opportunities for guests to engage with your museum, they can also provide some challenges not found during typical museum visits. Younger visitors and those with sensory sensitivities can become overstimulated by all the additional noise, activity, or extreme weather temperatures. The Colorado Railroad Museum works to accommodate various special needs at events by setting aside a quiet space for young families with babies needing to breastfeed or for visitors who just need a break, incorporating multiple water stations, and working with the region's d/Deaf and visually impaired communities to provide accommodations when possible.

Noise is another element that can be a significant factor at a railroad museum. Trains have been using bells, whistles, and horns to signal their movement to the public almost since they were first invented. Today, trains moving goods across the country or transporting passengers from stop to stop within a city are required by law to sound their horns at crossings in order to alert people to their presence. For safety's sake, these signals are necessarily loud, but for some visitors who are sensitive to sound, this can be quite uncomfortable. Blowdowns, where surface water is deliberately bled off the boiler using steam pressure in order to get rid of scum and particles that accumulate in the water, is another explosive sound for which it is difficult to prepare people.[22] Railroad museums are addressing these issues in a variety of ways. Some provide sound-canceling headphones upon request. Others notify the public of the situation on their websites and through on-site signage. (For more ideas on how to deal with scheduled loud noises, see chapter 4.)

A FAMILY'S DAY OUT WITH THOMAS

In 2019, the museum's collections curator Stephanie Gilmore was asked to assist a family composed of two legally blind parents, their fully sighted child, and their nanny (who is also legally blind) to navigate the museum's annual Day Out With Thomas™ event. This is one of the museum's most heavily attended events of the year. This licensed event includes a series of activities, entertainers, and a train ride behind a "life-sized" Thomas the Tank Engine. Unfortunately, the family had not made prior arrangements, but luckily Gilmore was available. Three years later, this has become an annual tradition for the family, who now calls to arrange for Gilmore to help them enjoy the event. That first year, she was asked to warn them about sharp corners and potential tripping hazards and to give specific verbal directions such as "move forward" or "move right or left." Gilmore quickly noticed that the family was startled by loud noises and that they preferred her to ask them to take their arm and lead them. When she took them on the event's train ride, they happened to prefer an open-air car and wanted the passing landscape described to them. When they first came to Day Out With Thomas™, their son was two years old and was skillfully helping to lead his parents around potential obstacles. Gilmore now encourages him (today at five) to describe the things he

Figure 10.2. A family enjoys a Day Out With Thomas™ at the Colorado Railroad Museum. *Photo courtesy of Stephanie Gilmore.*

sees to engage him, which she then uses as a model for her own efforts in guiding his parents and nanny. While she found it a bit awkward that first year, Gilmore has developed a friendship with the family over the years and looks forward to their visit.[1]

_____

1. Stephanie Gilmore, curator and librarian at the Colorado Railroad Museum, June 8, 2022.

FINANCIAL ACCESSIBILITY

Affordability is yet another thing that can create barriers to a positive museum experience. It is easy to assume that everyone who wants to can afford the admission price, but this is simply not always the case. The Colorado Railroad Museum approaches this issue in a few ways. The museum offers various free days for the community using local partnerships that the museum has developed over the years. They have been able to work with libraries to provide regional library membership passes. On a national level, the Colorado Railroad Museum has joined museums across the country to participate in the Blue Star program, which offers free admission to active-duty military families. The Blue Star Museums program is a partnership between the National Endowment for the Arts and Blue Star Families, in collaboration with the Department of Defense and museums across America.[23] In addition to the various free days and admissions, the Colorado Railroad Museum consciously prices its admission low in order to be more accessible to visitors. The museum is able to do this by adjusting pricing for its higher-end events such as Day Out With Thomas™ and The Polar Express Train Ride™ to offset these costs.[24]

ACCESSIBILITY THROUGH GOOD COMMUNICATION

Conveying just what efforts your museum is taking to ensure better accessibility not only helps to shape visitor expectations but also creates a partnership between the visitor and the museum experience. One of the best places to introduce a museum's resources and manage guest expectations is via the museum's website. The Colorado Railroad Museum in Golden, Colorado; the California State Railroad Museum in Sacramento, California; the B&O Railroad Museum in Baltimore, Maryland; the Railroad Museum of Pennsylvania in Strasburg, Pennsylvania; and Steamtown National Historic Site in Scranton, Pennsylvania, are just a few of the railroad museums that have taken this obvious step to help visitors better access their programming and exhibits. Ranging from an accessibility statement consisting of a simple sentence to a web page devoted to accessibility with downloadable maps and special program listings, these accessibility statements all help visitors plan their visit. Additionally, by having an accessibility statement, museums affirm their commitment to being accessible and encourage visitors to contact the museum with any questions. The Galveston Railroad Museum website offers a simple statement under the ADA accommodations bullet on its Visit page that "the Galveston Railroad Museum actively works to ensure all guests will enjoy the museum."[25] The longer statements or those museums devoting an entire page of their website to this effort may include sections on everything from sensory awareness, parking, service animals policy, mobility accommodations, medical and emergency assistance, where breastfeeding spaces are located, restrooms, and more.

The Workshops Rail Museum in Ipswich, Australia, discusses mobility barriers at its site and also provides a downloadable Sensory Map that identifies noisy, low-light areas and bright exhibit spaces that may flash, along with toilets, water fountains, and a baby changing room. The map also identifies where visitors can pick up sensory kits and earmuffs (noise-canceling headphones). The Workshops Rail Museum website's accessibility page also explains when visitors can find a quieter time to visit the museum, how they can avoid lines when purchasing tickets, locations for changing table facilities and feeding areas for young families, and where free Wi-Fi can be accessed for visitors with a Wi-Fi-enabled device.[26]

On-site communication and staff buy-in are critical as well. Once visitors arrive on site at the Colorado Railroad Museum, staff provides a central entry point for guests. Guest service staff are able to communicate with the rest of the museum team through radio, telephone, and Slack. It is these staff members who are often the point of contact for addressing any accommodations that may be needed. These front-line employees connect visitors with the best ways to access the site. The museum has also identified a daily manager to assist paid and volunteer staff in handling more challenging issues involving guest/staff safety and accommodation.

Regardless of their role, it is important that museum staff have familiarity with what access means and are appreciative of what their museum is doing to provide that access. Without that staff buy-in, visitors and their museum experience will suffer.

THINKING OUTSIDE THE BOX

At the Colorado Railroad Museum, improving accessibility is a priority. According to Executive Director Paul Hammond, "Our goal is to make the Colorado Railroad Museum available to as many as possible."[27] In order to continue to build on its efforts, the museum must bring new perspectives to this issue, to look outside the box.

One place to look when trying to think outside of the box about accessibility issues is to explore commercial organizations with a similar mission. For railroad museums, Disney theme parks are one such organization. The Disneyland Railroad's eighteen-minute ride around the perimeter of the park is legendary, being seen as one of the best methods for getting around the park. Yet even after all these years, even Disneyland is still not fully accessible to visitors who use mobility devices such as wheelchairs. The railroad provides three accessible stops in Tomorrowland, New Orleans Square, and Mickey's Toontown, but its Main Street Station remains accessible only to those guests who can climb stairs.

Despite this, Disneyland has poured time, money, and effort into making its theme parks accessible to all its guests. In fact, one Disney enthusiast named Angela created a website to "help people with disabilities and special needs plan and achieve the best Disneyland trip possible."[28] Her website, *All Access Disneyland: Magical Planning with Special Needs*, discusses various tools the parks have made available to visitors.[29] The site provides a number of links to helpful information for those who experience challenges when trying to access the parks. There are videos featuring virtual rides and planning links and a downloadable *Disneyland Park Guide for Guests with Disabilities*.[30] This helpful pamphlet included mobility, visual, and hearing sections providing information on tools that were complimentary or could be rented, phone numbers for further information, and safety issues associated with each category. Special breakout sections discuss service animals, magnetic fields, and areas where people may experience photosensitivity. The guide also provides an accompanying map. While it is unlikely that most museums can provide the detail Disney and its dedicated fans have, it certainly provides ideas for those wishing to up their game.

Railroad museums have a unique effect on people. By immersing guests in an environment filled with the unique smells, sights, and sounds of their collection, they are able to transport people of all ages back to another place and time. It is an experience worth having and sharing with all visitors. As the museum's Deputy Director Rob Kramer, put it, "We don't call anyone's disability into question, we just accommodate everyone as best we can."[31] And while it may seem that by doing so the museum is investing a lot of resources on just a few visitors, by making the museum more accessible to those visitors who need accommodation, it is actually making it more accessible for all visitors.[32]

NOTES

1. Railroaddata.com, accessed June 29, 2022, https://railroaddata.com/rrlinks/Tourist_Railroads_and_Railway_Museums_USA/.
2. Railroaddata.com, accessed June 29, 2022, https://railroaddata.com/rrlinks/Tourist_Railroads_and_Museums_International/.
3. Adam Burns, *Railroad Museums: A Complete Guide*, revised June 25, 2022, accessed June 29, 2022, https://www.american-rails.com/museums.html.

4. Railway & Locomotive Historical Society, Inc., "History of the Railroad & Locomotive Historical Society," accessed June 30, 2022, https://rlhs.org/WP/indexphp/history-of-the-rlhs/.
5. Railway & Locomotive Historical Society, Inc., "History of the Railroad & Locomotive Historical Society."
6. Merriam-Webster, "museum" definition, accessed May 25, 2022, https://www.merriam-webster.com/dictionary/museum.
7. International Council for Museums, "museum" definition, accessed May 25, 2022, https://icom.museum/en/resources/standards-guidelines/museum-definition/.
8. Paul Hammond, executive director of Colorado Railroad Museum, interview, May 1, 2022.
9. Heritage Rail Alliance, "Frequently Asked Questions," accessed May 10, 2022, https://heritagerail.org/faq/.
10. Paul Hammond, "Recommended Practices for Railway Museums," Heritage Rail Alliance, April 25, 2019, https://heritagerail.org/wp-content/uploads/2019/10/HRA_Toolkit_April_25_2019_FINAL.pdf.
11. Hammond, "Recommended Practices for Railway Museums," 32.
12. Drew Meek, "Displays Inside Railroad Equipment vs. the ADA," Railway Preservation News, February 26, 2006, accessed April 9, 2022, http://rypn.org/forums/viewtopic.php?f=1&t=30329.
13. Randolph R. Ruiz, "Displays Inside Railroad Equipment vs. the ADA," Railway Preservation News, October 19, 2006, accessed April 9, 2022, http://rypn.org/forums/viewtopic.php?f=1&t=30329.
14. Hammond interview.
15. Rob Kramer, deputy director at the Colorado Railroad Museum, interview, April 9, 2020.
16. Conservation By Design for the Colorado Railroad Museum, Golden, Colorado, *Interpretive Master Plan*, December 2020.
17. Kramer interview.
18. Hammond interview.
19. Steamtown National Historic Site Pennsylvania, "Steamtown National Historic Site Announces Accessible Exhibit Improvements," November 2019, accessed April 9, 2020, https://www.nps.gov/stea/learn/news/steamtown-national-historic-site-announces-accessible-exhibit-improvements.htm.
20. Sina Bahram, Corey Tompson Design, and Melanie Fales, "Inclusive Design: and Accountability: A Methodology of Museums for All Shapes and Sizes," American Alliance for Museums Annual Meeting, Boston, Massachusetts, May 21, 2022.
21. Bahram, Tompson Design, and Fales, "Inclusive Design: and Accountability."
22. Kramer interview.
23. Blue Star Families museum program, accessed May 10, 2022, https://www.arts.gov/initiatives/blue-star-museums/frequently-asked-questions.
24. Kramer interview.
25. The Galveston Railroad Museum website, accessed May 20, 2022, https://galvestonrrmuseum.org/visit/.
26. The Workshop Rail Museum, accessed May 20, 2022, https://theworkshops.qm.qld.gov.au/.

27. Hammond interview.
28. All Access Disneyland: Magical Planning with Special Needs, "About," accessed May 28, 2020, https://allaccessdisneyland.com/about/.
29. All Access Disneyland: Magical Planning with Special Needs.
30. Disneyland Park Guide for Guests with Disabilities, accessed May 28, 2020, https://disneyland.disney.go.com/media/dlr_nextgen/SiteCatalog/PDF/Disney land_Disabilities_Guide_09112015.pdf.
31. Kramer interview.
32. Hammond interview.

11

Accessibility at the Intrepid Museum

CHALLENGES AND OPPORTUNITIES

Charlotte J. Martin

Intrepid was not built for everyone.

When it commissioned *Intrepid* in August 1943, the US Navy was focused on getting sailors, aviators, and aircraft to the Pacific as quickly as possible. The aircraft carrier would make it possible for aviators to attack Japanese enemy aircraft, ships, and other targets and help turn the tide of World War II. The over three thousand young men who served on board all had specific roles in supporting this mission, and the ship's design, with its steep narrow ladders, raised doors, fuel supply, crowded berthing, and heavy machinery, helped make this work possible.

Intrepid would continue to serve in the Navy for over thirty years. Since 1982, though, the ship has served a different mission. As the centerpiece of the Intrepid Museum, it is now a vessel to advance the understanding of the intersection of history and innovation in order to honor our heroes, educate the public, and inspire future generations.

That mission cannot be accomplished without a commitment to accessibility and inclusion, including for those individuals with disabilities and their communities. The very features that made *Intrepid* so effective as an aircraft carrier now present both challenges and opportunities to those goals. This chapter explores how museum staff and key partners address those barriers to accessibility while trying to take advantage of the strengths of the historic site and its major artifacts. Essential to this work is a mix of stopgap efforts and, more recently, embedding accessibility into projects from the beginning, while working with key partners and self-advocates to ensure choice and a continuum of opportunities for engagement.

THE WHY: BARRIERS AND OPPORTUNITIES

Like many historic sites, the Intrepid Museum presents numerous barriers to accessibility. Mobility wise, the only preexisting elevators on the ship were for aircraft and bombs. Spaces can be tight and may require ladders or stepping through raised narrow doorways. The Cold War submarine *Growler*, another major museum artifact, is even more compact with smaller doorways between compartments. On a sensory level, the hangar deck (the ship's "garage" and now the main exhibition space) is cavernous and made of steel, so sounds carry and reverberate. Uneven surfaces and other hazards are scattered throughout. The flight deck is subject to the extremes of weather and the smells of the tide, and in the submarine, the diesel smell could never be fully cleaned out of the engine room. The vessels can also be unfamiliar, with roundabout ways to get places and names used only in the Navy. Moreover, as a battle site, *Intrepid* can stir difficult memories for some visitors.

At the museum, we have a responsibility to address these physical, sensory, communication, intellectual, and emotional barriers. The museum's existence is based on the idea that the ship, submarine, aircraft, spacecraft, artifacts, and crew member stories have public value. If we exclude people with disabilities—whether intentionally or not—by neglecting to address problems with accessibility, then we both fail to meet our mission to "educate the public" and devalue the site and its stories. Accessibility and inclusion must be core values and we must proactively engage with those most likely to be excluded.

Fortunately, like many historic sites, the Intrepid Museum already has quite a few accessibility strengths. As an immersive environment, the museum presents opportunities to make concrete connections to the past and to technological innovations, complementing and supplementing the learning that takes place in schools and other venues. Storytelling takes on added dimensions. The sounds, smells, navigation, and feel of the site may present challenges but can also provide a direct link to content for visitors with disabilities.

CONTINUUM OF OPPORTUNITIES

Every museum or historic site needs to start somewhere. For the Intrepid Museum, the ship's reopening, in 2008, after an extensive renovation and exhibition update provided a jumping-off point for new approaches. These efforts started by identifying accessibility gaps or challenges, developing potential solutions through research of best practices at other sites, and seeking the input of disabled self-advocates and experts. The foundation of this work is based on making sure people have actual choices in how they engage with the museum. If choice and comfort are key to any visitor's experience, this needs to extend to those with disabilities and their companions. If there are limits to when these choices are available, then the museum needs to make extra effort to welcome the impacted communities through free or reduced admission and specific outreach when those opportunities are actually available.[1]

For example, one of the museum's early accessibility efforts was in addressing the communication barriers for visitors who are d/Deaf or with hearing disabilities. At a minimum, this means ensuring that all audio content in the museum is available in other formats: videos have open captions (and those without sound are clearly marked as such) and transcripts of audio-only tracks are readily available. Automated captioning is available for virtual programs and meetings, with live captioning available for large on-site programs or by request. Box office ticket desks have hearing loops for visitors with hearing aids with t-coils (where audio is transmitted directly to the hearing aid), as does audio in exhibitions.[2] These are a baseline.

For d/Deaf visitors whose primary language is American Sign Language (ASL), though, the museum needs to address the language barrier. Some of the first programs offered by the museum were both spoken tours with ASL interpretation and tours led by a specially contracted d/Deaf educator in ASL. These were offered for free at intervals throughout the year. Now the museum offers ASL interpretation at museum festivals and major public programs, such as Astronomy Nights, with ASL users able to register for free admission on those days. ASL interpretation is also available at no additional cost for tours, with advance request, and fully funded programs are available for school groups. However, not everyone who comes to the museum wants to come for a tour or special event or may not have planned the visit in advance. Therefore, when the museum developed a new audio guide after reopening, one of the languages offered was also ASL on an iPod Touch available to borrow. (At the time of writing, the museum is not using the audio guides, in favor of a more flexible interactive mobile guide, described later.)

An early priority was also addressing major barriers for visitors who are blind or have low vision. The museum is full of things to look at: artifacts, restored spaces, labels, signs, and hazards. But there is also a tremendous opportunity for nonvisual learning. As artifacts, the aircraft carrier and submarine present visitors with a sense of scale beyond numbers; visitors move through alternating large and small spaces, hear the way sounds travel, and even smell the materials. In addition, we are fortunate that there are readily available models of many of the aircraft and spacecraft and replicas of certain smaller artifacts. Access educators also worked with the aviation curator to determine aircraft in the museum's collection that guided visitors would be able to touch and potentially go inside. Educators observed verbal description programs at other museums and also arranged for department trainings led by blind self-advocates and experienced verbal description educators. Tours incorporate description, touch, movement, and additional context. For an aircraft, the educator might begin by describing its dimensions, shape, and coloration, as the visitor touches a scale model. The group will walk along and around the real plane to get a sense of the scale and touch features within reach. Depending on the theme of the tour, the educator will share different aspects of its history and answer questions. All of this creates an experience stronger than one using only words or only touch.

Any visitor who is blind or has low vision can reach out in advance to arrange a customized verbal description and touch tour at no additional cost (local schools and organizations are also eligible for funded programs and an introductory previsit lesson). Educators have led tours for visitors from around the world, including the writer of this email from Denmark (lightly edited for spelling): "We are so so pleased with the experience. The girls were excellent guides, did perfect on all that was going on particularly guiding, but also had a wonderful way of showing things to us, let us touch and discover and this was for sure a fantastic day. [. . .] Museums like this are a pleasure and need to be seen."[3] In cases like this, families and friends can have an equitable travel experience with each other. There are also local visitors who have returned for multiple tours, including a couple who had such a good time on an earlier tour that they decided to arrange for another touch tour for themselves and a few friends to celebrate their City Hall wedding earlier that morning.

The staff tries to accommodate last-minute requests for verbal description and touch tours, but there is not always someone available. Knowing that staffing levels will always be a potential challenge to day-of tour requests and wanting to ensure that visitors who are blind have the choice and tools to explore on their own, the museum has developed different tools to make this possible. As a baseline, the museum has printouts of large-print labels available at the entrances of all special exhibitions and, increasingly, online. Developed with Touch Graphics, a tactile guide with a talking pen is also available for any visitor to borrow while at the museum. The guide contains raised line maps and tactile photos of artifacts to assist with wayfinding, as well as information on artifacts. When a user presses the pen to a tactile image in the book, the pen shares different layers of information through a built-in speaker or headphones: the object name, then a detailed visual description, then additional historical context. Users have shared positive feedback on the tactile guide, but it is also very challenging and expensive to make updates to it, so it is not practical for temporary exhibitions and artifacts that move locations. As a result, the museum prioritized visitors who are blind when developing its interactive accessible mobile guide, in 2020, and has worked to increasingly build description and tactile elements into exhibitions, as discussed later in this chapter.

Early in the development of the access initiative, educators noted that groups with developmental disabilities, such as self-contained special education classes and day habilitation groups, were already interested in visiting the museum but were not necessarily getting the most out of the experience. The museum is a natural draw for people with a wide range of interests, including ships, military history, aviation, transportation, and space travel, but if the in-

Figure 11.1. As part of a verbal description and touch tour, children who are blind or have low vision feel the outside of a small propeller plane. The relatively small size of the airplane means that participants can feel the entire plane, which educators supplement with scale models, detailed descriptions, and additional context. *Courtesy Intrepid Museum*

formation is not accessible or the museum is not hospitable, that interest will not translate into a rich experience. Educators developed a menu of programs, called All Hands programs, specifically for groups of students and adults with developmental disabilities, autism, learning disabilities, and emotional-behavioral disabilities, adapted to meet the specific academic and social-emotional goals and needs of the group. For example, the Life at Sea theme can focus on connecting the daily lives of sailors with our own daily routines and making comparisons, or the theme can focus more on the types of jobs on *Intrepid*, how they worked together, and how they compare to jobs in our communities. A group's main goal may be to practice being out in the community, so educators will make sure to acknowledge positive behavior, while still covering the content and having fun.

Initially, and sometimes still, teachers and group organizers could be reluctant to share information about their groups, concerned that we would turn them down for a program, oversimplify the content, or treat them with a negative attitude. These concerns were valid and based on experiences with field trips elsewhere. Staff communicating with group organizers learned to explain why they were asking for the information, not to weed them out or remove content but rather to ensure that educators were prepared to support their communication needs/preferences, bring along the most helpful teaching resources, plan accessible routes, tap into participant interests, and focus on the group's goals within the scope of the theme.

Of course, that means educators and colleagues need to follow through. Educators send social narratives—photo-illustrated, plain language, step-by-step guides of what to expect while at the museum, from entry through the end of the program—in advance to address concerns or anxieties about a change in routine. These were initially created for students with autism, but we have gotten feedback that a wide range of students and adults appreciate the preparation support. Groups come in knowing what to expect and are ready to jump right into the program, excited when they recognize their educator or a particular airplane from the social narrative. Educators often start by distributing visual vocabularies (a grid of nine keywords or ideas with a corresponding image) that they use to show the next stops, task students with finding the next object, remind students of previous topics, and give anyone who does not communicate verbally another tool to share responses. To support participants with auditory processing delays, language disabilities, ADHD, and hearing disabilities, educators supplement spoken information with images, touch objects, and visual vocabularies. For those with intellectual disabilities, educators scaffold information, make connections to previous references, break down complex questions, and share concrete examples. They have noise-reduction headphones available for students with sensitivity to noise, to help counter the many noises that reverberate through the museum, so students can better focus and/or feel more comfortable. They are ready to hand a simple fidget to a student who seeks out touch or needs to hold something to focus. Every self-contained class or corresponding adult group has its own museum educator so that participants can get the same level of attention at the museum as they do in the classroom or group.

Initially, it was easy to tell when an educator was preparing for an All Hands program versus a general school program. The All Hands educators would have bags full of models, replica objects, fidgets, and binders of supplementary images, while other educators would be empty handed. As the access and school programs teams collaborated more on trainings and as more educators came on board, the best practices used in All Hands became integrated into all school programs. This transition has helped ensure that students with disabilities in general education or inclusion classes still get the tools they need and are not blocked from accessing the same learning goals as their peers. The museum's exhibits are still the core of all guided programs, and these additional materials and pedagogical techniques help learners get the most out of their short time at the museum. Again, the museum has the advantage of not being a school and can provide a hook for learners who struggle in other settings.

Although organized groups are a significant portion of the museum's one million annual visitors, most visitors come with their families or friends in their free time. The next step was to ensure the museum could be welcoming and a positive experience for individuals with developmental disabilities and their families. The museum started offering two specialized programs, first, Access Family Programs for children with developmental or learning disabilities and their families, and soon after, Early Morning Openings for children with autism and their families.

Access Family Programs take place on select Sundays with an hour-long guided tour, followed by related activities in the Education Center. Each program has a different theme, so families can come every time or pick and choose the topics that interest them most. Themes have focused on traditions on the ship, in comparison to our own traditions; Intrepid's role in the space race and the experiences of astronauts; aircraft design; and many more. The hands-on tours are meant to engage the whole family, so they can have a shared experience. Educators plan the post-tour activities for families to do together, to build off the tour content and focus on different skills and interests. For example, one activity might require more fine motor skills, while another encourages socialization through a game, and another is a more open-ended creative project. Visual instructions at each activity allow families to work at their own pace, with educators available to assist too. A variety of materials, such as adaptive scissors and multiple drawing options, allow participants to choose what works best for them or to try something new. When the theme fits, the educators will work with the volunteer department to arrange for an Intrepid former crew member to participate, share stories, and act as a bridge to history. Educators prepare illustrated question prompt cards for any participants who are shy, not sure what to ask, or do not communicate verbally.

Even with these supports, the museum can be overwhelming for many children, particularly those with autism. Working off a small seed grant, the access team piloted an Early Morning for children with autism and their families, with the support of Autism Friendly Spaces and a new Parent Advisory Council (since renamed the Autism Advisory Council). If the program succeeded and made an impact, the museum could use the pilot as leverage for additional funding, which it did. Like the sensory-friendly programs at many other museums, these programs take place before the museum opens to the public to address some of the major barriers that our advisers put forward:

- Sensory overload—Educators could turn off sounds and videos that play while the museum is open and also provide a designated quiet space where families can take a break (Access Family Programs also have a designated quiet space near the activities).
- Crowds—Without loads of other visitors, participants who are sensitive to crowds could be more comfortable, and families with children who tend to elope, or wander, could feel secure that their child would not get lost in a crowd.
- Uncertainty—Educators send out a social narrative and visual vocabulary and visual schedule in advance, so families can prepare for the visit, ease

concerns, and set expectations. Without other visitors or programs going on, there are fewer surprises.

- Attitudinal—We often hear from families about the dirty looks they received from fellow visitors and even staff at other sites and they are worried about going to another museum with the general public.
- Financial—Living with a disability or caring for someone with a disability comes with added expenses for therapies, adaptive technology, and other things. In addition, for the reasons listed previously, families may be hesitant to pay for transit or parking for a program they think they might need to leave after only a few minutes. (This program and the Access Family Programs and most others described here are free or very lost cost.)

The program has evolved a bit over the years, always with support from the Autism Advisory Council, as we learn lessons and adapt to changes, such as the impacts of the COVID-19 pandemic. Throughout, though, the goals have been to help families feel more comfortable and confident in going to museums. Like with Access Family Programs, themes rotate over the course of the year, with specific content and social-emotional goals. For many years, programs began

Figure 11.2. Participants at an Early Morning Opening for children with autism and their families design mission patches for a program about astronauts on Intrepid. Visual instructions on the table include both photos and text to describe the steps of the project. The visual vocabulary for the program is also on the table. *Courtesy Intrepid Museum*

with a wait activity to help get families excited about the theme while they waited for enough people to start a tour. Educators then led small groups of families on a multisensory tour related to the theme. Now families receive a welcome bag with a fidget and checklist, and they explore at their own pace. Educators are stationed in key areas to facilitate related activities, such as going inside a helicopter, teaching some basic swing dance moves, or introducing a former crew member. In both formats, families finish in the museum's interactive Exploreum, which stays closed to the public for an additional hour. Families can play in all of the hands-on exhibits and check out additional activity stations until 11:00 a.m. Afterward, they are welcome to stay in the museum as long as they like.

As successful as these programs are, having only specialized programs does not represent real choice, a true continuum, or a full range of entry points for people with disabilities. For example, families that start by attending Early Morning Openings might feel comfortable enough after a while to attend an Access Family Program, but our Autism Advisory Council noted that they might also want to attend on a random day or to check out the festivities during Fleet Week. What were we doing to reduce barriers to these events? How were we ensuring that adults with autism or developmental disabilities could also access the museum?

We started to look more holistically at the museum and our programs. With the support of the Autism Advisory Council, we created a general social narrative and posted it on the museum's website. We could then adapt the social narrative for festivals and public programs. We also looked to other museums, such as the Franklin Institute in Philadelphia, for examples of sensory guides that would illustrate key sensory considerations, such as loud noise and the ability to touch. In our version, we expanded beyond that to note the physical accessibility of spaces, places where visitors are allowed to eat (this is not always obvious), and bathroom locations, because those are not evenly distributed but may be essential information. Both of these resources are tools to help visitors, not just those with autism, decide if this is what they are looking for and, if so, to plan their experience with the information they need. The council also vetted objects for a sensory bag that would be available for anyone to borrow from the information desk. The bags include a few different fidgets, noise-reduction headphones, nonsticky clay, and some visual vocabulary sheets.

At the same time that the Autism Advisory Council brought up concerns about offerings beyond childhood, the Museum, Arts and Culture Access Consortium (MAC), in New York City, launched an initiative, Supporting Transitions, to foster opportunities for adults with autism in cultural organizations as both visitors and employees, especially once they age out of school and many services at age twenty-one.[4] The museum hosted an early MAC focus group for adult self-advocates, and we soon recruited some of these self-advocates to serve on our own advisory council. We also started offering adult versions of our Access Family Programs more regularly, taking care not to merely replicate the children's version but focus on the adult audience. Soon after, we also piloted an Early Morning Opening for teens and adults. After a couple of tries, we recognized that teens and adults, with or without autism, are often less eager to wake up early on a Saturday than families with young children. We then piloted Sensory Friendly Evenings, which we have continued to offer and tweak over the past several years.

Around the same time, in 2016, we started All Access Maker Camp, a weeklong day camp for children with developmental disabilities, ages eight to fourteen. The New York Transit Museum's Subway Sleuths program (described in chapter 7) provided some of the inspiration for this program, particularly the idea that fostering campers' passions can be a springboard for trying new things, building skills, and connecting with others. The camp is application based and educators select campers based on aligned interests, goals, past camp experiences (particularly those with no prior or negative experiences), potential financial need, and a mix of strengths and areas needing support. That mix is important so that educators can give campers the appropriate attention and so that campers have opportunities to shine and support one another at different points. All projects are inspired by the museum's history and collection and scaffold over the course of the week, with both low- and high-tech components. The campers also get some real-world experience through a project developed by the aircraft restoration team, using real tools. Each session concludes with a showcase, where campers get to show off their work to their families and educators can introduce campers' adults to one another, especially if their campers made a connection. Groups are small and sessions take place when students in year-round school have off. Each year also includes a special session for returning campers, as well as a winter "reunion" so campers can stay connected with the museum and one another and continue to grow their skills.

One parent whose son has participated in a number of access programs recently wrote, "Thank you for the opportunity to be a part of the access program. My son has been a part of this program for several years. Regardless of his autism diagnosis he was able to speak about his interest in aeronautics and experience and was accepted in our local middle school with a great STEM program that will focus on his abilities and interest in piloting. We have so many pictures at Intrepid and they all speak for him!"[5] When accessibility is a priority, museums and historic sites can start to fulfill their public value.

This content hook also applies to the growing population of individuals with dementia and their care partners. Since 2012, the museum has hosted programs for this audience, beginning with The Stories Within, which focused on storytelling, handling artifacts, and discussion. As Intrepid's years of service (1943–1974) coincide with the formative years of those most likely to be experiencing or caring for someone with memory loss, materials covered during the programs could prompt a participant to share a story (whether true or not) for the first time or feel a general sense of comfort. As with other

Figure 11.3. At All Access Maker Camp, children with developmental disabilities, including autism, use tools with the help of the Museum's aircraft restoration team to complete a project for the team's workspace. *Courtesy Intrepid Museum*

programs, former crew members would sometimes join to share stories and photos from their time on board, further enriching the experience. Educators also started to experiment with incorporating music and smell, particularly during post-tour activities. This work was inspired initially by the important work with this audience taking place at art museums, especially the Museum of Modern Art, and was supported by training from colleagues at CaringKind and other cultural organizations.

More recently, with support from The Mellon Foundation, the museum has tapped into a specific aspect of *Intrepid*'s history—the daytime "tea dances" that would sometimes take place on *Intrepid*—to bring music and dance to the museum, in partnership with Rhythm Break Cares, an organization specializing in dance for people with dementia. We also sought funding to address the challenges of traveling to the museum, especially in poor weather, so that we can arrange car service for registrants from anywhere in New York City, while also increasing off-site programming at memory care centers and other facilities.

INFRASTRUCTURE

While the Intrepid Museum's access initiative was and is based in its education department, it is also a cross-departmental, institution-wide effort. This is essential to ensuring that the infrastructure of the museum is increasingly

Accessibility at the Intrepid Museum   **139**

accessible, accessibility is built into exhibition design, the development team includes accessibility in all proposals, managers are prepared to support staff with disabilities, and staff and volunteers are ready to welcome visitors and coworkers with disabilities.

Establishing buy-in takes time. Early on, access educators would make a point of inviting other museum staff to stop by and observe programs, so they could see for themselves how impactful these programs could be. Educators would compile thank-you notes and emails and share them widely. Access team members have always been active in professional networks, gathering and sharing back best practices, demonstrating to colleagues what could be possible at our own site. Over the years, we have brought in experts, including disabled self-advocates and experts of veteran mental health, for trainings across the museum and have organized both formal and informal internal trainings tailored to specific departments. We have identified colleagues in different departments who are allies and advocates and encouraged them to be a resource for their colleagues.

VISITOR SERVICES, SECURITY, AND VOLUNTEERS

With attitudinal barriers a major concern for potential visitors with disabilities, it is important that staff and volunteers are prepared to welcome visitors professionally and kindly. For visitor services staff, the access team coordinates with supervisors to lead trainings in tandem with their daily morning meetings at different times of the year. There are a number of seasonal staff members, so we cover an introduction to disability, the social model of disability, language, and basic etiquette whenever there is a large batch of new hires. We also delve more deeply into specific topics, such as service animals, basic verbal description, or demonstrating the many accessibility resources (lightweight stools, sensory bags, assistive listening devices, etc.) available at the museum. We always emphasize avoiding making assumptions and instead offer visitors clear information about their options. Because there are some staff members who have been at the museum for a long time, we invite them to share their expertise and experiences with different scenarios. These are professional development opportunities that increase confidence and expand their toolkits for welcoming visitors.

The access team has also worked with the volunteer managers to lead some informal trainings for volunteers and to provide resources that managers can pass along. At the Intrepid Museum, volunteers have different roles, including being stationed at key points in the museum to answer content questions and greet visitors. For volunteers who specifically assist with access programs, such as former crew members sharing their stories or general volunteers assisting with check-in, access educators provide additional context and support. Often, once a volunteer assists with an access program, they are eager to do so again. In some cases, they have then felt comfortable actually registering for programs for their family members with disabilities.

At the Intrepid Museum, visitors' first interactions with staff are typically with a member of the security team during the mandatory security screening (metal detector and bag check), so these interactions are crucial to setting the tone for the visit. Security officers are also scattered around the museum, tasked with ensuring the safety of both people and artifacts. Setting up training sessions for the security team was more challenging based on their schedule and staffing level requirements. As a result, the access team schedules a burst of small intensive training sessions, usually just a few officers per two-hour session. In addition to the general introduction to disability and why we focus on accessibility, we spend much of the session working through scenarios, particularly around deescalation. We go through different reasons why a visitor might behave in a way that seems erratic or potentially unsafe and how a security officer's response, even just their uniform, may influence the situation. These sessions are opportunities for mutual learning and building up best practices.

DEVELOPMENT AND FINANCE

Accessibility accommodations (especially when applied retroactively), programs, and trainings cost money. Early on, access managers worked with the development team to support proposals specifically for accessibility and for including accessibility in larger grants. Now the development team is proactive in seeking out funding opportunities for accessibility. By factoring accessibility into budgets and funding requests early on, we commit to following through on improving accessibility. During budget season each year, department heads increasingly reach out for recommendations on budgeting for accommodations, such as ASL interpretation or captioning. This has to be an active two-way process.

EXHIBITS AND THE PHYSICAL ENVIRONMENT

Like many historic sites, the Intrepid Museum is a challenging physical environment, with certain areas accessible only by stairs or ladders. Three elevators and a couple of lifts added to the former aircraft carrier make much of the museum physically accessible, but certain areas cannot be fully accessible. In addition, the ship can be confusing for anyone to navigate (even former crew members describe getting lost during their first couple of weeks on board), especially so for visitors with sensory or developmental disabilities. The museum has addressed this challenge through a mix of assistive supports, bringing the interpretation out of inaccessible spaces, updating exhibitions, and digital technology. As disability advocate Emily Ladau noted during a convening hosted by the museum for a project on sensory interpretation in historic sites, she has no interest in going to another historic site just to stay in a room and watch a video.[6]

For physical access, the museum has long had lightweight portable stools available for visitors to borrow so visitors can take a break wherever they are. Over the past few years, the museum has also added new benches and distributed them more strategically around the museum.

When the museum reopened in 2008 it included the Exploreum, an interactive space with hands-on exhibits. This area allowed visitors to touch replica or relocated parts of the museum, such as a small version of the ship's helm, crew bunks, a replica Gemini space capsule, and, more recently, a scaled-down version of parts of the submarine. This not only gave visitors an important hands-on experience but also made content from inaccessible spaces available to visitors. However, the early Exploreum exhibits were not fully accessible. They needed to be easily moveable to make room for special events, and so all had a raised platform. Several years later, with the formation of an Exploreum working group, which included a member of the access team, we identified accessibility as a priority for all Exploreum exhibits, with all new components designed to be physically accessible, while also moveable, and clearly explained through both text and images.

New and temporary exhibitions also presented an opportunity to increase accessibility in meaningful ways. Like many museums, the Intrepid Museum brings together working groups, led by a curator, for each temporary exhibition. Designers would also bring in the access team at different points to double-check font and color choices, display heights, potential obstacles, multimedia features, and other design choices. Over the years, these consultations moved earlier and earlier in the process, with the exhibits team creatively working best practices into plans from the beginning. For example, for a temporary exhibition called *Navy Cakes: A Slice of History*, the team designed a full-size tactile replica of *Intrepid*'s twenty-fifth-anniversary cake, a huge cake to serve all three thousand crew members. In addition, the display cases in the exhibition looked like cakes with a color "frosting" trim. The trim corresponded with the subthemes of the exhibition, each theme with a different color and texture, accounting for color blindness and other factors. The design choice was fun, thematic, and a tool for accessibility.

One of the biggest challenges at the Intrepid Museum has been the submarine *Growler*, which is a narrow, one-way experience that requires using stairs and stepping through multiple extremely small raised doorways. Besides one label and some audio guide content, there was almost no interpretation outside of the submarine. When the museum got to work preparing an exhibition on the submarine and its Cold War context, to open in the spring of 2018, this was an opportunity to plan for accessibility from the beginning. The exhibition would be fully physically accessible in a tent on the pier with ramps to enter and exit. The communication and interpretation inside the space would also be more accessible than before. Submariner oral histories would be presented at stations with both audio and full transcripts available. The illustration of the arch of the Regulus missile launch would be raised so that visitors could both look at and touch it.

The team also collaborated with the Stevens Institute of Technology to develop two interactive elements: an area that would replicate the sounds and vibrations of the submarine in different situations and a station about sonar. Modeling after colleagues at Access Smithsonian, the Museum of Science (Boston), the Institute for Human Centered Design, and other organizations, we decided to test these prototypes early on with disabled user/experts, recognizing that following guidelines or best practices is not enough. We installed early prototypes of the two interactive elements in another section of the museum, and we invited different groups to try out the prototypes and then share feedback in a brief interview. We invited members of the Museum's Autism Advisory Council and reached out to local advocacy groups (such as the local Hearing Loss Association of America chapter) and networks to bring in testers who are d/Deaf, blind, or with physical disabilities. Members of the evaluation or access teams observed the testers as they used the exhibits, making notes of sticking points or unclear tasks, and then asked participants about the experience. This feedback led to crucial improvements in the design, implementation, and effectiveness of the interactives.

The museum expanded on this work by bringing together historic sites from across the country, disability advocates, and the New York University (NYU) Ability Project for a project, Developing Sensory Tools for Interpreting Historic Sites, funded by an Institute of Museum and Library Services National Leadership Grant. This project looks beyond basic accessibility and accommodations to address how historic sites of all sizes and budgets can integrate multisensory design and exhibit elements to improve interpretation at their sites, particularly for visitors with disabilities. The participating historic sites receive funding to attend in-person and virtual convenings, work with NYU Ability Project students as they develop proposals, and then test prototypes at their sites. The disability advocates receive honoraria for contributing their time and expertise at all stages of the project. In the summer of 2021, the Intrepid Museum opened *Making History Accessible*, which featured prototypes for addressing different challenges proposed by the project group, including the interpretation of artifacts and spaces behind glass, fully inaccessible nonpublic spaces, and other interpretation challenges. The prototypes were developed by the Intrepid Museum's exhibits team and Ability Project students, in consultation with the historic sites and disability advocates. Prototypes used touch, smell, sound, and digital tools. The museum then invited additional user/experts with disabilities to explore the exhibition and share feedback and gave two free tickets to return to the museum to each person. The other historic sites then each selected one or two elements to develop and test at their own sites. These findings have been compiled into a free toolkit, "Making History Accessible: Toolkit for Multisensory Interpretation," with a focus on practical low-cost solutions, available on the Intrepid Museum's website.[7]

WORKPLACE AND HIRING

Improving accessibility for visitors is essential but only part of the work toward inclusion. Recognizing the much higher un- and underemployment rates for people with disabilities, the museum stayed involved with MAC's Supporting Transitions project as it shifted focus to fostering employment opportunities for adults with disabilities, particularly those with autism. In 2016, with support from the FAR Fund, the museum hired two part-time paid interns on a three-year grant that has since been renewed twice. The museum works with service providers with customized employment programs that help match organizational needs with job candidates and provide support for both the individual and the organization. We identified areas where we could use extra help and the partner organizations (originally Birch Family Services and now JobPath) identified clients with corresponding strengths, such as organizational skills, an affinity for repetition, or computational skills, to bring in for interviews. Birch and JobPath provided resources for managers ahead of interviews, including the recommendation to share interview questions in advance, and supported both the new hires and the managers in establishing routines and communication systems. Over time, the job coaches become less directly involved but remain available if needed.

This project has been mutually beneficial. The interns gain new skills, hone their strengths, and have potentially their first stable, long-term job. Managers get help they need to keep their work going and also develop their management and hiring skills. For example, it is now more common for hiring managers to provide job interview questions in advance, resulting in more prepared job candidates and productive interviews. Job descriptions are also more descriptive of the actual job requirements, work environment, and where there is flexibility. Of course, two internships are only one step. With almost all staff offices located on the former aircraft, barriers around physical accessibility, climate control, and sound bleed present major challenges to a fully inclusive workforce. Remote work options for positions that do not require being on the museum floor and individual accommodations can help, but this is an area where we are growing.

ADAPTING TO A NEW REALITY

With the explosion of the COVID-19 pandemic in March 2020, the museum, like most others, was suddenly forced to adapt to a new reality. Although some programs needed to be canceled, such as the spring session of All Access Maker Camp, educators quickly converted almost all programs to virtual formats, both live and asynchronous. Educators and their program participants lost access to the immersive aspects of the museum—its physical space, tactile exhibits, and original artifacts—but gained opportunities for more equitable programs.

Educators maintained many best practices, such as sending social narratives to All Hands groups ahead of time, and applied them in new ways. For example, educators at the museum often make connections between technology on the ship with technology in our own lives (for example, comparing a propeller with a handheld fan). Now, with program participants immersed in "everyday life," educators could use that as an opportunity to make even more concrete connections. Educators also sought to maintain multisensory learning, continuing to incorporate movement in programs and identifying common household items participants could use for touch. Educators took advantage of not being in the space to include video and audio content, such as oral history clips, that is difficult to use in a noisy steel ship, and chose to focus on topics and spaces that are not fully accessible on site. For example, on-site programs about the submarine are never fully equitable because not everyone is able to enter the submarine. However, a Virtual Verbal Description Tour or Access Family Program means that all participants in that program have access to a similar experience. Once automated captioning became more common in applications like Zoom, accessibility for meetings and programs also improved (with live captioning still hired for larger or more specialized programs). We also sought out resources and feedback on creating accessible digital documents for asynchronous materials.

With virtual programs, educators also took advantage of digital resources that had not been fully utilized beforehand. The museum had already had a Google Arts and Culture page with 360-degree views of most museum spaces before the pandemic, but educators put these to use more than ever before. We appreciated more fully how that site, as well as a full 3-D scanning project of the museum, could open up opportunities for engaging with nonaccessible spaces. These are not replacements for physical access but can give a much richer sense of the space and exhibitions than only photos or a narrative video.

At the same time, the Developing Sensory Tools for Interpreting Historic Sites team at the Intrepid Museum and NYU Ability Project came together to address concerns for the museum's eventual reopening about crowding and distributing shared audio guides. The team decided to develop an interactive mobile guide that users can access on their own smart devices via a web browser. Early on, the team decided that the guide should be accessible, fully compatible with the accessibility features on an individual's device, easy to update, easy for other museums to implement, and a tool for planning a visit and wayfinding in complicated spaces. We also saw this as an opportunity to bring together preexisting content divided across different platforms: print labels, the audio guide, the tactile guide, the museum's YouTube channel, and digital archives.

The team selected around fifteen artifacts and spaces as a starting point and developed an initial site map. The site is easy to navigate, including for screen reader users. All stops include a visual description, the label text, supporting historical images (with description), short captioned videos, and additional historical context or statistics. Each stop also includes a map and a link to detailed wayfinding instructions to assist with navigation. The NYU Ability Project team worked with the museum on the design and WordPress coding in a way that would be easy for the museum to update. They did informal tests with screen reader users and then conducted some user interviews once the site was close to completion. They also advised on the placement of QR codes around the museum and observed visitors using them after the museum reopened. The mobile guide became one of the key components of the Sensory Tools project, with several historic sites selecting the mobile guide as their site's project for the prototyping phase. Because of its flexibility and accessible design, the mobile guide, now available on Bloomberg Connects, has also been a core component of the museum's efforts to expand the stories we tell, particularly those that are less represented in the museum's collections around sailors of color and LGBTQ+ sailors.

LOOKING AHEAD

Even with all of this progress toward accessibility and inclusion, we recognize that these are ongoing processes and the museum has to remain proactive. For example, we are aiming to build off the advisory group of the Sensory Tools project and the Autism Advisory Council to more regularly and formally include people with disabilities in exhibition, education, and web projects at all stages, with funding to recognize their time and expertise. With turnover, both seasonal and general, always a factor, trainings and the sharing of professional development resources need to remain active and adapt to evolving best practices and advocacy.

The museum is building off the lessons learned from the Sensory Tools project in the development of new and upcoming exhibitions. For *On the Mend: Restoring* Intrepid's *Sick Bay*, curators introduce the history of the ship's sick bay, along with efforts to restore the space for eventual public access. The exhibition has been an opportunity to begin implementing the 3-D digital scans of the space and also test ways to address the barriers presented by using those scans. The exhibits team worked closely with a vendor to develop a tactile map of the sick bay with both large text and Braille labeling, taking heed of the complaint we heard from advisers who read Braille that museum and public Braille signage is often inaccurate and poorly executed and maintained. We are also testing out safe ways to display authentic tactile objects, in this case, surgical equipment,

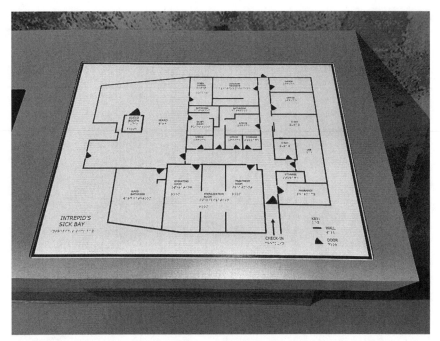

Figure 11.4. For On the Mend: Restoring Intrepid's Sick Bay, the exhibits team worked with a vendor to create a durable, accurate and meaningful tactile map of Intrepid's sick bay, which will one day be opened to the public. With *On the Mend*, the team is starting to prototype ways to make sick more accessible, both within and outside the space. *Courtesy Intrepid Museum*

and for the first time, have recorded audio descriptions (recorded using Zoom for this version) of some key artifacts available to anyone by scanning a QR code. Labels and object descriptions are available in the space, in the large-print label book, and online. The work in this exhibition will grow as we prepare sick bay for opening to the public and grapple with its limited accessibility.

Programmatically, the museum will continue to offer an array of access programs for specialized audiences but is working to ensure that all on-site and virtual public, family, and education programs are inclusive. Programs increasingly include ASL, description, previsit resources, and sensory-friendly supports. This work requires ongoing collaborations on staff training, resource development, and financial planning, as well as the inclusion of disabled perspectives at all stages.

The ship *Intrepid* may not have been built for everyone, but the Intrepid Museum can and will continue to move toward that goal.

NOTES

1. Much of this work at the Intrepid Museum was pioneered by Miranda Applebaum Hoffner and then Barbara Johnson Stemler, who built the museum's access initiative and team and worked to establish buy-in across the institution.
2. The steel ship can interfere with the copper loops, so we have mostly switched to loops hanging from the ceiling rather than placed on the ground under a mat.
3. Letter to Brigid Tuschen, *Re: Accessible Tour for Blind Visitors*, March 28, 2017.
4. MAC, the New York City Museum Educators Roundtable (NYCMER), and the Kennedy Center's Leadership Exchange in Arts and Disability (LEAD) had long provided essential networks of peer support in the museum's access work.
5. Letter to Charlotte Martin, *Re: Survey & Thanks for Attending Intrepid's Access Family Program!* June 30, 2021.
6. Emily Ladau to Developing Sensory Tools for Interpreting Historic Sites Convening, December 10, 2019.
7. The toolkit can be found here: https://www.intrepidmuseum.org/access

12

Building a History

RELATIONSHIPS AS ACCESSIBILITY

Jennifer L. Crane

For the assisted living staff member or special education teacher on a bus headed to a museum for a field trip, it is a day filled with the potential for new experiences and excitement, as well as apprehension. Employees whose days are spent in these settings know the specifics of the people with whom they work. They also know that a change in routine or surroundings might lead to an unfortunate disruption at their destination, fewer future outings, and lost connections with important community resources. Museums want to attract and retain visitors while keeping their exhibits and other offerings intact; visiting groups want to explore and enjoy museums along with other visitors in a smooth, uninterrupted fashion. Yet even with good intentions on both sides, field trips gone awry can still result in misunderstandings, missed opportunities, and lost connections.

One important way to avoid this dilemma is for the staff of historic sites to purposefully seek out and cultivate relationships with one another and with outside organizations. Educational and senior living institutions and historic sites can learn a lot from one another, with lasting beneficial outcomes for all involved. With thoughtful work and imaginative preparation by museum staff, they can enable visitors with diverse needs to enjoy positive experiences and view museums as welcoming friends. Additionally, all the staff members of partnering sites can reap the rewards of such connections. There are several effective ways in which museums and other historic sites can connect with educational and senior living organizations, which are likely to regularly bring groups needing accommodations or modifications during their visits.

THE JOHNSON COUNTY MUSEUM

The Johnson County Museum in Kansas is a premier example of an institution that has consistently prioritized relationships with outside organizations. At the time discussed in this chapter, in the early 2010s, the museum operated three sites: the Johnson County Museum and the adjacent 1950s All-Electric House in Shawnee, and the Lanesfield Historic Site in Edgerton.[1] With only ten employees, the museum not only cultivated strong relationships with multiple educators at other historic sites in the Kansas City metro area, but it also easily maintained connections specifically with teachers and assisted living staff. The creation of these networks naturally initiated the sharing of knowledge and led to lasting bonds with those community groups who often needed modified experiences at the museum's three sites.

The Johnson County Museum's main exhibit at the time, *Seeking the Good Life*, conveyed the story of its home county, located in northeastern Kansas. The 1950s All-Electric House was a 1954 model home originally situated in nearby Prairie Village, and subsequently acquired by the museum and moved to their property decades later. Some thirty miles away, the third site was the last remaining building in what had been the small town of Lanesfield, a one-room school from 1904.

Figure 12.1.   The Johnson County Museum in Shawnee, Kansas, in 2016. *Courtesy Jennifer Crane*

Smaller, restored buildings related to the schoolhouse as well as a modern visitor center completed the site's offerings in what is now Edgerton, Kansas.

SITES AND PARTNERS

This trio of compelling perspectives on Johnson County's history made for very attractive destinations for area schools and senior living establishments. As the museum's sites were situated in two cities several miles apart, visitors in different locales had easy access to them. Visitors who perhaps were limited in their ability to travel a great distance hopefully could at least make a shorter trip to one of the sites. Additionally, the museum, house, and one-room school were low- or no-cost field trip options suitable for any budget. Perhaps most importantly, it is likely that the school district and assisted living staff each logically reasoned that the students and older adults in these settings would greatly benefit from the wholesome combination of educational content and relatively quiet surroundings of each site.

Visitors of nearly any age and comprehension level could reasonably take in at least some of the wealth of information housed at each location. Museum education staff had synthesized and organized programs and hands-on interactives from exhibits and collections content, making them readily available for area school children. These school field trip experiences also offered memorable, interesting alternatives to the limitations of school textbooks and a classroom. To serve the other end of the age spectrum, each site's exhibits and programs covered the Johnson County history that was already woven into the memories of many older county residents. In particular, the more recent history of the 1950s All-Electric House and the *Seeking the Good Life* exhibit encapsulated the living memories of older visitors who walked into these sites with a more personal connection to the subject matter. Given all these factors, it was easy for both the teachers of area students and the staff of senior living facilities to view the Johnson County Museum's offerings as valuable community resources and appealing destinations worthy of their time and travel.

WHY ACCESSIBILITY?

With this set of circumstances in Johnson County, its museum's staff (and that of any other community destination) had even more reasons to consider and plan for visitor populations who have diverse needs. These reasons have only become more pressing as the twenty-first century continues. The changing demographics of the American population along with the shifting perspectives of individuals with disabilities mean that a museum's potential visitor population has new and different identities and expectations. Not only that, museums and historic sites will increasingly encounter a diversified pool of potential employees due to these changes, meaning that the very makeup of these institutions is undergoing a change as well. Amid their work of looking into the past, staff of any historic organization must regularly pause and consider the implications of future developments as well.

The world of the twenty-first century is an encouraging one for individuals who experience a disability. With the passage of the Americans with Disabilities Act (ADA) in 1990 and the Individuals with Disabilities Education Act (IDEA) in the rearview mirror, multiple generations have now been born into and lived within a framework of much greater understanding and opportunity in this country. The ADA is a federal civil rights law intended to prevent discrimination against individuals with disabilities. The IDEA, passed in 1975, established a free, appropriate, public education for all, providing services for those needing specialized education.[2] Adults and children who experience disabilities now navigate a world in which they have more mandated rights, and therefore more autonomy and confidence. Now that the stigmas associated with disability, while not totally gone, are fading away, individuals need not hesitate to ask for accommodations and modifications as they venture into public spaces.[3] Amid this major societal shift, museums and historic sites have the opportunity and responsibility to attract and support visitors who experience disabilities.

STATISTICS AND BACKGROUND

It is important for museum staff to examine the situations of the sites with whom they create partnerships. They, too, have histories that impact their present and the needs of the people they serve. Understanding their perspectives is key to building meaningful relationships with them. It is well worth the time of any historic site to consider and learn more about their area schools and assisted living facilities, for example, two significant audiences for the Johnson County Museum.

More and more, children with disabilities are included in the mainstream classroom and educated with their typically developing peers as much as possible. In the past, special education students usually received much of their instruction in separate classrooms (or even separate schools) with only one another as peers. It is more common in recent decades for special education teachers to collaborate with classroom teachers on inclusion, meaning instruction is often conducted for all students together, sometimes by either or both educators. According to the US Department of Education, "in 2018–19, more than 64% of children with disabilities were in general education classrooms 80% or more of their school day."[4] In these cases, a school's general education and special education staff are often providing services to all students; consequently, all staff are aware of and advocate for the needs of students with disabilities. The inclusion of children with disabilities also means these students commonly participate in field trips with their peers, with accommodations and modifications tailored to each child's needs. These needs are as varied as the children themselves. For example, children with disabilities may require more direction, wait time, physical assistance, a quiet space to escape stimulation, or even an extra teacher or paraprofessional to accompany them, or they may not. Again, each child and their disability is unique. If the staff at historic sites take the opportunity to reach out to school personnel ahead of a visit, they could learn helpful information that may guide them in planning a field trip for that group.

Increasing numbers of the aging American population means an increasing need for historic sites to be aware of and consider this demographic's needs as well. Based on recent projections from the US Department of Health and Human Services, by the end of the current decade, "all baby boomers will be older than 65. This will expand the size of the older population so that one in every five Americans is projected to be retirement age."[5] Going forward further in time, "by 2060, nearly one in four Americans will be projected to be an older adult," that is, sixty-five or older.[6] These population changes are poised to generate major ripple effects reaching every facet of American society, historic sites included. Community organizations must work together to anticipate these demographic developments and their implications.

More people are living longer than ever with disabilities that historically have cut short people's lives or severely limited their opportunities. Individuals with disabilities are now able—and have the expectation—to be included in a wider range of community activities. These changing expectations extend to the workplace as well. Individuals with disabilities own their own businesses, travel for work, and make valuable contributions to a variety of fields. This includes the history field, which will inevitably see the same changes in its practitioners as it will in its visitor and audience demographics. This, too, points to the need to focus on accessibility at historic sites and museums. After all, some of these visitors will join historic organizations as employees. Their unique perspectives will certainly change the direction of the field in ways yet unknown. As the aforementioned legislation has ensured equal rights for people with disabilities, these individuals rightfully have more reason to confidently self-identify as people who experience a disability and advocate for their own perspectives in the field of history.

Many other aspects of communities are changing to accommodate both the aging American population and those of any age with disabilities. Local leaders gather to discuss the growing need for universally designed homes in their neighborhoods. City and county entities offer assessments of older citizens' residences to offer personalized recommendations. They hold public workshops on senior household safety to enable residents to comfortably age in their own homes. In some areas, school districts with declining populations of school-age children close emptying school buildings as new retirement homes break ground. Public transportation systems expand to offer specialized local travel services expressly for older residents and people with disabilities. All these scenarios have unfolded, for example, in Johnson County, Kansas, where the sites outlined in this chapter reside.

As though speaking to historic organizations specifically, a report from the US Department of Health and Human Service's Administration for Community Living even points out:

> Inclusion of older adults and people with disabilities also offers many benefits to communities themselves. Communities miss out on valuable voices and perspectives when people with disabilities and older adults are left out. . . . When older adults are excluded, communities lose wisdom collected over many decades, and their connection to history.[7]

This special connection of older residents to history, so valued by the Johnson County Museum, lays the groundwork for all museums and historic sites to build meaningful relationships and benefit their communities.

OUTCOMES FOR SITES

All these developments within local communities emphasize the pressing need for historic sites to also adjust to coming demographic changes and evolving expectations of audiences. Sites can take a variety of proactive steps to support and prepare for a more diverse visitor population, as disability is one component of diversity. Taking such steps speaks volumes about a historic site and invites connections with new and varied partner organizations. It also paves the way for a future in which museum professionals are as diverse as the population of the general public. This in turn means their workplace's efforts and offerings will reflect this coming diversity.

RELATIONSHIPS BETWEEN HISTORIC SITES

One step toward this optimistic future involves staff of historic sites reaching out to one another to build relationships. By establishing a bond between organizations with similar goals and issues, these sites pool expertise and create opportunities. The Johnson County Museum frequently initiated and supported these types of connections. Their educator and other local museum educators met regularly as a group called Museum Educators Roundtable (known more commonly in the museum field as simply MER) to discuss accessibility in addition to other education-related topics. This was an important way for staff to form professional networks but also to discuss common experiences and look for new ideas. Each MER meeting was hosted by a member's own site, which enabled other meeting participants to see firsthand the potential issues and challenges associated with a location. Members shared and learned strategies for accommodating crowds of varying ages, modifying tours and content, and communicating effectively with all visitors.

Through the efforts of MER, these Kansas City area sites (including the Johnson County Museum, National World War I Museum, Nelson-Atkins Museum of Art, and others) organized and held a Coalition for Museum Learning symposium. During this on-site gathering, museum professionals shared knowledge and insights with staff of other sites. In particular, MER members from two different sites copresented on *Special Populations and Museum Engagement*.[8] Their presentation provided current findings and background on various types of disabilities and outlined best practice approaches for accessibility.

REACHING OUT TO SCHOOLS

As for cultivating relationships with nonmuseums, the Johnson County Museum remained in regular contact with schools and leveraged the knowledge of teachers in several ways. The potential for a relationship between schools and historic sites is a natural one; they often have similar goals and outlooks. Both types of organizations contain vast repositories of information and expertise. Both stand ready to serve the public with the intention of providing education for those who enter. They both often must contend with underfunding and understaffing issues while making the most of their available resources. Historic sites are trusted partners for schools; they tend to offer low-cost access to an abundance of content that easily aligns with school curricula. Schools in turn are typically a ready and willing audience for historic sites, as they have large numbers of students of varying ages who are open to and benefit greatly from formative experiences with community institutions like museums.

The popularity of the Johnson County Museum's sites with area schools made it easy to form relationships with them and even individual school staff members using a variety of approaches. As the museum's curator of education was a former teacher, this meant that this staffer had an insight into how to best communicate with other teachers as well.

On one occasion, the museum invited an area special education teacher to give a presentation to the museum staff about accessibility strategies for their visitors. This teacher also was a regular volunteer and tour guide at the museum and consequently had insight into the museum's layout and general processes and had interacted with its staff and visitors. The program, therefore, was not only about accessibility in general but also was tailored to the specifics of their sites. Museum staff learned various ways in which they could further make their sites more welcoming to visitors with diverse needs, all while forming a genuine, lasting connection with this teacher and volunteer.[9]

For several years, the museum's Lanesfield Historic Site had regularly offered a popular living history program, specially created for upper-level elementary-age children. Many area fourth- and fifth-grade students participated in the daylong program each school year. A visiting class would receive a warm welcome and introduction in the visitor center by a museum staffer dressed as

Figure 12.2. Lanesfield Historic Site, the more distant of the Johnson County's Museum's sites, is located in Edgerton, Kansas. *Johnson County Museum*

an early twentieth-century school teacher. Teachers and students would then make the short walk from the visitor center to the one-room school and await the arrival of the schoolmaster or schoolmistress. Upon entering the school, the staffer would also assume the character of a 1904-era one-room school teacher, a stern educator handing out small reading primers and firmly leading the class in basic educational exercises and expectations of the era. A final wrap-up session at the end of the turn-of-the-century school day would find the visiting children more relaxed, with the museum staffer answering questions and explaining what school, education, and the small, long-lost town of Lanesfield were like in a bygone era. Often, staff members noted that students with anticipated behavioral issues or other challenges found the living history program so removed from their everyday routine that it motivated their enthusiastic participation, and this helped make it accessible to them.

The curator of education continuously worked with teachers to ensure that living history programming met their instructional needs (including outlining it with the Common Core curriculum, which had been initiated in 2010 and adopted state by state). By maintaining regular email correspondence with area teachers, the museum made a useful, education-friendly connection with these school personnel. Over time, museum staff naturally got to know teachers individually, which encouraged the teachers to continue bringing their classes year after year, and the living history experience became a tradition and rite of passage for many local elementary students. Within this type of comfortable relationship, it was easier for teachers to feel they could communicate needed accommodations or modifications ahead of time or upon their arrival at Lanesfield.

For classes or schools that could not make a trip to any of the museum's sites, the museum also offered outreach programming. Museum staff compiled groups of reproductions of related historical items and supplemented each group with a corresponding PowerPoint presentation on a flash drive. Each selection of items was placed in a trunk, which could be used in two different ways. A teacher could rent a trunk for a predefined period of time for use in their classroom or sign up for a museum-staffed trunk program for their class or school. An educator who requested the latter type of trunk experience would welcome a museum education staffer into their classroom to present to students on a given aspect of Johnson County history. There were other advantages of this type of program; it utilized three-dimensional objects to hold (an experience not always offered in museum settings), along with an expert speaker to interact with kids. Outreach programs like these were yet another practical and valuable method of building relationships with area schools, whose students might experience varying types of disabilities.

These trunk programs easily enabled accessibility for all students to participate in museum-related activities without leaving their school building. Students with disabilities especially benefited from these programs brought directly to their classroom, as their school day schedule was largely left intact and there was no travel required. Best of all, students could physically handle objects, making for a rare hands-on history lesson that broke through the abstract concepts of time and vicarious experience.

Additionally, the museum invited local teachers to the main site on a regular basis to serve on an educational advisory board and offer feedback about upcoming programming and exhibits. Regular meetings were held after school on weekdays, to cooperate with an educator's typical workday. The curator of education, sometimes along with the museum director, would discuss future initiatives and museum offerings with attendees. This type of meeting enabled area educators to have a say in how programming could be derived from anticipated exhibit content. Once again, it invited a personal connection with area teachers, who now had all the more reason to bring their students for class field trips and maintain a relationship with the museum.

Yet another method of building relationships with schools took the approach of offering meaningful professional development opportunities to area teachers. Educators must regularly fulfill their state's requirements to remain certified or licensed, a condition of employment by school districts. This means that educators are continuously looking for classes that meet the requirements of recertification or relicensure for their state. Of course, many teachers tend to prefer to spend their time, effort, and money on classes that are interesting and significant to them.

The Johnson County Museum had a ready, enjoyable answer for this common situation. The museum offered an annual weekend course through Ottawa University titled "Recreating History in the Classroom," in which teachers could enroll for the all-important continuing education credit. Participating teachers met one day at the main museum location and the next day at the Lanesfield Historic Site for instruction, discussion, and activities conducted by the museum's curator of education. Over the two days, they experienced firsthand the Johnson County Museum's array of exhibits and programs. Most importantly, they also learned how to incorporate museum materials and visits to each location in their instruction. This was a very productive method of cultivating connections with area educators and demonstrating in person how experiences at all the museum's sites could be tailored to individual students, particularly their students with disabilities.

REACHING OUT TO SENIOR ORGANIZATIONS

As for senior or assisted living facilities, they, too, have a natural connection to museums and historic sites. They both contain vast reserves of information about the past. With this shared awareness, they each have a vested interest in ensuring a community's ties to its history are maintained and valued. Similar to the relationship with schools, historic organizations are a low-cost alternative for field trips, and of course they specialize in the content of particular interest to many senior residents.

Senior living organizations tended to be one of the museum's main audiences for outreach programs. This segment of the population understandably had a greater need for community experiences that could easily be brought to their door, as residents often had reduced mobility due to health or disability-related conditions. Much like the in-school trunk programs, a museum educator would travel to a facility and give a presentation about some facet of county history or about the Johnson County Museum itself. This required a ready knowledge of not only historical content but also the awareness of how to conduct an accessible program for residents with disabilities. The presenter needed to be nimble in accommodating the immediate needs of residents, including using a microphone if requested, accepting varying levels of audience participation, and fielding sometimes unusual or very specific questions. Museum staffers who had the ability to accept and empathize with residents' needs often received repeat invitations to those senior living facilities.

As outlined earlier, the development of outreach programs and similar offerings is a particularly important strategy for building relationships with senior living communities, as this audience is more likely to have mobility-related disabilities. By participating in outreach programs, the facility saves transportation costs and time, and it also avoids the possibility of a resident having an accident or emergency at a site. Initiating connections with older adults in the community acknowledges the human expertise and resources within a locale who hold a personal memory of museum and historic site content, and whose lives reflect the work of said staff.

Additionally, museums that take the time to highlight the existing personal associations between local history and the younger members of that community facilitate relationships in innumerable ways, for example, through local, trusted publications. In the fall of 2011, the Johnson County Museum's curator of education wrote a piece for *The Best Times*, the county's free magazine regularly mailed to residents sixty years of age and older. This magazine featured general interest articles and news about the county. In her piece, the educator reflected on her personal recollections of family to extoll the value of grandparents in the transmission of history to grandchildren.[10] This was an exciting, more personal way to reach many area residents, all while acknowledging and validating their points of view.

Furthermore, the curator of education and her staff worked with local senior living facilities to enable their residents to participate in tours with modifications and accommodations. Sometimes these changes were made in advance; other times they were made at a moment's notice. Upon the arrival of a group, education staff met with the facility's accompanying staff member to assess needs and break them up into smaller groups. It was important for museum staff to confer with group leaders upon arrival and to make immediate changes depending on the needs and abilities of visitors that day. As the Johnson County Museum had two sites very near one another, a group could tour the exhibits of the main museum building while another group (or groups) toured the 1950s All-Electric House next door.

Figure 12.3. The living room of the 1950s All-Electric House, a major stop for tour groups, and one of the more accessible rooms. *Johnson County Museum*

Visitors whose health and feeling of wellness may easily change from day to day require flexibility in their activities. Accordingly, it was important for the museum's staff to anticipate, recognize, and empathize with the specific needs of visitors to ensure the success of an on-site visit. Often tour guides needed to be creative about accommodating the physical abilities of visitors. This sometimes meant showing an available video of the house in lieu of a physical tour. Other times, a group would only approach the location, with the guide giving a tour of the outside and discussing the site's history from that vantage point. These alternative ways of giving tours were inclusive of everyone and gave each visitor a meaningful experience of the house while respecting his or her needs.

Visitors who were capable of venturing further and longer might enter the house but not be able to fully tour the interior due to difficult-to-access areas. As the house had been built in the mid-twentieth century, it had not been envisioned nor constructed with accessibility for disabilities in mind. Stairs, carpeting with runners, difficult-to-maneuver corners, narrow hallways, and other small areas prevented some visitors from taking the typical, full tour route through the home. Near the conclusion of a tour of the All-Electric House, the guide normally opened a door in the kitchen to allow visitors to walk a few steps down into the garage. (The garage normally marked the end of the tour, as it featured a small exhibit with more recent photos and text about the home's owners through the years and the laborious process by which the house had been transported to the museum grounds.) Visitors who were unable to navigate the steps could still receive pertinent information from the experienced tour guide who would open the door for a glimpse of the garage interior and discuss the history of the home since the 1950s.

Tours of the All-Electric House focused on a time period which many of the residents of assisted living facilities not only remembered but remembered as adults. Understandably, the tours with these groups were often very different from tours with younger visitors, whose perspective on the decade could not have been shaped through firsthand experience. Older adults' comments and questions reflected their personal knowledge and deep connections to the subject matter presented at the site. In these instances, an effective tour guide had to be open to receiving information rather than positioning oneself as the all-knowing source of information. Staff had to be able to gracefully receive constructive criticism, respond to much more detail-oriented questions, and still offer an informative tour while surrounded by people who remembered the era firsthand. This type of open, nonjudgmental listening was a necessary ingredient for maintaining relationships with senior living organizations.

Time is another factor in accessibility, and the recognition of this aspect of a visit was vital in providing a positive experience for these visitors. What was normally a half-hour house tour was sometimes only fifteen minutes, depending on the needs of the group. On other occasions, modified tours took up most of an hour. More time was needed for logistics, allowing visitors to move around the sites, perhaps focusing on exhibits for which staff-guided tours were not normally offered. Museumgoers who are often unable to travel to many public places may want more time in a place in which they are able to visit and are accommodated.

As can be gathered from these scenarios, accessibility often means opening staff members' minds to new perspectives. This can take the form of responding appropriately to visitors whose needs may seem unusual or whose behavior and communication may not follow social norms. Or it might take the form of visitors whose expression of their personal perspectives and memories might appear to question a historic site's messaging or storylines. Again, the ability and willingness of Johnson County Museum staff to acknowledge and respect differences and make last-minute changes created trust with assisted living facility staff and their residents. Visitors are more likely to gain a meaningful experience when tours and experiences are created with their perspectives and needs in mind. Museums and historic sites that value and maintain an atmosphere of acceptance and empathy build lasting relationships and can anticipate repeat visits from facilities.

When historic exhibits, sites, collections, educational programming, and other offerings more closely match the experiences and backgrounds of the surrounding community, everyone benefits. Staff members have opportunities to explore new directions in their work, and hopefully enjoy greater job satisfaction as a result. Visitors who routinely fail to see themselves in exhibit text and images or have to make special requests for on-site accommodations now feel validated and welcomed. The museum experience, often stereotyped as full of high-level content and reminders to not touch anything amid a hushed silence, is accessible to all.

For the museum professional anticipating the arrival of a school or assisted living group at the museum for a field trip, there are a lot of potential unknowns. Staff working in museums and historic sites understand that many outside community groups often have limited time and funding for such outings and must consider these excursions carefully. Therefore, sites that wish to make the most of the opportunity to welcome large groups need to learn about and connect with them as much as possible. Investing in the valuable relationships to be made with specialized groups of visitors enables museums and historic sites to lay the groundwork for consistently successful visits and the meaningfulness of their sites. The outcomes of these extensive strategies are limitless. Ultimately, the history field stands to gain a more diverse population of visitors and draw in a new generation of equally diverse professionals who are ready to contribute innovative and exciting perspectives to the field.

NOTES

1. In 2016, the Johnson County Museum moved from Shawnee to its current location in Overland Park, Kansas, and placed the 1950s All-Electric House inside the museum. This new location opened in the spring of 2017.

2. This law was originally named the Education for All Handicapped Children Act, or EHA. First passed in 1975, the IDEA was renamed and reauthorized in 1990. For a complete history, see Kim E. Nielsen's *A Disability History of the United States* (Boston, MA: Beacon Press, 2012).

3. Generally speaking, accommodations are alternative ways of presenting information to others, while modifications refer to changes to the content itself to make it easier to comprehend. For example, within a museum setting, accommodations might refer to a shortened tour, large-print versions of text, or the option to listen to content rather than read it. As far as making modifications, museums may use simpler wording in written materials or during a tour, or offer different programming for specific groups.

4. US Department of Education, "A History of the Individuals with Disabilities Education Act," last modified January 11, 2023, https://sites.ed.gov/idea/IDEA-History.

5. Jonathan Vespa, Lauren Medina, and David M. Armstrong, "Demographic Turning Points for the United States: Population Projections for 2020 to 2060," US Census Bureau, https://www.census.gov/library/publications/2020/demo/p25-1144 .html#:~:text=Introduction&text=The%20year%202030%20marks%20a,to%20 be%20of%20retirement%20age.

6. Vespa, Medina, and Armstrong, "Demographic Turning Points for the United States," 25.

7. Administration of Community Living, "About Community Living," last modified September 29, 2020, https://acl.gov/about-community-living.

8. Amy Duke and Jennifer L. Crane, "The Museum Experience for Special Populations," presentation at the Greater Kansas City Coalition for Museum Learning, Shawnee, Kansas, March 2013.

9. Jennifer L. Crane, "Special Needs Overview: Information and Accommodations for the Museum Setting," presentation at the Johnson County Museum, Shawnee, Kansas, January 2009.

10. Jennifer L. Crane, "Forebears and Museums Both Provide Adventures in History," *The Best Times*, September 2011, 28.

13

Creating Access for Patients and Caregivers Through Museo-Medical Partnerships

Kristy Van Hoven, PhD

> Organizations that more closely resemble the population they serve, and furnish these inclusive connections, can be more responsive to the needs and interests of their visitors.
>
> —Heather Pressman and Danielle Schulz[1]

There is a whole field of study dedicated to understanding, defining, and refining the idea of accessibility and access to community resources. In many fields, there are also specialists that study accessibility in the context of the industries they serve. Medicine and museology are no different. In fact, accessibility to resources in medicine can mean life or death, while accessibility to museum resources can mean the difference between an actual or perceived acceptance or rejection within a community.[2] Recognizing the need for accessibility and understanding the role accessibility plays in wellness and well-being is the bridge that brings many museum and medical professionals together in museo-medical partnerships.

It is in that vein that accessibility, through museo-medical partnerships, will be explored in this chapter followed by ideas on how historic houses, sites of significance, and other museums and community institutions can utilize

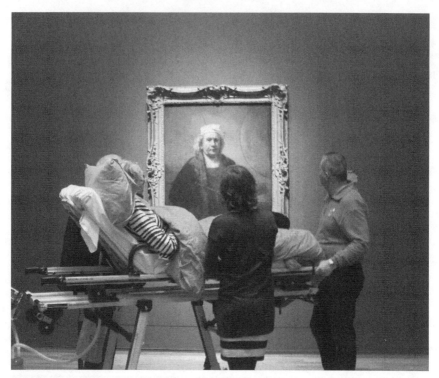

Figure 13.1. A terminally ill patient visits "Late Rembrandt" at the Rijksmuseum in 2015. *Courtesy Ambulance Wish Foundation*

museo-medical partnerships to increase their ability to serve their audiences and engage new visitors and stakeholders.

Museums are unique partners in well-being and communities, providing patients, caregivers, and their families opportunities to engage with their communities. From large history and science centers to historic homes and sites of significance, museums are places people can turn to understand the community and the natural world around them. Through partnerships with medical professionals, museums can build relationships that support acute and chronic patients' ability to participate in and enjoy museum experiences, as well as experience the benefits of museum visits and participation like other members of their communities. With a keen eye for opportunities to support and promote healing and well-being, museums can build relationships that secure their future as supportive partners in community and individual well-being.

To provide safe and considerate access for patients, caregivers, and their families, museums often partner with medical professionals and institutions in what has become known as museo-medical partnerships. These dedicated partnerships are generally formed around opportunities and programs that promote health and well-being for museum visitors. Special accessibility considerations help make museum experiences successful for the patients and other stakeholders. As a growing body of knowledge is produced by museum and medical scholars, historic sites and sites of significance are starting to chart their own courses to successfully and sustainably support health and well-being in their communities and engage new audiences through wellness and therapeutic-driven experiences.

In 1973, the Rehabilitation Act was passed and is considered the first disability civil rights law enacted in the United States. It set in motion an era of federal projects taking disability into account when implementing new projects and programs. In 1990, the United States Congress passed the Americans with Disabilities Act (ADA) into law, ensuring individuals with disabilities will not be discriminated against in any aspect of public life. The purpose of the law is to make sure that individuals with disabilities have the same rights and opportunities as those without disabilities, including access to public accommodations; employment; transportation; federal, state, and local government services; and telecommunications addressed in five "titles" (or sections) that relate to different areas of life (see chapter 2 for a more detailed explanation). Although the law outlines generalized requirements for access, they are often left to the interpretation of those implementing accessibility strategies. Museums and medical centers are dependent on an individual or community's ability to use the facilities they manage. To maintain accessibility, many museums, medical centers, and other services turn to the ADA to help develop in-house policies and programs that support further accessibility to their resources. The ways in which museums and medical centers need to be accessible can be a nearly endless list. In this chapter, the list will be consolidated into three main points that are addressed as primary goals in the museo-medical partnerships explored in this study. These three areas are (1) mental accessibility, (2) physical accessibility, and (3) socioeconomic accessibility.

BUILDING COMMUNITIES FOR HEALTH AND WELLNESS

It is important for historic homes and sites of significance, as well as other types of museums, to understand the roles they can play in supporting their communities and visitors' health and well-being. The therapeutic activities of museums are one of the easiest gateways for museums and sites to enter museo-medical partnerships and provide access to a variety of patient groups and their caregivers. From physical therapy activities like walking around spaces and galleries to handling objects on tour or through outreach programs, historic sites and museums that invite their visitors to participate in the experience are inherently delivering physical therapy opportunities through their day-to-day activities. Mental and intellectual therapeutic activities can be a little more challenging for museums to conceive and integrate into their programming on their own. This is where museo-medical partnerships with local patient advocacy groups,

Figure 13.2. Visitors to a historic site engage in discussion with museum staff about indigenous culture. *Courtesy Kristy Van Hoven*

clinics, or medical groups can help museums build their programming to support patient health and well-being.

A growing number of museums, historic houses, parks, and sites of significance across North America are engaging in partnerships with physicians that provide prescriptions for museum visits to their patients. These "museum on prescription" partnerships are rooted in the idea of encouraging patients seeking therapeutic interventions to engage in self-directed or museum-led programs that support the health objectives of the patients and their healthcare teams. As others have explored in this book, visitors can experience a number of barriers to accessing museum and museum-based resources. From socioeconomic to physical barriers, patients can face the same stigmas and barriers to access as other visitor groups, with the added pressure of being acutely or chronically ill or in the middle of their healing journey. We probably all felt this barrier during the coronavirus pandemic as we had to run errands with a tickle in the throat and the thought "it's just allergies, it's not COVID, I swear!" rolling in our heads. By prescribing museum visits, literally in some cases on a prescription pad, physicians are removing some real or perceived barriers to museum participation and access for patients and their caregivers.

In the following sections I will review some opportunities for historic homes, sites of significance, and museums in general to create unique expe-

Figure 13.3. Veteran Participating in art program at the Veterans Art Center at the Museum of Modern Art in New York. *Courtesy MoMA (1944.3_MA2331_CCCR)*

riences for patients and to participate more fully in public health initiatives in their communities.

MENTAL ACCESSIBILITY

For our purposes here, mental accessibility is understood as the ability for someone to connect through thoughts, emotions, sensory experiences, and intuition to an opportunity or experience. Mental accessibility can be limited due to injury, medical or chemical interventions, medical treatments, biological or genetic alteration, or age. Mental barriers to access are generally harder to see and remain taboo in cultures and societies across the globe. Although more groups are putting effort into understanding and advocating for mental accessibility across industries in the twenty-first century, there is still a great deal to be understood about the brain, its health and diseases, and its accessibility needs when less than optimal conditions exist.

One of the earliest museum-based programs in North America that focused on mental healing was the "War Veterans' Art Center" started in 1945 at the Museum of Modern Art (MoMA) in New York City: "The principal object of the Center was to help veterans adjust themselves [in preparation for a return to civilian life] through the creative process."[3] This program lasted for four years culminating in an exhibit of participant works in 1948 before being morphed into a more inclusive program for civilian visitors. Through this program, MoMA recognized a need within the community and developed a program that made art and the museum's collections accessible to a group of nontraditional visitors who needed help in achieving wellness after serving in World War II. MoMA continues this tradition with expanded accessibility programs including cornerstone programs like Meet Me at MoMA, a program developed for dementia visitors and their caregivers, and has been the program other museums across North America study and use for inspiration in the creation of their own memory engagement programs.

In recent years museums like the Museum of Fine Art in Montreal and museums in England have conducted research programs on the effectiveness of prescribed museum visits. Through ongoing research, museum researchers have reached the preliminary conclusion that museums, at the very least, provide an opportunity to get out of the house and engage in an extracurricular activity. The researchers have discovered that in some cases, organized programs and visits for patients help stimulate self-confidence, encourage physical engagement, and promote feelings of inclusivity that promote a sense of well-being, which in turn supports more effective healing and prolonged wellness.

PHYSICAL ACCESSIBILITY

Physical accessibility is understood as the physical ability of an individual to participate in an opportunity. Barriers for patients to physically participate in museum experiences can include individual physical limitations (including, but not limited to, visual or auditory impairment and/or physical ability to move and manipulate oneself or other objects) or group limitations, such as patients that need external medical equipment and/or caregivers to assist in their daily activities. Physical barriers can also include geographic barriers (usually in reference to a patient's ability to travel to or partake in a program away from their current location), which can affect individuals, care teams, and communities. Last, physical accessibility can refer to the ability to access resources (for example, transportation or caregiver support that may be necessary for a museum visit). With a vast range of challenges presented by physical accessibility for patients looking to engage in museum experiences, museo-medical partnerships help overcome these barriers. It is important for museo-medical partners to clearly

Keep Calm and Wash Your Hands!

Discover how pandemics have shaped emergency medical response since the the 18th century

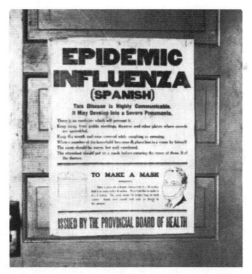

Figure 13.4. Virtual Exhibition homepage Keep Calm and Wash Your Hands! Curated by the National EMS Museum explored pandemics and public health lessons learned with their virtual visitors during the COVID-19 pandemic closures. *Courtesy Kristy Van Hoven*

identify the physical barriers they can tackle when developing programs for patients. In some cases, physical barriers are ones that cannot be removed, but alternatives to access may provide a pathway to participation with creative solutions developed by the museo-medical partnership.

In the past thirty years since the ADA was passed into law, museums have worked closely with communities to make great strides in removing physical barriers to their galleries, collections, sites, and structures. Historic sites around the country have embarked on partnerships to remove barriers to access for their visitors through partnerships with patient networks and disability advocacy groups. Buildings were altered, where they could be, to allow for easier access for those who used mobility assistance devices such as wheelchairs and walkers, and lights were added to hazardous areas or areas of low natural light to facilitate visitors with low vision. Eventually, tactile tours and other sensory programs allowed more visitors to access the museums and historic sites. As a result, visitors feel more included, welcome, and wanted when visiting museums that have accounted for varying visitor experiences. Today, promoting the role historic museums can play in public health education, well-being, and patient care is moving to the forefront of partnership planning for many museums, including historic sites.

As museums work to redefine their role in their communities post-COVID-19 pandemic, providing access and a welcoming environment for nontraditional visitors is front of mind.

> There is an authoritative voice in there . . . ways that museums have told people to think about what they are seeing, but we are stepping back from that, and we are welcoming multiple voices . . . community folks are coming in and talking about their experiences.[4]

Debra Hegstrom and her team oversee programs and education at the Minneapolis Institute of Arts. They are responsible for identifying areas where the museum can offer patient-centric and accessible opportunities to participate in the museum or engage with its collections. In addition to gallery tours, Hegstrom and her team have identified and piloted programs that engage nontraditional museumgoers in the museum experience. Examples include citizen curator projects to promote cultural identity and build community well-being and resilience; brain health programs that engage patients with chronic and acute brain injury along with their caregivers in art and discussions around history and art; and the Minneapolis Institute of Art provides a physical meeting place for therapeutic and debrief sessions for soldiers, civic employees, and other groups seeking alternative meeting places for group health programs.

Historic homes and sites of significance can also provide physical meeting spaces and therapeutic programming and other such resources to their visitors and communities. From handling historic objects in situ and discussing memories and lessons around such objects, to literally walking in the footsteps of previous generations and experiencing the sights, sounds, smells, and feelings of a bygone era, historic sites can be unique partners in grounding discussions on the human experience and memories. All museums, large or small, contemporary building or historic site, need to have staff prepared to lead discussions that can be hard, triggering, and/or traumatic for the visitor. Through museo-medical partnerships with health professionals and patient advocacy groups, many museums are supporting a growing number of programs that engage the five senses in a journey of healing, well-being, and reliance for many patient visitors.

SOCIOECONOMIC ACCESSIBILITY

Unlike mental and physical accessibility, socioeconomic accessibility is not usually at the forefront of museum planning. Many museums in North America have unwittingly limited accessibility to their sites and programs by simply charging a fee to participate, placing age limits on exhibitions or galleries, or requiring travel to sites that may be challenging or even unreachable by public transportation. In their book *Museum Basics*, Timothy Ambrose and Crispin Paine outline some of the socioeconomic barriers to museum participation, "one of the main reasons that people do not visit museums is that they think they will not feel comfortable there."[5] They go on to state some other perceptions that limit people visiting museums:

> The idea of visiting a museum may not have even occurred to them.
> Too often museums seem to have opening hours to suit the convenience of museum staff rather than that of visitors.
> It's easy to get tired in museums, especially for senior and children visitors [and I would add those visitors who are experiencing ill health].
> Is the museum designed with children in mind?
> Many museums are in the richer parts of towns or are convenient for car drivers, while the majority of the local population may not have daily access to cars.

Additionally, with the increasing number of digital opportunities presenting themselves in the first part of the twenty-first century, and then grown exponentially from 2019 to 2022, digital accessibility (and access to technology) has presented itself as a barrier to participation in museums for patients and other economically challenged visitors, and subsequently museo-medical partnerships. As Pressman and Schulz note, "When accessibility is overlooked during the digital design process, not only are countless websites, mobile applications and documents made unavailable, but the online experiences in general can become a source of frustration and alienation."[6]

These barriers can be magnified for patients and their caregivers when health concerns and limitations come into the equation, and so it falls to museums and their partnerships with patient groups and medical professionals to create opportunities to remove some, if not all, of these barriers to participation. Institutionalization can have a lasting and detrimental effect on the quality of life, health, and well-being of a patient. To reduce feelings of isolation, particularly for hospital-bound and visitors living in long-term care facilities, cultural and historical encounters create a sense of shared belonging, even if through outreach programs or other nontraditional media to reach patients at their bedside, as I have witnessed through my experiences with hospital and care facility partnerships with museums in which I was employed or volunteered.

Historic sites are some of the most community-based museum institutions I have worked in. They can be closely tied to their immediate community while neglecting relationships with communities farther away. As others have mentioned, partnerships with funders, community advocacy groups, and families help bridge that gap. Another essential partner in bringing groups into the site is the caregiver.

In many instances, caregivers or care teams are the ones who make decisions for their ill family member, friend, or client. A caregiver needs to be able to bring their charge to a museum easily and be assured their visit will be safe and in accordance with the activities and experiences the patient is allowed and able to do according to their medical directives. Historic sites are challenging in many respects, as we have previously explored, but that doesn't mean that barriers to site access cannot be overcome through partnerships. From creat-

Figure 13.5. Preparing to present a patient bedside program in a local hospital. *Courtesy Kristy Van Hoven*

ing special free and reduced days or times to providing outreach programs to community hubs, clinics, or hospitals, to working in partnership with patient advocacy groups to coordinate group excursions where costs can be shared across many families and visitors as opposed to the burden of one. All these opportunities allow for socioeconomic barriers to be reduced or removed.

As part of their study in 2019, Helen Chatterjee and her team at the University College London looked at museum hospital schools and the programs local museums created for pediatric patients who spent days, weeks, and months in hospitals and care facilities receiving treatment. These hospital-based outreach programs brought museum experiences to the students through their archaeological, archival, and historic hands-on collections.

Engaging with the patients at the bedside, although presenting unique challenges of their own, removed several barriers to access for these students and their caregivers. Knowing the museum experience took place in a care facility with physicians close at hand in the event of an emergency, some students were able to receive their continuous chemical treatments while participating in a program and engaging in well-being conversations with museum staff. This helped the students feel like a part of their community even though they were removed from the day-to-day activities of school and field trips *to* museums. For many historic homes and sites, educational outreach programs are a great way to start offering in-patient museum experiences. With a bit of training to ensure program leaders are comfortable with the sights, sounds, and smells of the clinical setting and working directly with patients and their care teams, historic sites have a wonderfully unique opportunity to provide greater access to their stories through museo-medical partnerships and patient programs.

CREATING ACCESSIBLE OPPORTUNITIES THROUGH MUSEO-MEDICAL PARTNERSHIPS

"Linkage to helpful resources is a first step to self-care," and museums "serve as agents of public health and mobilization as they enhance health care environments."[7] When embarking on a partnership, museum and medical partners evaluate the needs of their users. When intersections of those needs emerge, partnerships are born. Understanding barriers to participation is key to understanding some of the driving forces behind museo-medical partnerships.

The first step to approaching accessibility in any setting is understanding that "disability is a natural part of the human experience"[8] and entering the partnership with clear and achievable goals.[9] To ensure accessibility is at the forefront of a museum or medical center's mission, many have dedicated staff that participate on development teams to ensure accessibility is a consideration throughout the planning and implementation process.[10] Whether it be mental, physical, or socioeconomic access, museo-medical partnerships have plenty of opportunities to maintain and increase access to programs for their patient-visitors.

While it is tempting to talk about projects that tackle one or two accessibility issues, it is safe to assume that, in actuality, many barriers to accessibility are interrelated and can be removed through dedicated project management. For example, sensory inclusion programs can benefit not only those on the autism spectrum but also those who have experienced loss or grief and may need momentary pauses from stimulation to process their emotions. Additionally, we traditionally think of tactile experiences as assisting visitors with vision challenges, but sensory experiences can also spur memories in brain trauma and dementia patients.

At The Henry Ford a special program was developed to bring art to life for those seeking sensory opportunities at the museum. In the museum's collection is a set of prints by artist Norman Rockwell called *The Four Freedoms*. To engage the community and the patient-visitors in the artwork, The Henry Ford partnered with the Detroit History Museum to curate a community quilt project in conjunction with the exhibition of the prints across their two sites. As Bree Boettner described in 2018, the project allows visitors, and specifically Alzheimer's and dementia patients and caregivers, to explore the idea of the four freedoms represented in the art, allows a hands-on opportunity to interact with the artwork by creating textile art, and allows the participants and visitors to reflect on what those four freedoms are today. According to Boettner the program "was well received and in fact, people are still talking about it, remembering the program."[11]

Another fantastic program of which I was a part was the Museum on Wheels program at Baycrest Hospital in Toronto, where volunteers would take a collection of thematic artifacts to a variety of brain trauma wards and use the objects to stimulate memories, speech, and physical rehabilitation for acute trauma patients as well as long-term cognitively degenerative patients. On a few occasions, patients would recognize volunteers or staff presenting the program and seemingly pick up conversations where they left off days or weeks prior.

Some programs invite participation from the community by offering unique opportunities to engage in ways individuals feel are more comfortable and familiar, like photography competitions open to the public at the Royal Ontario Museum and the Art Gallery of Ontario:

> By bringing [patients] to places like the ROM it became a positive experience for everyone. It's been helpful in the sense that it is reducing a lot of stigma and bringing forth acceptance. And with those competitions that they have out there, like at the ROM and the AGO, where they are inviting all to participate.

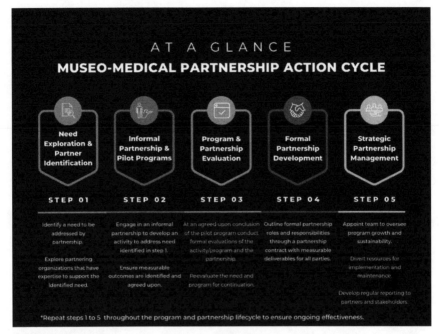

Figure 13.6. Table created by the author to help museums start their journey on museo-medical partnerships. *Courtesy Kristy Van Hoven*

> Like the ROM where anybody can send in pictures. Some of our guys did. It's just that normal, that normalization they are craving.[12]

Other programs encourage community members to choose their participation by offering free and reduced days and designated nights where the museum stays open to visitors who may otherwise not have the time to visit during regular operating hours.

By allowing partnerships to grow while serving other needs at museums, museo-medical partnerships not only serve the needs of their patients in unique and engaging ways but grow and sustain themselves through positive impacts on the community's well-being and become leaders in demonstrating social responsibility.[13]

NOTES

1. Heather Pressman and Danielle Schulz, *The Art of Access: A Practical Guide for Museum Accessibility* (Lanham, MD: Rowman & Littlefield, 2021).

2. Francesca Rosenberg, "What Does It Mean to Be an Accessible Museum?" *Medium*, November 16, 2017, https://stories.moma.org/what-does-it-mean-to-be-an-accessible-museum-9e9708254dc9.
3. Rosenberg, "What Does It Mean to Be an Accessible Museum?"
4. Debra Hegstrom, senior educator, interviewed by Kristy Van Hoven, 2018.
5. Timothy Ambrose and Chrispin Paine, *Museum Basics: Second Edition*, pg 20.
6. Pressman and Schulz, *The Art of Access*.
7. Lois Silverman, *The Social Work of Museums* (New York: Routledge, 2009).
8. US Department of Education, "Rehabilitation Act of 1973," accessed January 16, 2020, https://www2.ed.gov/policy/speced/leg/rehab/rehabilitation-act-of-1973-amended-by-wioa.pdf.
9. Pressman and Schulz, *The Art of Access*.
10. Hegstrom interviewed 2018.
11. Bree Boettner and Anne O'Rear, former manager of education programs, Detroit Historical Society, and community connect coordinator, Alzheimer's Society of Michigan, interviewed by Kristy Van Hoven, 2018
12. Kristen Ireland, recreational therapist, interviewed by Kristy Van Hoven, 2018.
13. Richard Sandell, *Museums, Society, Inequality* (London: Routledge, 2002).

14

Breaking Barriers to History

Selena Moon

In college, I took an American studies course called "Narratives of Internment" where we studied the history, impact, and aftermath of the Japanese American incarceration during World War II.[1] We read memoirs, poetry, and novels written by former incarcerees, such as Miné Okubo's *Citizen 13660* (the first book about the incarceration by a Japanese American, published in 1946), John Okada's *No-No Boy*, and Hisaye Yamamoto's poetry. Except for a classmate from Hawaii, none of us had learned about the incarceration in school and I only knew about it because I had Yoshiko Uchida's children's fiction books about Japanese American children as a child.[2]

Six weeks after the attack on Pearl Harbor, on February 19, 1942, President Roosevelt signed Executive Order 9066, declaring the West Coast a military exclusion zone. Although a specific group was not mentioned, the order applied to Japanese Americans living on the West Coast who would be forcibly removed.[3] Most were sent to temporary "assembly centers" in fairgrounds and racetracks across the West Coast, while some went directly to Manzanar incarceration camp in California.[4, 5] While the camps were being constructed, incarcerees lived in "makeshift barracks from a horse stable" or in a large building in a stockyard.[6] When the ten camps were finished, incarcerees were moved to incarceration camps at Heart Mountain, Wyoming; Manzanar and Tule Lake, California; Topaz, Utah; Minidoka, Idaho; Poston and Gila, Arizona; Granada (Amache), Colorado; and Rohwer and Jerome, Arkansas.[7]

In my college course, one of the books we read was Jeanne Wakatsuki Houston's *Farewell to Manzanar*, about her family's experiences at Manzanar as a child. While discussing the book in class, our professor told us about an annual pilgrimage to the site. In 1969, 250 activists and students made an impromptu pilgrimage to Manzanar that had since become an annual event, held on the last Saturday in April. Manzanar was declared a National Historic Site in 1992 thanks in part to efforts led by Sue Kunitomi Embrey, who was incarcerated there and who attended the inaugural pilgrimage.[8] Through a series of serendipitous events, half of my class attended the 2007 pilgrimage.

2007 VISIT

On the last Saturday in April 2007, we joined former incarcerees on the round-trip bus ride from Los Angeles. Manzanar is about four hours north of Los Angeles, in the Mojave Desert, at the foot of the Sierra Nevada Mountains in Owens Valley. Our first stop was the visitor center, which provided a background of what led to the incarceration, the history of the incarceration, and preservation efforts. There were many exhibits with explanatory plaques, newspaper clippings, and photographs.

After that, we went out to watch the program. There was a large tent, but the majority of the guests sat in the sweltering heat to learn about the history of the war, the camps, and preservation efforts. It was hot and dry, and just sitting in the sun was tiring. After the speeches and commemorations, there was an *ondo*, a Japanese folk dance. Even we college students were drained—though exhilarated—and I wondered how the elderly visitors were doing (even those born during the war would have been in their sixties). Besides the tent, there was little shade, and though there was plenty of water provided, it was still exhausting being out in the heat.

The pilgrimage and program was a moving albeit frustrating experience for me. Despite being visually impaired, I gave little thought to accessibility, except to briefly wonder how the elderly visitors got around on the sandy ground and be irritated at how inaccessible much of the material was to me because of my visual impairment. Little did I know that my fleeting thought about the site's accessibility during the pilgrimage would turn into a career.

Despite being fascinated with history since childhood and ultimately being a historian, I generally do not enjoy museums because of how inaccessible they are for people with disabilities. In many cases, the artifacts are in dimly lit rooms and the label text is small and at feet level. Even if the label is well lit and at eye level, the text is frequently still minuscule. This was somewhat the case at the Manzanar visitor center. Some of the exhibits were well lit and had fairly large black text on a white background. However, others did not. Some of the text was black on a gray background or black text superimposed on black-and-white images. Occasionally the text was red or light gray on a white background or even white on a red background. This lack of contrast on top of the lack of lighting made the text and the pictures difficult to discern. Some of the exhibits were only partially lit or near doors and windows, also making the text difficult to read because it was either too dim or too bright. At the back of the museum was a large wall listing all of the incarcerees. Between the height (it reached almost to the ceiling), the dim lighting, and the text being superimposed onto a picture, it was impossible for me to read. What should have been the most impactful part of the visitor center was made less so by its inaccessibility. The dim lighting also made navigating the exhibits difficult, especially with obstacles such as benches scattered throughout the room.

One of the interactive portions of the exhibition was the ID tag station with pictures of incarcerees with replicas of the tags worn when they were forcibly removed. The explanatory text was white on a red background and the text on the tags was small. This is also a frequent problem with similar exhibits that provide visitors with a more personalized experience, such as a card containing information about people who experienced the event where the font is often very small.

The visitor center itself was fairly physically accessible, with a wheelchair ramp from the main parking lot and a flat one-floor exhibit. However, the accessibility, especially for people with mobility disabilities, changed upon leaving the visitor center. There was a wheelchair ramp out the back door and a sidewalk that only extended a short way, which was later expanded. The rest of the site was gravel and sand. Though I did not see any visitors including former incarcerees using any mobility aids, I wondered whether they had difficulty navigating the uneven path. To say nothing of anyone wanting to go beyond what had been the camp boundaries, whether they had mobility disabilities or used a guide dog or cane. There was no accessible path, the ground was uneven and covered in plants.

DISABILITY IN THE INCARCERATION CAMPS

Several years after my visit to Manzanar, I began researching Japanese American disability history, initially focusing on their experiences in the camps. My interest began after reading two interviews with Deaf Japanese Americans, Nancy Ikeda Baldwin and Ronald "Ron" Hirano, both children during the war.[9] Nancy and her family were Deaf, while Ron was the only Deaf person in his family, though he had a hard of hearing brother. Ron was among several Japanese American students attending the California School for the Deaf (CSD) when Executive Order 9066 was issued. He received an exemption, but all other Japanese American students were incarcerated. Nancy recalled that "as a Deaf family we stayed together [in camp], and I recall a sense that we were quite helpless."[10]

It was several years before I learned the extent of how disabled people were treated during the incarceration. In the 1980s, many incarcerees talked about their experiences during the redress hearings and through oral histories over the following decades. Margie Motowaki Wong recalled her family was sent to

Manzanar: "When I saw they were taking this man . . . he was an invalid. He was an old man and they rolled up a sheet or something. They were carrying him . . . onto the bus. 'Cause he couldn't walk and they didn't have a wheelchair I guess."[11]

Though some efforts were made for various needs at the "assembly centers," little was done to make daily life easier for disabled and elderly people. Bill Hosokawa wrote that "the distance to the lavatories, more than 100 yards in some parts of Puyallup [Assembly Center in Washington], posed a problem for the elderly and families with small children. Chamber pots became a highly valued commodity."[12]

After several months, incarcerees were moved to the camps. On top of the distance between various parts of the camp, the extreme weather made life difficult as well. The camps were in isolated locations, mostly in the desert. Incarcerees lived in barrack apartments built of wood and tar paper. Temperatures ranged from negative 35 degrees Fahrenheit in winter to 115 degrees Fahrenheit in the summer. There were also frequent dust storms.[13] The kitchens "were often located in the administration complex," Eiichi Sakauye recalled, "far from the residential area; the sick and the elderly had to walk as much as a mile three times a day to get their special food."[14]

Figure 14.1.1. Temporary hospital. *Photo by Dorothea Lange, Courtesy of the National Archives*

Chapter 14

Figure 14.1.2. Manzanar Hospital. *Photo by Dorothea Lange, Courtesy of the National Archives*

Initially, one of Manzanar's barracks served as a temporary hospital. However, the building appears not to have had a ramp and was perhaps only accessible by a set of stairs without railings.[15] There were wooden outhouses beside the hospital, which also had stairs without railings.[16] Presumably, those who were bedridden or had mobility disabilities had chamber pots or other more accessible toilet facilities. The permanent hospital building, completed around July 1942, included a ramp.[17]

I have found few records and especially images relating to disability in the camps. The WRA hired Dorothea Lange and Ansel Adams to document the incarceration and life in the camps.[18] Adams's photographs include Tom Kano in his wheelchair and nurse Aiko Hamaguchi with other incarcerees outside the hospital.[19]

People with less severe mobility disabilities and ailments were able to get around to varying degrees. Wong's sister, Betty, had osteomyelitis, which meant that "one leg was shorter."[20] Though she could walk, including going to the block mess hall for meals, Betty spent much of her time in a wheelchair in the hospital with other disabled children.[21]

But even if incarcerees had mobility aids, they were sometimes useless in camp. Takato Hamai suffered an infection and had an operation that shortened his left leg, and he used crutches. He and his family were sent to Gila River,

Figure 14.1.3. Hospital latrines, for patients, between the barracks. *Photo by Dorothea Lange, Courtesy of the National Archives.*

Arizona. There he made a pair of crutches. He had difficulty navigating the barrack stairs and wrote in his diary about how the uneven ground was hard for him to walk on.[22]

John Inazu interviewed his grandmother Lily about her family's experiences at Manzanar. She recalled: "My mother-in-law was in a wheelchair, and we couldn't even push it because the place was so sandy."[23] She was not the only one with such difficulties.

The Sakurai family lived in Troutdale, Oregon. They were sent to the Portland assembly center. Betty Sakurai had "multiple[,] multiple handicaps," including cerebral palsy, and used a wheelchair. Neither the assembly centers nor camps had bathroom facilities in the barracks. At the Portland Assembly

Figure 14.2. Nurse Aiko Hamaguchi and patient Tom Kano and others. *Photo by Ansel Adams. Courtesy of the Library of Congress.*

Center, her brother Richard gathered scrap lumber and built "a chair and cut a hole in the seat . . . so that the chamber pot would just slip underneath."

The Sakurai family was transferred to Minidoka, where Richard made Betty another special chair to accommodate a chamber pot. He also "design[ed] a chair in such a way . . . [that] it will still be stable and won't wobble and fall apart. . . . And years later I discovered that I had re-invented a famous chair called an Adirondack chair."[24] The family also modified their apartment. They "put a little porch outside the door so [Betty] could come out and be outdoors. She couldn't go any further than that because the wheelchair wouldn't go up and down the stairs of that porch. And if she got down to the ground, of course it was either muddy or something like that so she couldn't leave the room."[25]

Other incarcerees made modifications as well. John Nakada and his family were initially incarcerated at Heart Mountain. His mother, who had multiple sclerosis, was paralyzed from the waist down and used a wheelchair. She was "basically confined to the room 'cause, it was pretty terrible," but "it was too cold to go outside anyway." The family transferred to Gila River, which was "a lot better . . . for [his] mother." There, "We made an arrangement and made a ramp and so she could go in and out, she could even go to the mess hall, she could go to the bathroom, everything like that. But my father still had to, you know, push her [to] get there so in that respect it was a lot better."[26]

Other disabled and elderly people could not leave their barracks at all. Travis Mita recalled his grandmother Yoriko and great-grandmother Kise's experiences at Topaz. The family, who lived in San Francisco, initially did not believe that the incarceration would happen. When they did, "the stress of it caused Kise to have a stroke. During her whole time throughout camp, she was . . . an invalid." Yoriko, who was also physically disabled, cared for her mother in camp. She spent "all of her waking moments, whenever she was awake, she was taking care of her mom." She brought food from the mess hall where she worked, and as Kise was incontinent, Yoriko would "clean her up, take all the dirty clothes out. You didn't have a bathroom inside of your barracks. You had to take the clothes out to the middle of the washroom."[27]

While there was some information about physically disabled incarcerees, blind and visually impaired people are often overlooked. One of the few documented is Tokinobu Mihara. Three generations of the Mihara family were forcibly removed from their home in San Francisco to Pomona Assembly Center in California, then Heart Mountain, Wyoming. Tokinobu became blind in camp due to untreated glaucoma. His blindness "sharply curtailed his ability to earn income and get around Block 14. Eating at the mess hall was difficult and required Sam and Nobuo, his older son, to guide him there, so he ate in the barrack more often than not."[28]

Interestingly, another issue of navigating the camps and the identical barracks, that visually impaired people probably faced, comes from Nancy Ikeda Baldwin. She recounted the time she got lost at Tule Lake.

> One night, very late, I went to use the bathroom. On my return I got lost. I could not find my barrack, and I wasn't able to read numbers. . . . Eventually, after walking around aimlessly, I finally saw my mother stood out waving her arms to get my attention. Because my dad didn't want this to happen again, he placed a big USA flag on the roof, a USA flag! Of all the things he could have chosen instead. He wanted to make sure I'd find my way when I saw it. Looking back on it there are many ironies about that. I couldn't see it at nighttime. And there I was locked up inside an internment camp.[29]

Other families did not use such drastic measures to personalize their homes. Some made decorative nameplates that they put up by the door.[30]

MANZANAR'S ACCESSIBILITY PLAN

Through various projects over the last few years, I have learned more about accessibility. The year after visiting Manzanar for a second time, I organized a session for the National Council on Public History's annual meeting titled "Breaking Barriers to History: Making History and Historical Research Accessible." One of the panelists worked at Ingenium, Canada's Museums of Science and Innovation. They were renovating and using the opportunity to make the museums more accessible and had created a report, "Ingenium Accessibility Standards for Exhibitions," that included a detailed description of exhibit components, including measurements, font spacing and margins, and lighting levels.[31] Ingenium does include embedded American Sign Language (ASL) and Quebec Sign Language (LSQ) in their videos, along with bilingual captions.[32]

Between this detailed report and other materials, I have learned about many accessibility considerations and features. This includes many that I had not thought of, such as proper line breaks, using shapes and letters and not just color-coded information, the size of handles for interactive exhibits, the best lighting levels for visually impaired visitors while still keeping fragile objects from being damaged, minimizing sounds to allow videos to be heard, and even how to phrase verbal descriptions of object locations. I think that all museums should become aware of and incorporate these elements into their exhibits.

There were many changes at Manzanar between my first visit in 2007 and my second visit in 2019. A World War II–era mess hall was moved to Block 14 in 2002 and was restored. Additional exhibits were added in 2011.[33] Two barracks buildings were reconstructed in 2010 and exhibits were installed within them in April 2015.[34] A replica women's latrine was reconstructed in 2017.[35] All of these new additions included wheelchair ramps.

However, it was not until after most of the new exhibits and components were installed that NPS began looking at accessibility. By 2016, a "new accessible sidewalk [that] links the visitor center, barracks, and latrine" was added.[36] In 2017, NPS released the "Accessibility Self-Evaluation and Transition Plan Overview" (Accessibility Overview, for short), a detailed plan to improve accessibility. They evaluated physical accessibility, programmatic accessibility, and park-wide accessibility, including issues relating to missing signage and illegible content.[37] The renovations were divided between immediate (0–1 year), short term (1–3 years), midterm (3–7 years), and long term (>7 years).[38] Breaking accessibility projects into smaller chunks like this makes them easier to complete in a realistic way. In the case of the Accessibility Overview, each section of the site and each portion of the exhibit had notes regarding improvements to exhibits. The report was not as detailed as some others I have seen and did not include any pictures of the exhibits, making some aspects difficult to visualize. However, some of the accessibility components were more detailed than I had seen elsewhere.

The visitor center section of the Accessibility Overview contains a detailed description of the accessibility features, including a ramp, seating, signage, and exhibit and bookstore layout. It notes that "exhibit information is delivered with strong color and contrast, and horizontal panels can be approached from the front or side." It also includes information on tactile portions of the exhibit. "Objects not encased can be touched and are within reach range" and that "most all objects are accessible by wheelchair and include sufficient room for transferring from a wheelchair onto a barracks bed."[39] Other improvements include relocating or altering exhibits "to ensure they are cane detectable" for visitors who are blind or have low vision and providing audio descriptions.[40] The plan also includes open captioning and "audio description of all images being shown on the videos throughout Visitor Center (three total)."[41] The Accessibility page for Manzanar lists captioning and "audio descriptive devices" for the film *Remembering Manzanar* shown at the visitor center.[42] Audio description verbally describes key visual elements in TV or movies "when the images and actions on screen are described during natural pauses in the dialogue."[43]

While I did not view *Remembering Manzanar* on site, I did view it on Manzanar's YouTube channel, which had captions but no audio descriptions.[44] The captions include each speaker's name, which is especially helpful as they are mostly not on screen. The speakers' names are in sentence case but the dialogue is in all capitals. The Described and Captioned Media Program (DCMP) recommends that "mixed case characters are preferred for readability" and that "1. Captions should have a minimum duration of 40 frames (1 second and 10 frames). 2. Captions should have a maximum duration of 6 seconds. (Background music notation is an exception to this guideline)."[45]

The National Deaf Center on Postsecondary Outcomes (NDC) explains that "there is no universal sign language. In America, the d/Deaf community uses ASL. ASL is a complete, grammatically complex language . . . ASL is not a communication code designed to represent English."[46] NCD says that ASL interpreting "does not provide equivalent access because the interpreter and video cannot be viewed at the same time." A paper transcript does not solve the problem either because "the viewer is asked to read along while watching the video."[47] But as ASL and English are separate languages, some may have difficulty with English captions. Some museums and historic sites are starting to include ASL video translations alongside the video being shown; however, this is not very common yet.

Like many museums and sites, the Manzanar website has a page dedicated to accessibility, which explains what accessibility and features are available in each exhibit. The page also has text-only and audio versions of the park's brochure. Unfortunately, the text-only and downloadable audio links do not work well. The text-only version is riddled with typos:

Manzanar National Historic Site
<!—description—>
Overview
This is the audio-only version of the parkâ€™s [*sic*] official print brochure. It tells the story of Manzanar, located in California, and provides information related to your visit.[ ] Side one includes quotes, historic photographs, and photographs of artifacts.[48]

The typos continue intermittently throughout the page. People who use a screen reader would have an especially difficult time understanding this text. The audio version requires users to download the files first rather than being able to stream them from the internet.[49] The audio brochure features a monotone voice that makes it difficult to understand.

The Accessibility Overview contains a lot of detail about making signs and printed materials legible. Changes include "easy to read fonts, such as sans-serif options Arial or Frutiger."[50] It encourages alternative formats for printed material including Braille and large-print publications as well as audio-described publications and tactile maps. It even details things such as a "minimum readable typeface" of eighteen-point font, aligning left justified, using a black or white type color with graphics and text "with at least 70% contrast," and avoiding hyphens, red, underlined, and italicized text.[51]

Also in the Accessibility Overview, there was a note to include information about accessibility in all publications by providing multiple formats.[52] It is good to know that there are both large-print and Braille options and that NPS staff understand the difference. I have been to museums and even tours at government facilities and asked for large print only to be handed Braille materials, which the guide did not seem to understand that I could not read. It is important to note that not all people who are blind or visually impaired can read Braille, and like ASL, this is a language that is not a direct one-to-one translation from English.

2019 VISIT

In 2019, I attended Manzanar's fiftieth annual pilgrimage. The site had changed significantly since my visit in 2007. Since then, there had been many renovations and additions, as mentioned earlier, including a replica barrack and other buildings, a latrine, and a dining hall. The buildings and artifacts simulated conditions during the war and the other buildings had oral histories, displays, and pictures. A concrete path now connected all of the buildings, making them physically accessible to mobility device users. While the changes to increase accessibility were substantial and wide ranging, there was a varying degree of success and implementation.

While the site was more accessible, many of the changes suggested in the 2017 report had not been implemented and accessibility continued to be a problem in a number of areas. The written material on the exhibits appeared to be the same as it had been in 2007 and continued to be visually inaccessible. This ironically included text relating to disability education in one of the barracks. The type was still small and in Times, or a similar font, and written directly on a wooden table with the grain still visible. The captions on the pictures and newspaper clippings were in small print against dark backgrounds. There was one part with a larger font mimicking handwriting in chalk on a blackboard that was slightly easier to read due to the size and contrast.

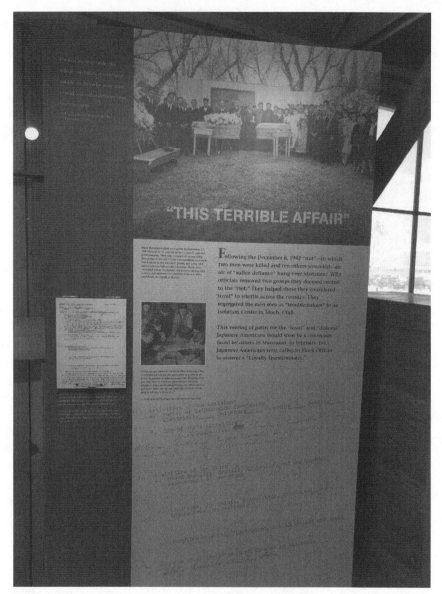

Figure 14.3.1. Panel on Manzanar "riot" and loyalty questionnaire. *Courtesy Selena Moon*

In the Accessibility Overview, there was a precaution to "avoid red text" and "provide graphics with at least 70% contrast."[53] I did not see any red text, but there were several exhibit panels throughout the visitor center and the site with black text on red or gray backgrounds, or gray text on gray or clear backgrounds, combined with a lack of lighting and small print. And there were still exhibits

Figure 14.3.2. Panel on education for disabled children at Manzanar.
Courtesy Selena Moon

with black text superimposed on black-and-white images.[54] The evaluation also notes, under programming accessibility, that "publications, videos, and tours did not have alternate formats in braille, large print, open captioning, or audio or electronic formats."[55] The brochure at least is in a "variety of formats including braille, audio description, and text-only," though large print is not mentioned.[56] I look forward to returning to the exhibit after the 2017 recommendations are fully implemented and being able to easily read the text.

According to Manzanar's Accessibility Overview, "Interpretive wayside" (the descriptive panels scattered around the site), should have a 24-point minimum font without the use of italics."[57] Despite stipulations that one of the immediate tasks (from 2017) would be that "when exhibits [inside Barrack 14] are replaced, ensure that text is 24-point minimum and use sans serif fonts."[58] It is wonderful that NPS has put so much thought into the font and font size. Unfortunately, this has not been implemented in any of the exhibits that I saw. Even the main explanatory text was frequently difficult to read. And the majority of the supplementary material was almost illegible. Newspaper clippings, captions, and quotes were either in small text, gray on white, were dimly lit, or otherwise difficult to read. Some of the signs were small, with black text on glass. The print on the photo captions was small and illegible due to a lack of light. There were also signs at floor level, where some of the print was quite large, but most was not. Even the panels discussing disability education in the camps did not meet NPS requirements. I am eager to see the revised panels that will allow more people to view especially this portion of the exhibit, which discusses an overlooked part of incarceration history.

There were many improvements regarding wheelchair access between 2007 and 2019. There is an acknowledgment of wheelchair users in all of the renovation plans, including a picture of a person pushing a wheelchair on site.[59] There was also a plan to add a bench and "stable path" in Merrit Park and to "maintain a firm and stable outdoor recreation access route," near the Arai Fish Pond through frequent raking.[60] There were also other mobility-related improvements that I had not thought of such as adding armrests "in the center of the bench providing support . . . while also allowing for ease of transfer from a wheelchair to the bench seat at either end."[61]

UNINTENTIONAL ABLEISM

Despite significant efforts to make the site accessible for wheelchair users and others, especially given the older population that is likely to visit, much of the site remains inaccessible and NPS still assumes an able-bodied visitor as the default. Not only that, but the text at the interpretive center and on NPS literature is ableist and exclusionary. While the site is accessible by car, there are suggestions to "stop occasionally and walk through the site" and reminders to "watch your step."[1] Much of the site remains still inaccessible to many users. The concrete path does not appear wide enough to allow two wheelchairs to pass each other. I also did not see any curb ramps allowing anyone using a wheelchair to get off the path.

One panel in the visitor's center, titled "A Place for History," describes how Manzanar became a National Historic Site, through Sue Kunitomi Embrey, Shi Nomura, and others' efforts and features a quote from Embrey: "No one could really learn from the books. You have to walk through the blocks, see the gardens, and the remains of the stone walls and rocks." While I am sure Embrey did not mean to be exclusionary, Embrey is correct in that history such as this must be experienced, much of the site—as it was during the war—is inaccessible to people with limited mobility and who use mobility aids. There is no indication when Embrey said this, but by the time Manzanar became a National Historic Site, many of the first and second generation were possibly in their seventies to nineties and it must have been difficult for them to navigate.

---

1. National Park Service, "Manzanar After-Hours Guide, 2011," accessed June 1, 2022, http://npshistory.com/brochures/manz/after-hrs-guide-2011.pdf.

Figure 14.4. Barrack 8 Tactile map. *Courtesy Selena Moon*

The garden tour map and the accessibility website acknowledge that only parts of the site are wheelchair accessible.[62] The Block 14 mess hall, cemetery, and monument "has limited access by wheelchair as the approach is sandy."[63] The cemetery is quite a distance from the concrete path and the ground is uneven. There was no seating around the cemetery, and despite plans to

I asked fellow members of the Disabled Academic Collective (DAC) whether such signage was problematic. Maria H. said:

> I need mobility devices through most events. I can walk some but not for a long period time. And I do get offended when I see signs saying I have to walk through things. I feel like it's a m[i]croaggression, like the organizers didn't even consider that maybe people can understand it just as well from mobility devices or in some other way. It's ableism through lack of imagination, in my opinion.[2]

Another member, Chariss agreed. "It also feels like one of those things where if you can easily make an adjustment to be more inclusive, why not do it? these could all be switched probably without too much trouble to say uneven sidewalk, wear comfortable attire (or removed? is this one necessary?), move through the site."[3]

---

2. Maria H., Discord message to author, June 30, 2022.
3. Chariss, Discord message to author, June 30, 2022.

provide it, it was still not implemented as of 2019.[64] The concrete walkway by the Block 34 garden is only on one side.[65] Anyone using a wheelchair wanting to see things such as the site of the Children's Village would have to navigate the sand, to say nothing of attempting to navigate beyond the camp's boundaries.

Despite my reservations, others see Manzanar as an accessible location. Several websites relating to wheelchair-accessible travel include Manzanar, and there are wheelchair users who have visited Manzanar and posted about their experiences. However, they did note that parts of the site were inaccessible to them. Gene Ogami and his father have visited Manzanar many times, including many times after his father was in a car accident and began using a wheelchair. Gene recalled that "I had to push my dad around backwards [in his wheelchair] because it was so sandy." However, he did note that NPS "are making an effort in the last years putting in ramps."[66]

Aside from wheelchair accessibility, there are several accessibility features that I have never seen. There are what I later learned were "orientation tactile maps" that the NPS website referenced attached to the door. I had never seen one and took pictures without knowing what it was. A white rectangular piece with raised edges represented the shape of the room and the inside of the room had raised dots, like a thin LEGO® piece. The portion of the rooms with exhibits were cut out and the audio descriptive kiosk was designated by a round piece on top of it. There was a star denoting "You Are Here" at the door. There is Braille beneath the words in the legend, but no text about the exhibits.

While the NPS website goes into detail about accessibility, the Manzanar Pilgrimage FAQ page does not discuss accessibility at all, either for the pilgrimage or Manzanar. Nor does it link to any NPS accessibility information. The pilgrimage is inaccessible to many, without ASL interpretation or captions. Even with a mic, given the size of the crowd and the space, it may be difficult for some patrons to hear. When the pilgrimage became virtual during the COVID-19 pandemic, there were automatic captions (albeit very badly rendered) and ASL interpretation for some events, which greatly increased accessibility.

Access for disabled people has significantly improved at Manzanar since the 1940s and even the early 2000s. While there is still work to be done, the site is vastly more accessible today than it was in 2007 and certainly more so than when the camp was functioning in the 1940s. It took nearly thirty years after the Americans with Disabilities Act (ADA) was adopted in 1990 for Manzanar to implement most of its accessibility features; however, the NPS is working toward greater accessibility as is evidenced by its Accessibility Overview for the site. As is the case with many historic sites, small changes could make the overall site accessible to many more. While I am excited to see the new features that will make this important landmark more accessible, I hope that one day, accessibility features will be part of the framework of historic sites and not an afterthought.

NOTES

1. Much of the terminology used to describe what happened to Japanese Americans during World War II is euphemistic and inaccurate. "Internment" has been the most widely used phrase, but it refers to enemy aliens legally detained during a war. However, most of the people sent to the camps were Japanese Americans born in the United States. Japanese immigrants were categorized as "aliens ineligible for citizenship" unable to obtain US citizenship until 1952. For more information, see "Terminology," https://densho.org/terminology/.
2. Uchida and her family were incarcerated at Topaz, Utah. She was accepted to graduate school at my alma mater Smith College and allowed to leave camp in 1943. In the 1970s, she began writing children's fiction books about Japanese American children that not only included major historical events such as World War I, the Great Depression, and World War II but also issues of racism, citizenship, and multicultural identity.
3. "Executive Order 9066: Resulting in Japanese-American Incarceration (1942)," National Archives and Records Administration, https://www.archives.gov/milestone-documents/executive-order-9066.
4. "Assembly centers" were facilities surrounded by fences and military police where Japanese Americans were sent after being rounded up by the military. For more information, see "Terminology," https://densho.org/terminology/.
5. The debate continues over what to call the camps. The government usually called them "relocation centers" and "internment camps," though some, including President Roosevelt, and modern historians call them "concentration camps" or "prison camps." For more information, see "Terminology," https://densho.org/terminology/.

6. Testimony, Toshiko Toku, Seattle, September 10, 1981, 39, and testimony, James T. Fujii, Los Angeles, August 6, 1981, 80, cited in Commission on Wartime Relocation and Internment of Civilians, Personal Justice Denied Part 1: Chapter 5: Assembly Centers, US Government Printing Office, 1983, 139, accessed April 14, 2021, https://www.archives.gov/files/research/japanese-americans/justice-denied/chapter-5.pdf.

7. John L. DeWitt, *Final Report: Japanese Evacuation From the West Coast, 1942* (Washington, DC: US Government Printing Office, 1943), 34, https://collections.nlm.nih.gov/catalog/nlm:nlmuid-01130040R-bk.

8. Harlan D. Unrau, "Chapter Sixteen: The Manzanar War Relocation Center Site, November 21, 1045–Present (continued)," in *The Evacuation and Relocation of Persons of Japanese Ancestry During World War II: A Historical Study of the Manzanar Relocation Center* (US Department of the Interior, National Park Service, 1996), accessed June 2, 2022, https://www.nps.gov/parkhistory/online_books/manz/hrs16d.htm.

9. Deaf with a lowercase "d" refers to being audiologically deaf, while Deaf refers to members of the Deaf community who are culturally Deaf, though not necessarily deaf, as this may include hard of hearing people, hearing parents of Deaf children, and others.

10. Ronald M. Hirano, "Ronald M. Hirano," interview by Lu Ann Sleeper, Oral History Center, UC Berkeley Library, June 6, 2013, transcript, https://digicoll.lib.berkeley.edu/record/218949?ln=en; Hannah Takagi Holmes, "An Oral History with Hannah Holmes," interview by Arthur Hansen, Oral History #1476, Transcript, Japanese American, Center for Oral and Public History, California State University Fullerton, Fullerton, California, August 27, 1981.

11. Margie Y. Wong, "Margie Y. Wong," interview by Richard Potashin, Densho Digital Archives, audio, 01:54:38, January 21, 2011, https://ddr.densho.org/narrators/598/.

12. Letter, Bill Hosokawa to Angus Macbeth, commission staff, September 14, 1982 (CWRTC 8800-16), cited in *Personal Justice Denied*, 142.

13. Report of the WRA, March 18–June 30, 1942, 10, and testimony, Eiichi E. Sakauye, San Francisco, August 12, 1981, 226; and testimony, George Matsumoto, San Francisco, August 12, 1981, 113, cited in *Personal Justice Denied Part 1: Chapter 6: Relocation Centers*, 161, accessed May 5, 2022, https://www.archives.gov/files/research/japanese-americans/justice-denied/chapter-6.pdf.

14. Testimony, Yasuko Ito, San Francisco, August 13, 1981, 54, cited in *Personal Justice Denied*, 162.

15. Dorothea Lange, Department of the Interior, War Relocation Authority Manzanar Relocation Center, Manzanar, California. Emergency hospital housed in temporary quarters at this War Relocation Authority center for evacuees of Japanese ancestry. The modern new hospital is almost ready for occupancy as shown in Photo C-851, Manzanar, California, July 2, 1942.

16. Lange, War Relocation Authority, Manzanar Relocation Center. Hospital latrines, for patients, between the barracks, which serve temporarily as wards. For the first three months of occupancy medical facilities have been meager but the new hospital fully equipped, is almost ready for occupancy." Manzanar, California, July 2, 1942.

17. Lange, War Relocation Authority, Manzanar Relocation Center. The new hospital at this War Relocation Authority center is almost ready for occupancy. It will be fully equipped to care for all the needs of ten thousand persons. There are accommoda-

tions for 250 beds. It is fully insulated, has double floors, inside heating, and with all-new equipment. This hospital will be staffed by evacuee doctors and nurses. Manzanar, California, July 3, 1942.

18. Library of Congress, "Ansel Adams's Photographs of Japanese-American Internment at Manzanar" (digital collection), Library of Congress, https://www.loc.gov/collections/ansel-adams-manzanar/about-this-collection/.

19. Ansel Adams, photographer, Nurse Aiko Hamaguchi, patient Tom Kano, Manzanar Relocation Center, California/photograph by Ansel Adams, California Manzanar, 1943, photograph, https://www.loc.gov/item/2002697851/.

20. Wong, interview.

21. Wong, interview.

22. Nancy Ukai, "Takato Hamai's Crutches," *50 Objects Stories* (blog), accessed August 10, 2019, https://50objects.org/object/takato-hamais-crutches/.

23. John Inazu, "Beyond the Legality of Executive Orders," *The Hedgehog Review*, February 16, 2017, https://hedgehogreview.com/web-features/thr/posts/beyond-the-legality-of-executive-orders.

24. Richard Sakurai, "Richard Sakurai Interview," interview by Richard Potashin, July 24, 2010, audio, 02:22:13, Densho Digital Repository, https://ddr.densho.org/narrators/536/.

25. Sakurai, interview.

26. John Nakada, "John Nakada Interview," interview by Richard Potashin, July 23, 2010, audio, 02:13:21, Densho Digital Repository, https://ddr.densho.org/narrators/532/.

27. Travis Mita, "An Oral History with Cheryl Gertler and Travis Mita," interview by Arthur A. Hansen, May 5, 2002, Oral History #528, transcript, Japanese American, Center for Oral and Public History, California State University Fullerton, Fullerton, California, May 5 2002, https://cdm16855.contentdm.oclc.org/digital/collection/p16855coll4/id/12413/rec/1.

28. Nancy Ukai, "The Mihara Braille Board," *50 Objects Stories* (blog), accessed August 10, 2020, https://50objects.org/object/the-mihara-braille-board/.

29. Nancy Ikeda Baldwin, "Nancy Ikeda Baldwin," interview by Lu Ann Sleeper, February 27, 2013, Oral History Center, UC Berkeley Library, https://digicoll.lib.berkeley.edu/record/218926?ln=en. While Nancy herself wasn't visually impaired, her challenge illustrates the struggle individuals who were blind or had low vision would have faced.

30. Nancy Ukai, "Nameplates," *50 Objects Stories* (blog), accessed August 7, 2021, https://50objects.org/object/nameplates/.

31. Ingenium, "Ingenium Accessibility Standards for Exhibitions," revised February 19, 2018, https://accessibilitycanada.ca/wp-content/uploads/2019/07/Accessibility-Standards-for-Exhibitions.pdf.

32. Ingenium, "Ingenium Accessibility Standards for Exhibitions," 21.

33. National Park Service, "Your Dollars at Work," *Manzanar National Historic Site*, updated May 14, 2020, https://www.nps.gov/manz/learn/management/yourdollarsatwork.htm.

34. National Park Service, "Manzanar National Historic Site Museum Management Planning Team," 2011, 5, 59, accessed June 1, 2022, http://npshistory.com/publications/manz/mmp-2011.pdf; Manzanar Committee, "Manzanar National His-

toric Site Wins Prestigious Award for Barracks Exhibit," (news release), *Manzanar Committee* (blog), April 14, 2016, https://manzanarcommittee.org/2016/04/14/manzanar-barracks-oah-award/.

35. National Park Service, "THINGS TO DO Explore Manzanar Block 14 Exhibits," accessed May 15, 2022, https://www.nps.gov/thingstodo/explore-manzanar-block-14-exhibits.htm.

36. Keith Wood, "Manzanar National Historic Site Hosts Record 105,307 Visitors in 2016," *Manzanar Committee* (blog), January 26, 2017, https://manzanarcommittee.org/2017/01/25/manzanar-visitors-2016/.

37. National Park Service, "Accessibility Service—Evaluation and Transition Plan Overview Manzanar," November 2017, 8, http://npshistory.com/publications/manz/accessibility-self-eval.pdf.

38. National Park Service, "Accessibility Service—Evaluation," 3–4, 17, 21.

39. National Park Service, "Accessibility Service—Evaluation and Transition Plan," 53.

40. National Park Service, "Accessibility Service—Evaluation and Transition Plan," 21.

41. National Park Service, "Accessibility Service—Evaluation and Transition Plan," 59.

42. National Park Service, "Accessibility—Manzanar National Historic Site (U.S. National Park Service)," *Manzanar National Historic Site*, accessed May 30, 2022, https://www.nps.gov/manz/planyourvisit/accessibility.htm.

43. Library of Congress, "Audio Description Resource Guide," National Library Service for the Blind and Print Disabled (NLS), accessed September 17, 2022, https://www.loc.gov/nls/about/services/reference-publications/guides/audio-description-resource-guide/.

44. National Park Service, "Remembering Manzanar," 21:51. https://www.youtube.com/watch?v=Spo1Khmp2U4&ab_channel=ManzanarNPS.

45. Described and Captioned Media Program, "Captioning Key—Text." *Described and Captioned Media Program*, accessed June 1, 2022, https://dcmp.org/learn/597-captioning-key—-text.

46. National Deaf Center on Postsecondary Outcomes, "The Deaf Community: An Introduction," *National Deaf Center on Postsecondary Outcomes*, accessed June 28, 2022, https://www.nationaldeafcenter.org/sites/default/files/The%20Deaf%20Community-%20An%20Introduction.pdf.

47. National Deaf Center on Postsecondary Outcomes, "Why Captions Provide Equal Access," *National Deaf Center on Postsecondary Outcomes*, accessed June 10, 2022, https://www.nationaldeafcenter.org/sites/default/files/Why%20Captions%20Provide%20Equal%20Access.pdf.

48. National Park Service, "Manzanar National Historic Site," *Manzanar National Historic Site*, accessed June 4, 2022, https://www.nps.gov/manz/planyourvisit/upload/Manzanar_National_Historic_Site.txt.

49. National Park Service, "Manzanar National Historic Site."

50. National Park Service, "Accessibility Service—Evaluation and Transition Plan," 21.

51. National Park Service, "Accessibility Service—Evaluation and Transition Plan," 57.

52. National Park Service, "Accessibility Service—Evaluation and Transition Plan," 57.

53. National Park Service, "Accessibility Service—Evaluation and Transition Plan," 57.

54. National Park Service, "Accessibility Service—Evaluation and Transition Plan," 54.

55. National Park Service, "Accessibility Service—Evaluation and Transition Plan," 57.

56. National Park Service, "Accessibility Service—Evaluation and Transition Plan," 54.

57. I think that Arial is easier to read than Times or Times New Roman because the letters are thicker, though some find Times and Times New Roman easier to read because letters such as capital "T" have hooks at the top. I had never thought of italics as hard to read, but thinking about it, italics compress the letters together and some are difficult to read. National Park Service, "Accessibility Service—Evaluation and Transition Plan," 23.
58. National Park Service, "Accessibility Service—Evaluation and Transition Plan," 25.
59. National Park Service, "Accessibility Service—Evaluation and Transition Plan," 56.
60. National Park Service, "Accessibility Service—Evaluation and Transition Plan," 47.
61. National Park Service, "Accessibility Service—Evaluation and Transition Plan," 21.
62. National Park Service, "Manzanar Japanese Garden Tour Guide—NPS History," accessed June 1, 2022, http://npshistory.com/brochures/manz/garden-tour.pdf.
63. National Park Service, "Manzanar Accessibility," updated May 19, 2020, https://www.nps.gov/manz/planyourvisit/accessibility.htm.
64. National Park Service, "Accessibility Service—Evaluation and Transition Plan," 3.
65. National Park Service, "Manzanar Accessibility."
66. Gene Ogami, phone conversation with author, July 1, 2022.

15

Creating an Immersive Accessible Experience at Mt. Cuba Center

Charlotte Barrows PLA
Jennifer Lauer

Gardens, as living relics of human ingenuity and connection to the natural world, are an integral part of our collective heritage. The impulse to tend and visit gardens to fulfill utilitarian, spiritual, recreational, and aesthetic needs is ancient: gardens as works of art have nourished human societies for more than ten thousand years. Today, as the effects of the COVID-19 pandemic continue to impact communities across the world, public outdoor spaces have taken on renewed significance as sources of mental, physical, and spiritual renewal. At the same time, public gardens have emerged as important places for public education and scientific research regarding climate change, ecological integrity, and conservation.

These spaces and experiences must be accessible to people of all abilities. According to the Centers for Disease Control and Prevention, mobility disabilities—defined as serious difficulty walking or climbing stairs—affect 13.7 percent of adults.[1] However, many historic gardens and outdoor spaces throughout the world were *not* built to accommodate people with disabilities. Landscape architects are professionals best suited to the task of adapting historic landscapes to meet the requirements of the Americans with Disabilities Act (ADA) and making outdoor sites accessible. Accommodating the needs of people with mobility disabilities requires rethinking historic gardens that lack accessible routes to key destinations. Accessibility can be achieved in historic landscapes through subtle design modifications, including manipulation of grade, pathways, and materials. Such changes allow all users to access qualities central to a garden's original design intent: the sequencing of movement through the space; key axes, thresholds, and arrival moments; and unique experiences created through arranged plantings, viewsheds, and materials.

ADA adjustments to the historic landscape also expand the opportunity to access gardens among other users, including parents pushing strollers. Because so many groups of people require these adjustments to access the landscape, such changes can open the possibility of intergenerational gatherings for people of all ages and abilities. This chapter will describe the process by which Nelson Byrd Woltz Landscape Architects (NBW) integrated sensitive ADA modifications to the historic landscape at Mt. Cuba Center, a nonprofit public garden and site listed on the National Register located in Hockessin, Delaware.[2]

Mt. Cuba Center aims to inspire public appreciation for the beauty, value, and conservation of northeastern native forest ecology—specifically focusing on plants of the Appalachian Piedmont. The 1,083-acre site is composed of ecologically rich landscapes and naturalistic gardens, with the visitor arrival centered around a 1930s Colonial Revival home surrounded by early to mid-twentieth-century formal gardens. With respect to Mt. Cuba Center's historic significance, NBW carefully analyzed the property's estate-era historic gardens and circulation systems to inform a thoughtful revision to the property's arrival sequence, with an aim to better serve public guests and accommodate growing visitorship. The proposed design, partially constructed as of this writing, integrates ADA-compliant slopes, ramps, and railings with historic materials from the early to mid-twentieth century, allowing all to access Mt. Cuba Center's important formal garden spaces without compromising the gardens' historic integrity.

These efforts were part of a larger comprehensive landscape plan to holistically reenvision the property's educational, garden, and production zones. This plan represents a visionary new chapter in Mt. Cuba Center's public educational offerings while carefully considering the needs of guests with mobility disabilities, who make up a significant portion of Mt. Cuba Center's visitorship. These goals were achieved in close partnership with the staff and board of Mt. Cuba Center, fulfilling the institution's mission: to inspire an appreciation for the beauty and value of native plants and a commitment to protect the habitats that sustain them.

HISTORICAL SUMMARY

The property originated as the private estate of Lammot du Pont Copeland and his wife, Pamela Cunningham Copeland, who purchased 126.7 acres of farmland near the village of Mount Cuba in 1935. Their home, a Colonial Revival structure designed by Victorine and Samuel Homsey, was built the same year. The surrounding formal garden beds, the Main and Conservatory Terraces, and a vehicular Forecourt were designed and implemented by landscape architect Thomas Sears during the mid- to late 1930s. In 1949, noted landscape architect Marian Cruger Coffin, who had worked on several other historic du Pont gardens, visited Mount Cuba for the first time. Coffin designed and implemented several additional formal gardens for the Copeland property during the 1950s, including the Tennis Lawn, Upper Allee, Round Garden, and Lilac Allee. These spaces created a series of garden "rooms" spreading southward on an axis with the Copelands' Colonial Revival structure ultimately providing an important arrival sequence to the naturalistic gardens later developed by landscape architect Seth Kelsey in the 1960s.[3]

The property began to open to public visitation by hosting docent-led tours of its designed gardens and conservation areas during the 1980s. In 2002 the estate officially became part of the 501(c)3 not-for-profit Mt. Cuba Center, Inc., and was added to the National Register of Historic Places in 2003.[4] Today, Mt. Cuba Center is nationally regarded as an important site for horticulture, ecology, and conservation research and education and is a significant destination among the historic public gardens and landscapes of the Brandywine Valley in Pennsylvania and northern Delaware.

Mt. Cuba Center's formal gardens, including those of Sears and Coffin, are today referred to as the "Core Gardens." They are the focus of this essay's examination of the balancing act between historic integrity and current accessibility for a site like Mt. Cuba Center—a former private estate, now dealing with challenges generated by growing visitor use. The following analysis puts the formal garden rehabilitation projects within the context of the larger comprehensive landscape planning efforts in progress.

PROJECT BACKGROUND: COMPREHENSIVE LANDSCAPE PLAN

The transition from private estate to public accommodation has been incremental. The Copelands began planning for eventual public visitation as early as the 1960s, and the public was invited to tours and special events in the 1980s and 1990s.[5, 6] In 2010, the site opened for general admission. Despite efforts to make adaptations to existing facilities and infrastructure to accommodate the growing visitation and programming, many space and circulation conflicts emerged. Visitor pressure overwhelmed existing parking capacity and staff time was inefficiently used to manage the flow of visitor vehicles.

In 2015, Mt. Cuba Center created a strategic plan to address its growing visitorship, its expanding staff and programs, and its aspiration to merge the historic Mt. Cuba property with the adjacent 501-acre Red Clay Reservation, which would bring the property's holdings to 1,083 acres. *The Mt. Cuba Center Strategic Plan 2016–2020* identified several goals for the organization, including a Comprehensive Landscape Plan to guide the evolution of Mt. Cuba Center's landscape and facilities. The Comprehensive Landscape Plan aspired to protect the scenic character of the gardens and grounds and address visitor circulation and wayfinding, parking, and accessibility while preserving the intimacy of the visitor experience.[7]

In 2017, Mt. Cuba Center's property merged with the Red Clay Reservation. The same year, Mt. Cuba Center hired NBW and a team of consultants to conduct a Comprehensive Landscape Plan to envision the necessary site alterations to address ongoing institutional challenges and expanded acreage by focusing on operations, circulation, facilities, programming, and conservation.

The yearlong planning process, which drew upon the knowledge of Mt. Cuba Center's staff and board members through interactive workshops, resulted in the consensus that too many programmatic needs were crowded within the Main House. The Comprehensive Landscape Plan addressed multiple conflicts by proposing a separation of staff areas from public routes and spaces; an emphasis on the Main House as one of many destinations rather than the main attraction; an expansion of the types of gardens and plants featured; and an introduction of the public experience to the newly acquired conservation land. Three main project focus areas emerged:

- The Core Gardens project area is composed of sensitive alterations to the formal gardens that link visitors to other key horticultural spaces as well as the Main House, where Mt. Cuba maintains adaptable program spaces, restrooms, and refreshments. (Phase 1 is complete at the time of this writing.)
- The Education Courtyard and Gardens project area adapted the Chauffeur's Complex into a series of indoor and outdoor hands-on learning spaces that include demonstration gardens, classrooms, a wet lab, and a library. (Phase 1 is complete at the time of this writing.)
- The Greenhouse Complex project area envisioned expanded support for the horticultural operations, additional vehicle storage, and offices for horticulture, propagation, and maintenance staff. (Phase 1 is under construction at the time of this writing.)

NBW linked these project areas with an expanded circulation network, separating staff and visitor traffic while improving internal maintenance access. A proposed connected path network accommodates people of diverse physical abilities so that every visitor can easily and intuitively access the main destinations and features of the gardens.

LEGAL AND VALUES-BASED DESIGN CONSIDERATIONS

During the planning and design process, Mt. Cuba Center considered many factors, including the financial and experiential impact of construction. Mt. Cuba Center also considered its legal obligation per the ADA to provide at least one accessible route to each site element open to the public. The ADA accommodations address:

- Building egress and entrances
- Routes from buildings to parking
- Parking
- Interior routes and access to building services and restrooms
- Communication features, such as signage

Mt. Cuba Center is subject to Title III of the Americans with Disabilities Act (ADA), which requires the removal of architectural barriers in places of public accommodation constructed or altered prior to the passage of the ADA (1990), where such removal is readily achievable. Determination of whether the removal of a barrier is readily achievable is the responsibility of the institution and is based on several factors, including the institution's overall finances. Even heritage landscapes like Mt. Cuba Center, which is listed on the National Register of Historic Places, must comply with 2010 ADA Standards to the maximum extent feasible.

Mt. Cuba Center faced challenges in providing ADA-compliant parking—including accessible parking spaces, access aisles, accessible passenger loading zones, and an accessible route to facilities—and in providing access to the Formal Gardens, which are terraced into the sloping topography around the Main House and accessible by stairs only. Per the ADA, the maximum allowable slope for pavement is 1:20, or 5 percent, with a cross-slope of no more than 1:48, or 2 percent. Pavement that slopes more than 1:20 in the direction of travel is considered a ramp, which has ADA requirements for maximum length, landings, and handrails. The ADA also stipulates that for a route to be accessible, the surface material must be stable, firm, and slip resistant. Many of the paths leading to and through the Formal Gardens were grass, gravel, and mulch, materials that are not sufficiently durable and stable to support public accommodation.

The necessary accessibility improvements were also supported by Mt. Cuba Center's 2018 Core Values: "We deliver remarkable experiences to our community and guests at every available opportunity. We do this by performing our roles with integrity and sharing our enthusiasm for our mission with everyone with whom we interact. . . . We treat every guest, student, and professional colleague as an important potential steward of our mission" and, "We welcome diversity in thought and outlook and encourage everyone affiliated with Mt. Cuba Center to express their unique views. We take great care to foster an environment of fellowship and community that embraces diversity and is inclusive. . . . Our staff, our board, and our committees respect differences, value diversity, and treat each individual with kindness and respect."[8]

With legal obligations as well as value-driven motivations, Mt. Cuba Center charged NBW with the challenge of designing sensitive alterations that would maintain the intimate scale and be in accordance with the materiality of the house and gardens. NBW's design approach prioritized the following tenets:

- Work within existing design logic of symmetry and axial organization
- Extend the existing material palette of brick and bluestone
- Preserve intimate scale and immersion in horticulture
- Extend the visitor experience to additional garden collections

ADAPTIVE REDESIGN OF ARRIVAL AND FORMAL GARDENS

THE FIRST ACCESSIBLE ROUTE FROM ARRIVAL TO THE FORMAL GARDENS

The first phase of the Comprehensive Landscape Plan is complete. This phase established an intuitive and accessible visitor arrival sequence from the Education Courtyard parking lot to ticketing to the gardens. This phase completed Mt. Cuba Center's first accessible route through the Formal Gardens and to the Main House.

These interventions significantly altered the public arrival experience, especially the experience of a person with a mobility disability. Before Phase 1 was implemented, visitors with mobility disabilities would have arrived at Mt. Cuba by parking in the Forecourt directly adjacent to the house. Though part of the house is accessible to guests with mobility aids, the historic gardens were inaccessible due to stairs, steep slopes, and inaccessible groundplane materials.

Visitors with mobility disabilities are now able to arrive and park in a single lot equipped with accessible parking spots, share the same ticketing experience as other visitors, and access bathroom facilities. Everyone enters the gardens along a carefully designed accessible path—The Overlook Path—along which an immersive journey through a woodland glade progresses to a dramatic view of the rolling hills typical of the region. This horticultural experience grounds the visitor in the landscape of the Delaware Piedmont by immersing visitors within the wider context of Mt. Cuba Center and encouraging engagement with Mt. Cuba Center's mission: to inspire an appreciation for the beauty and value of native plants and a commitment to protect the habitats that sustain them.

The area selected for the insertion of the Overlook Path had been underused and off limits to the public for decades. It consisted of several specimen trees—American hollies (*Ilex opaca*) and a yellowwood tree (*Cladrastis kentukea*)—along with an expanse of spring beauty (*Claytonia virginica*), a woodland wildflower. The character of the grove's bright shade, which did not exist elsewhere at Mt. Cuba, presented an opportunity to weave a new garden collection into the existing woodland. The new path, made of permeable pavement, was routed through this zone to preserve the existing vegetation and minimize grade changes while artfully moving the visitor along arcing geome-

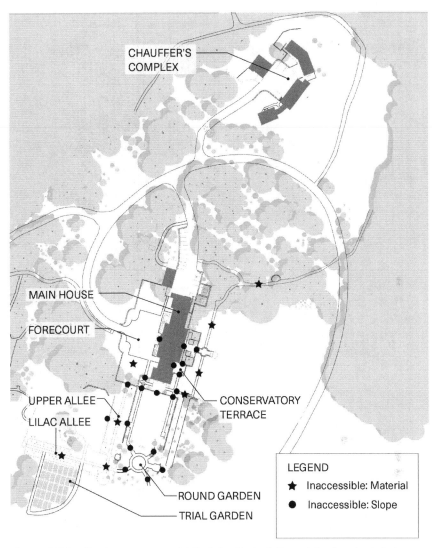

Figure 15.1.1. Barriers to access at Mt. Cuba Center's Formal Gardens included inaccessible ground plane materials such as grass, gravel and mulch; inaccessible grade changes including slopes over than 1:20 (5%); and terraces accessible by stairs only. While these barriers may be acceptable in a private garden with limited visitorship, they are not appropriate for public accommodation. *Courtesy Nelson Byrd Woltz Landscape Architects*

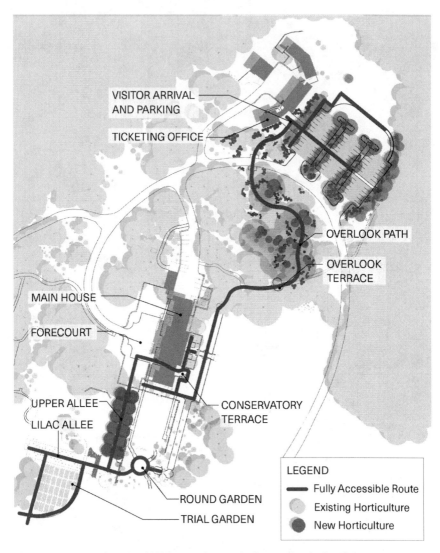

Figure 15.1.2. Nelson Byrd Woltz Landscape Architects worked with Mt. Cuba Center staff, administration, and board members to design Phase 1 of the implementation of the Comprehensive Landscape Plan, which creates the first accessible route from arrival, parking, and ticketing to the Main House and Formal Gardens. The design sensitively alters the historic fabric by respecting scale, proportion, and materiality of the original terraces and paths and prioritizes the display of native plants throughout the experience. *Courtesy Nelson Byrd Woltz Landscape Architects*

tries and robust, diverse native plantings to a fifteen foot by twenty foot blue-stone terrace. The design called for doubling the size of this Overlook Terrace to more adequately serve the public. Pavement material and pattern decisions for the extension of this terrace took cues from the original terrace: natural cleft bluestone in sizes that match the original seamlessly meets the edges of the terrace, increasing the size of the space to comfortably accommodate large numbers of visitors entering the gardens.

From the Overlook Path, visitors travel along a newly built accessible brick path in front of the Main House, from which they can access the Main Terrace and the ground floor portion of the Main House via the Conservatory Terrace.

ALTERATIONS AT THE FORMAL GARDENS—CONSERVATORY TERRACE

Before the renovation, access to the Conservatory Terrace entailed the usage of stairs, and a six-inch step prevented access to the Main House for anyone who could not step up. The NBW design called for the Conservatory Terrace, part of the Thomas Sears series of terraces around the Main House, to be raised six inches to meet the grade of the door threshold. The original pavement was har-vested (carefully removed and saved), the grade was raised, and the bluestone was relaid per the original pattern. The design added an additional riser to the remaining brick stair and a sloping accessible path replaced the two-riser stair

Figure 15.2.1. Thomas Sears's design of the Conservatory Terrace and the Main Terrace beyond did not accommodate people with mobility disabilities. *Courtesy Nelson Byrd Woltz Landscape Architects*

Figure 15.2.2. The renovation raised the elevation of the Conservatory Terrace, requiring a fourth riser at the stair in the foreground. In the background, a new sloping path replaced the two stair risers. A sloping path connecting the Formal Garden accessible pathway network meets the new finish grade of the Conservatory Terrace. Not shown here is the accessible threshold at the Conservatory door, which allows people with mobility disabilities to access the Main House from this side of the gardens. *Courtesy Nelson Byrd Woltz Landscape Architects*

between the Conservatory Terrace and the Main Terrace. Last, an accessible sloping path connecting the Conservatory Terrace (and by extension the Main Terrace, Main House, and route to the Upper Allee) was added to the side of the Conservatory Terrace. The design modification preserved the large saucer magnolia (*Magnolia* x *soulangeana*), which one approaches along the ramp; the magnolia is a contributing design feature of the terrace, adding a distinctive character and providing shade, scent, and beauty.

After crossing the Conservancy Terrace, visitors can move through the Main House into the Forecourt, and from there arrive to the Upper Allee via a newly built accessible path.

ALTERATIONS AT THE FORMAL GARDENS—UPPER ALLEE

NBW carefully redesigned the Upper Allee as a space to host small events, informal gatherings, and dining—programming that Mt. Cuba Center desired but lacked space for throughout the property. The original Marian Cruger Coffin design was a rectangular grass plane, planted with two lines of boxwoods and an allee of gum trees. Mt. Cuba Center replaced the gums with oaks in 2003. However, the oaks were in sharp decline, so NBW's design replaced the trees with new sweet gums, matching the historic spacing and height.

Key axes and views within the garden guided the layout of accessible routes. The new terrace maintains the centerlines of the original garden, the long axis centered on *The Gardener* statue (purchased by the Copelands in 1950 from Crowther of Syon Lodge in London).[9] Likewise, the short axis is centered on the Tennis Lawn, a space original to the Coffin design. These axes are emphasized by new brick paths with soldier courses, a pattern that matches other brick paths in the Formal Gardens. The scale of these paths is reminiscent of Coffin's narrow grass path between the boxwoods.

To accommodate public programming, fields of compacted stone dust between the brick paths extend to the trunks of the newly installed trees and to the edges of the original terrace, maximizing the accessible ground plane and providing a flexible space for both walking and gathering. Shrub and perennial beds at the ends and edges of the allee frame the space and, as envisioned by Mrs. Copeland, immerse not just a few members of a private estate but rather large numbers of visitors engaged in a commitment to conservation. Accommodating visitor seating included careful consideration of furnishings;

Figure 15.3.1. Before the renovation, the trees of Marion Cruger Coffin's design of the Upper Allee were in decline and the boxwoods were overgrown. Visitors with mobility disabilities could not easily access or travel through this garden due to its grass groundplane and inaccessible slopes. *Courtesy Nelson Byrd Woltz Landscape Architects*

Creating an Immersive Accessible Experience at Mt. Cuba Center 209

Figure 15.3.2. Nelson Byrd Woltz Landscape Architects worked with Mt. Cuba Center to design a significant alteration of the Upper Allee. Of importance was maintaining the central axes, overall proportions, and quantity and spacing of the canopy trees while extending the accessible groundplane to accommodate a growing population of visitors. Upgrades also include site lighting and furnishings to accommodate events and dining, programming that had been missing at Mt. Cuba Center. *Photo Courtesy of Mt. Cuba Center, www. mtcubacenter.org*

Mt. Cuba Center provided ADA-compliant café tables and expanded site lighting to safely extend program opportunities into the evenings. The result of this design layout is a simple and elegant terrace inspired by Coffin's work that serves all members of the public.

ALTERATIONS AT THE FORMAL GARDENS—ROUND POND

From the south end of the terrace, visitors can visit three additional garden areas that are newly accessible: the Lilac Allee, where a brick path replaced an inaccessible grass path; the Trial Gardens, a key destination for garden enthusiasts; and Coffin's Round Pond. Here the design called for demolishing one of the inaccessible arcing spoked paths and replacing it with an arcing ramp. The new path respected the scale and proportion of the original Coffin path and stairs, matching the materials and seamlessly meeting grade at the top and bottom of the insertion.

CONCLUSION

The National Park Service refers to seven aspects to describe the term "historic integrity": location, setting, design, materials, workmanship, feeling, and association. Mt. Cuba Center exhibits a high degree of historic integrity as it meets these factors in the following ways.

Location and *setting* refer to the particular point or position where the historic property was constructed and the character of the place where the historic resource is located. Mt. Cuba Center's Main House and Formal Gardens are in the same location where they were originally constructed. The fabric of the remainder of the property and adjacent properties continue to exhibit the agrarian and wooded land use of the 1930s. Topography, viewsheds, roads, paths, and fences are relatively unchanged.

Design is defined by the National Register as "the combination of elements that creates the form, plan, space, structure, and style of a property."[10] The spatial organization, massing, color, and materials of the Main House and Formal Gardens remain largely unchanged.

Materials is defined as "the physical elements that were combined . . . during a particular period of time and in a particular pattern or configuration to form a historic property." Mt. Cuba Center's Main House and Formal Gardens retain their character-defining exterior materials.

Workmanship is defined as "the physical evidence of the crafts of a particular culture or people." Craft is defined as "an occupation requiring special skill," and workmanship refers to "the quality of the craftsman's product."[11] The carefully constructed brick and stone masonry of the exterior of the Main House and of the Formal Gardens' pavement and walls continue to be reflective of the era in which they were constructed.

Feeling is a "property's expression of the aesthetic or historic sense of a particular period of time."[12] At Mt. Cuba Center, the Main House and Formal Gardens materials and workmanship are not the only aspects that deliver the sense of its era. Enormous canopy trees planted in the Copeland era survive to greet the public throughout the Formal Gardens and throughout the site. The understory planting at the Formal and Naturalistic Gardens is also in keeping with the Copeland's well-tended, carefully designed display garden—diverse in color, texture, and seasonal interest. In addition, the patina of time displayed on the surfaces of the masonry—pavement worn down under the footsteps of the Copeland family and friends, moss growing on cracks and crevices, surfaces bleached by a century of sun—contribute to the sense of the passage of time and the importance of this place.

Association is the link between an important person or event and a historic property. Mt. Cuba Center retains association through its connection to the Copelands and through its support of Mrs. Copeland's vision for the gardens as a center of conservation, open to the public.

NBW asserts that alterations to improve accessibility from arrival to the Main House to the Formal Gardens were sensitively made with regard to all of the previously discussed aspects of integrity. Around the Main House and at the Round Garden, surgical changes made via subtle grade changes and ramp and path insertions allow for physical movement along accessible pavement. Design decisions regarding materials and masonry patterns were based on Formal Garden precedents. Any disturbance of planting beds during construction resulted in a collaborative effort between the design team and the horticultural team at Mt. Cuba Center with regard to the selection and installation of new plants.

Changes to the Upper Allee, while significant, successfully balanced the historic design intent with the pressing need for an institution to accommodate the public. Providing public gathering, seating, and dining options outweighed the desire to preserve the groundplane of Marion Cruger Coffin's design. This design was inaccessible due to its slope and groundplane materials and its plantings were no longer contributing to Mt. Cuba Center's mission. As described earlier, while the NBW design took liberties to make changes to the Upper Allee's groundplane, the new pavement is in keeping with the original design in terms of scale, geometry, views, and material and horticultural selection.

Overall, the NBW-designed alterations transformed the experience for all visitors to Mt. Cuba Center. A beautiful, horticulturally focused arrival sequence, easily accessible historic gardens, and spaces that allow for improved public programming indicate that the site planning of this important garden is now in accordance with the ethos of the institution and Mrs. Copeland's vision. Moreover, NBW has determined that additional accessibility improvements at the Formal Gardens and elsewhere to fulfill Mt. Cuba Center's mission to inspire conservation action can be made without compromising the site's historic integrity. For instance, many routes need additional segments so that they are accessible at all times, regardless of whether or not the Main House is open. Looped routes, routes that do not require a person with a mobility disability to "double back" the same way that he or she came, are required. Additional phases of design could offer access to additional garden destinations, including the South Lawn and the Naturalistic Gardens. Accessibility improvements at the Main House could also extend access throughout the first floor and outside to the Main Terrace. Making these alterations while continuing to respect the scale and material qualities of the formerly private estate is imperative to achieve comprehensive, attentive public accommodation.

CREDITS/ACKNOWLEDGMENTS

The authors would like to acknowledge and thank the following team members whose contributions to the planning and design efforts were critical to the success of the project: Thomas Woltz, FASLA, principal, NBW; Chloe Hawkins, project manager and project director, former NBW employee; Jeffrey Downing, executive director, Mt. Cuba Center; George Coombs, horticultural director, Mt. Cuba Center; executive board, horticultural team, facilities and operations teams at Mt. Cuba Center; Beyer Blinder Belle Architects and Planners; revision architects; Bancroft Construction; and Jensen Hughes Code Consultants.

GLOSSARY

Axes: Plural of axis

Axis: A line connecting two points; often a centerline about which garden features are organized symmetrically

Allee: A designed path flanked by two (or more) rows of trees

Grade: Refers to the level of the land or landscape features such as pathways or walls

Grading: Sculpting or leveling the land to achieve specific design goals

Groundplane: The ground, pavement, or horizontal surface

Threshold: Arrival moment often signaled by an architectural feature such as a doorway, archway, or gateway

Understory: Perennials, shrubs, and small trees that are adapted to the shade of canopy trees

Viewshed: An important scenic moment, usually located at an expansive view, or at a designed axis

NOTES

1. Centers for Disease Control and Prevention, "Disability Impacts All of Us Infographic," September 16, 2022, https://www.cdc.gov/ncbddd/disabilityandhealth/infographic-disability-impacts-all.html.
2. Nelson Byrd Woltz Landscape Architects (NBW) is an internationally recognized landscape architecture firm with studios in New York City; Charlottesville, Virginia; and Houston, Texas. Dedicated to aesthetic and environmental excellence, social commitment, and innovation, NBW is designing major public landscapes across the United States and abroad. Through an approach rooted in ecological and cultural research as the foundation for meaningful contemporary landscapes, NBW works to build a deeper understanding of place and history, inspiring connections between people and the natural world.
3. Mt. Cuba Center, "History," September 2022, https://mtcubacenter.org/about/history/.
4. Jody E. Cross and Nedda E. Moqtaderi, "A Landscape History of Mt. Cuba," *Mt. Cuba History Project*, no. 10 (2004): 326.
5. Cross and Moqtaderi, "A Landscape History of Mt. Cuba," 66.
6. Cross and Moqtaderi, "A Landscape History of Mt. Cuba," 28.
7. Mt. Cuba Center, "Strategic Plan 2016–2020," Internal/Institutional Document, 2015.
8. Mt. Cuba Center, "Core Values," Internal/Institutional Document, September 2018.

9. Mt. Cuba Center, "Core Values," 322.
10. US Department of the Interior, National Park Service, "National Register Bulletin: How to Apply the National Register Criteria for Evaluation," 1997, https://www.nps.gov/subjects/nationalregister/upload/NRB-15_web508.pdf.
11. US Department of the Interior, National Park Service, "National Register Bulletin."
12. US Department of the Interior, National Park Service, "National Register Bulletin."

Part III

Diving Deeper

For those who are ready to take a deeper dive and ask, what comes next?, this section is for you. While making changes to make your site more accessible is an important first step, making strides to make your site disability inclusive in its narratives is an important next step. Also included in this section is a list of resources to help you continue on your accessibility journey.

16

Toward an Accessible Future

ACCELERATING DISABILITY JUSTICE IN HISTORIC PRESERVATION

REPAIR: Disability Heritage Collective
Featuring contributions by Shana Crosson, Gail Dubrow, Morgan LaCasse,
Laura Leppink, Perri Meldon, Sarah Pawlicki, and Chelsea Wait

WHO WE ARE

REPAIR's goal is clear: dismantle ableism in heritage conservation.[1] We believe
that moving issues of human ability and disability to the center of our thinking
offers an essential corrective to interpretive visions pitched toward the most
able-bodied, affluent, employable, autonomous, and privileged individuals. Because the experience of disability is complicated by race, gender, sexuality, and
class, this approach demands an intersectional perspective.[2]

The contributors approached this essay through intersectional and multi-
disciplinary lenses, all of which are necessary to understanding how ableism
operates systemically and identifying interventions required to make historic
properties and their respective disability stories accessible.[3] REPAIR draws
inspiration from Juliet Larkin-Gilmore, Ella Gallow, and Susan Burch, guest ed-
itors of the 2021 *Disability Studies Quarterly* issue on disability and indigeneity.
Larkin-Gilmore, Gallow, and Burch assert that coauthorship, collaboration, and
citational practices articulate "processes of cooperation, accountability, and
sustainability."[4] The collective authorship of this chapter builds on REPAIR's
ethos of mutual empowerment, allowing each writer to contribute according to
their particular abilities in their distinctive voice.

As a group of white scholars, activists, writers, practitioners, and artists,
we take the concept of repair—as in, reparations—seriously. How can we, as

a homogenously white authorship collective, advocate for the disability justice principles set forth by disabled, queer people of color in the predominantly white field of historic preservation? REPAIR tries to respond to calls made by racial justice advocates to address and deconstruct whiteness.[5] We recognize that studying whiteness is studying race and that white supremacy and ableism are interlocked systems of oppression. Our authorship collective's individual lived experiences of the social categories of disability, socioeconomic class, gender identity, sexual orientation, and religion bring intersectional perspectives to our work.

Work that has inspired REPAIR includes, but is not limited to, Sins Invalid's "10 Principles of Disability Justice," Leah Lakshmi Piepzna-Samarasinha and Stacey Park Milbern's "Disability Justice: An Audit Tool," MASS Action's "Readiness Assessment" and "Toolkit," and Sarah Marsom's work on dismantling historic preservation.[6] Sins Invalid's principles provide a clear compass for individuals and organizations committed to disability justice. These principles focus REPAIR's projects and ethical commitments. Piepzna-Samarasinha and Milbern's audit tool outlines theoretical and practical interventions organizations may take to foster disability justice, informing how REPAIR approaches historic preservation methodologies.

MASS Action's "Readiness Assessment" and "Toolkit" provide scaffolding for building organizational capacity to engage with justice-centered subjects and activities. MASS Action's resources focus on museums, while REPAIR tends toward a focus on historic places yet applies many of MASS Action's queries to the conservation side of preservation. Sarah Marsom's efforts to dismantle preservation, particularly through #DismantlePreservation Unconferences, provides a sharp reminder: "If historic preservation is not accessible, it is neither relevant nor revolutionary."[7]

REPAIR's emphasis on holistic interventions in preservation planning, documentation, interpretation, accessibility, administration, and maintenance is motivated by knowing that no single person associated with a historic site— whether an administrator, historian, interpreter, or custodian—can make the needed changes alone. Disability has too often been framed as an issue only relevant to a small minority of individuals, requiring an institutional response only from designated access specialists. However, if, as feminist theorist Alison Kafer posits, disability is best understood through a political/relational model in which "the problem of disability is located in inaccessible buildings, discriminatory attitudes, and ideological systems that attribute normalcy and deviance to particular minds and bodies," dismantling inaccessible systems through political action becomes a mission in which all concerned may take part.[8] A comprehensive agenda for action is needed. Thus, REPAIR strives to address the access needs of people with disabilities in the present day while simultaneously advocating for documenting and addressing disabled people's historic experiences and perspectives in site interpretation.

REPAIR's holistic approach to disability justice in historic preservation begins with the subject many preservationists likely think of first when imagining inclusion and equity for disabled people at historic sites: physical accessibility.

PHYSICAL ACCESSIBILITY

When initially considering accessibility in the context of heritage conservation work, many people will seek out relevant accessibility laws and guidelines.[9] As described in chapter 2, compliance with accessibility laws is not optional for public spaces. Accessibility is encoded in legislation, and institutions that fail to comply risk legal repercussions.

The systems built at the local, state, and federal levels to manage information about cultural resources were constructed with a narrower perspective on disability and physical accessibility than is currently accepted. The 1990 Americans with Disabilities Act (ADA) has had tremendous cultural impacts, influencing public perceptions of disability. Today, the ADA is the most comprehensive of all accessibility laws; therefore, federal agencies and private museums alike must comply with the ADA.

Since the ADA's passage, the National Park Service added *Preservation Brief 32: Making Historic Properties Accessible* (1993) to their collection of preservation reference documents. It focuses on interventions for people with mobility disabilities, emphasizing access measures like ramps, handrails, and modified doorways. The brief rightly asserts that "with the passage of the Americans with Disabilities Act, access to historic properties open to the public is now a civil right."[10]

Preservation Brief 32 successfully mirrors the Architectural Barriers Act (ABA) and ADA's original focus on physical accessibility standards but has not been updated to include further amendments and clarifications from the US Justice Department or from activists, practitioners, or scholars. Since its passage, the ADA has been amended to broaden the definition of "disability," and the Department of Justice has clarified that ADA "requirements apply to all the goods, services, privileges, or activities offered by public accommodations, including those offered on the web."[11] In 1993, when *Preservation Brief 32* was published, it was nearly impossible to imagine that so much about physical places would, in the near future, be navigated digitally.

Accessibility in digital space has become an increasingly pressing concern in recent years as preservationists face pressure to adapt conventional on-site practices to virtual formats. REPAIR has emphasized digital and design accessibility since its founding, primarily because of how ongoing pandemics have reshaped our professional lives and highlighted how virtual historic interpretation may be more accessible for us all.

Much as the simple act of installing handrails makes a critical difference for disabled visitors who require them for balance when climbing stairs, implementing digital accessibility measures expands site access for potential audiences at historic sites. Recent efforts to increase digital access to historic properties have included guidance in designing web interfaces for access to people with a wide range of disabilities; applying mobile technologies to expand access through language translation, audio description, and other means; and applying promising practices in the use of interactive digital technologies on site, such as those described in chapter 9.[12] REPAIR advocates for attending to issues of digital accessibility in charting the future of historic preservation as a field.

DIGITAL ACCESSIBILITY AND DESIGN

Design is integral to achieving digital accessibility. Good design goes unnoticed, but bad design inhibits a user's experience. The field of design encompasses many different aspects, but what is most relevant to digital spaces are the realms of information architecture (IA), user experience (UX), and graphic design of text and image.[13]

Digital spaces should be built with accessibility in mind. Accessible web design is nearly impossible to retrofit. Often, testing for accessibility is left until the end of a project when there is little time or budget remaining, and people not specifically trained to make digital content accessible rarely know what is needed. Designers and accessibility experts must be consulted from the beginning. Through incorporating appropriate programming and assistive technology, designers ensure that users can readily browse a site without growing frustrated.[14]

WHY PRIORITIZE DIGITAL ACCESSIBILITY?

A historic property's digital face is often the first thing seen by visitors, scholars, and members of the local community. Digital spaces include websites, social media platforms, online exhibits, event calendars, online stores, and more. Because a wide variety of people use and benefit from accessible digital spaces, leaving barriers in digital platforms is like locking a historic site's front door. Consider the following examples, based on real people, of individuals who rely on accessible digital spaces:

- Nine-year-old Joshua is interested in World War II and wants to visit a local exhibit about the war. Joshua has autism and needs to know what to expect when he is visiting so he feels comfortable. Fortunately, the fort's website features a page with information about the site's accessibility, including a video-based sensory tour. He and his family can watch this video together so they know what to anticipate.
- Lyssa is a graduate student who would like to do research at the historic home of a woman prominent in her field of interest. However, because

Lyssa is immunocompromised, traveling to this site would be risky. She was delighted to find extensive archival content about the home's former inhabitants posted on the site's webpage.

IA FOR A POSITIVE UX

Structuring a website's IA illogically is like letting visitors into a historic site only for them to encounter a maze, with no clear map of how they ought to navigate the space. Well-designed IA leads all visitors—disabled or abled—to the content they're hoping to find.

IA is relevant to accessibility as a design discipline involving organizing and structuring content so users can navigate information and effectively complete tasks. Content is the most important part of a website. When thinking about what kind of content should be featured in a digital space, it's important to anticipate what users might be looking for when they visit. Whether they seek to learn more generally about a historic place or find a specific piece of informa-

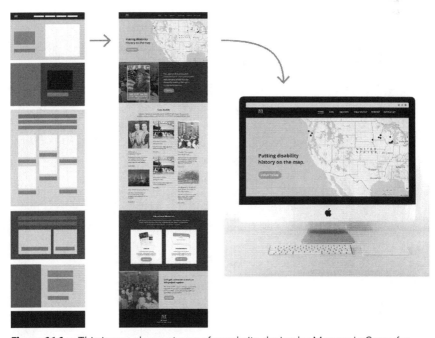

Figure 16.1. This image shows stages of a website design by Morgan LaCasse for REPAIR, including a user flow, a wireframe, and a prototype. To prioritize IA, user flows can help organize content and predict how a visitor might navigate a digital space. A wireframe represents a straightforward draft, and a working prototype can be used to test if the site meets the objectives.

tion, like about planning a visit, they need to be able to easily locate it. One component of IA is organizing information in a way that is logical and predictable.

IA features hierarchy and navigation much like the standardized structure of a book's layout. Information develops logically, with section and chapter divisions and labeling to divide and organize ideas. Nonfiction books are optimized for searching and wayfinding. A table of contents visualizes the book's structure and an index allows for keyword searching. Websites have more possibilities for different navigation paths and more content and therefore may generate greater confusion.

IA can provide a solid framework for organizing information, as opposed to treating a website as a place to simply house content. The UX design can then create a meaningful journey through the site: a strong introduction to the historic site that prepares an individual for a potential visit or content that complements interpretation learned at a prior visit. The web presence should serve as an extension of the historic site itself. Here are a few concrete steps that will help build IA:

- Be intentional about what content is included in the digital space and how the different areas of the digital space might be connected. What might a visitor be looking for? What might they expect to find? How might a user try to navigate to find this information?
- Use typography to create a hierarchy within the content. Headers and subheaders in a series of decreasing sizes can help group and organize sections of information. Headers allow screen readers to more clearly communicate the sections of a web page and make the content more readable for all audiences.
- Don't be afraid of "white" space (or negative space). It's important to not fill every pixel of a digital space with information and visual noise.

Once these steps are followed, to extend the house simile, visitors can open the front door (via digital accessibility) and locate what they most want to find (via well-designed IA). The focus becomes what is displayed in different rooms: the digital content.

CONTENT DELIVERY IN DIGITAL SPACES

How can digital spaces provide accessible venues for telling historic properties' stories?

- Create in-depth outreach and interpretive content about exhibits, tours, and programs to be posted to the website and social media. This type of content encourages people to visit, prepares those who need to know what to expect, and is useful for those who cannot physically tour the site.

- Include multimodal content, including text, images, video, and audio, that tilt toward a range of senses. Having content in a diverse array of media allows for more effective communication and increases visitors' engagement.
- Memorable stories are what most visitors treasure as takeaways from a site visit. Historical materials, like photographs and letters, are valued, but they want the stories of these objects, not just the catalog information.

As a historic property's digital presence is reexamined for accessibility, it's important to look at preexisting digital content, including e-newsletters, online collections databases, online ticketing and shopping, video, and interactive content. Legacy systems and websites built even a few years ago may not be accessible; evaluating them on a regular basis will ensure that they meet accessibility guidelines. These systems can be difficult to retrofit for accessibility and may require significant investment to rebuild, or even redesign, the spaces.

When using vendors for online collections databases, ticketing, and other similar functions, be firm in requesting a fully accessible product. Ask vendors to produce their Voluntary Product Accessibility Template (VPAT) and hold them accountable.[15] If they don't have a VPAT, insist on creating an accessible tool. When testing digital spaces, either independently or with a professional testing company, be sure to include testing of the vendor tools. Give any testing feedback to vendors to ensure a product that meets the needs of users with disabilities.

DIY approaches to accessibility are also readily available to organizations and individuals:

- Use accessibility tools like axe and WebAIM to highlight immediately fixable problems.[16]
- Instead of clicking through a website using a mouse, keyboard navigation using the "tab" or "next" key makes it possible to determine whether the order of information as presented is logical and consistent with the desired information hierarchy.
- Check for alt text describing the website's visual content to make the website more accessible to visually impaired users.

If budgets permit, expand beyond self-testing by hiring disabled usability testers and access specialists.[17] Budgetary constraints at many historic properties are an additional impetus for prioritizing digital and physical accessibility throughout the preservation planning process; designing for access from the start is more efficient than retrofitting access.

PRESERVATION PLANNING

Historic preservation once was a largely reactive field dedicated to saving individual historic buildings from demolition. Beginning in the 1970s, concepts from city and regional planning entered the field of preservation practice with the goal of systematically identifying properties within a district, neighborhood, city, state, or region predicted to be significant based on style, type, associations, or physical features.[18] Cultural resource managers at all scales of government engage in and support preservation planning activities from field surveys to theme studies.

Because most cultural resource plans were formulated without critical awareness of the experiences and perspectives of people with disabilities, it is an important first step to review existing guidance documents from the lenses of disability justice. Similarly, each aspect of new preservation planning initiatives would benefit from expertise that roots out the ableist assumptions built into standard planning processes, from how community partners are conceptualized to the many ways that properties currently focused on "other subjects" may contain unexamined disability histories.

National Historic Landmarks are often identified through theme studies conducted by the National Park Service. Theme studies identify and set a context for sites significant in various aspects of US history. Past theme studies, particularly those focused on histories of race, ethnicity, gender, sexuality, and other forms of social identity, provide models for making disability history more prominent in the landscape. These preservation planning documents have vastly accelerated the identification, documentation, designation, and, in selected cases, protection of underrepresented histories.[19]

In *LGBTQ America: A Theme Study of Lesbian, Gay, Bisexual, Transgender, and Queer History* (2016), editor Megan E. Springate argued for a methodological framework capable of integrating intersectional perspectives on history, positioning any individual as more than one relevant identity, and recognizing that no place represents a single social group's history. In the theme study's essay on LGBTQ identity and health, contributor Katie Batza wrote how Frank Kameny, a gay man, led the charge to halt the federal government's discrimination against homosexual employees. His and other efforts foregrounded the American Psychiatric Association's 1973 decision to remove "homosexuality" as a diagnosed mental illness—a victory for both the LGBTQ and disability rights movements.[20] In developing new approaches to planning for the preservation of disability histories at historic sites, it is critical to center the intersectional experiences of those with disabilities, including the stigmatization of their identities past and present.

Future planning studies that take intersectionality as a foundational principle must fully integrate the issue of disability through appropriate consultation with disabled site visitors, activists, and scholars. By centering disability as a critical issue in every aspect of preservation planning, places that previously made no mention of the subject become more relevant to a public that may not have intentionally sought information on disability histories. Major landmarks yet to be part of the inventory of known cultural resources will make it increasingly possible to tell all peoples' stories in the United States.

Because concerns about documenting and interpreting disability histories have emerged later than major studies on sites of women's history, civil rights history, and related topics, major gaps and omissions remain. As with individual nominations, revisiting and amending prior theme studies and the planning documents related to them will make it possible to uncover potential threads of disability histories meriting attention. Theme studies produced prior to the formation of disability studies as a formal field of academic inquiry, including War in the Pacific or guidance documents for Civil War battlefields, would benefit from a fresh view drawn from recent scholarship on disability. The inclusion of experiential and academic expertise about disability is relevant to any theme study or planning document, both in terms of access to the site and interpretive content.

Preservation planning requires collecting a base of primary sources through which a site may be interpreted. What sources are considered credible and worthy of study determine what stories are ultimately told at a site. Revealing disability histories at historic sites calls for creative, embodied documentation methods.

COLLECTION AND DOCUMENTATION

Documentation is a process of gathering, organizing, and synthesizing an array of evidence to be interpreted for public presentation. Documentation should be understood as a process rather than as a singular step in a static research project—it is the search for the many voices, the many experiences, and the many stories within a history of place. This process aims to amplify democratic participation and intersectional representation within historic preservation. Inviting community partners into the documentation process may reveal intangible heritage that practitioners had not previously considered. In documentation, REPAIR's goal is to amplify care, dignity, and access, particularly for those who have been excluded, historically and presently, from mainstream histories of place.

There are many voices missing from most histories of place because of shortcomings in the standard documentation process. Archival collections tend to preserve an official history, often prioritizing certain types of sources that bestow credibility on primarily white, male, upper-class, educated, abled perspectives. Standards of "credibility" merit reevaluation to account for a wider range of experiences produced from various standpoints: physicians, social workers, inmates of carceral facilities, and disabled people.

The field of historic preservation has long relied on written documents to analyze buildings and material culture. In turn, collection methods and material types have privileged particular sensory experiences through reliance on the visual, which results in sight-driven archival materials. Examples may include newspaper articles, governmental reports, citations, permits, and property assessments. These written documents can also implicitly create an expectation of literacy that may marginalize people of different learning abilities. Increasingly, however, practitioners have broadened their research methods to include oral history interviews, community memory sessions, and archaeological and ethnographic methods—all of which have served to unlock evidence inaccessible through the written record.[21] In addition to these methods, REPAIR advocates for a sensory-based approach. Expanding the archive to include awareness of the senses encourages a diversity of experiences regardless of the sensory orientation of a visitor.[22]

EXPANDING DOCUMENTATION AND COLLECTION METHODS

What is often absent in many of these commonly used methods are the sensory, embodied experiences of historical and present-day community members. Methods that explore sensory experiences elicit distinct place-based information and do not center exclusively on academic expertise. Sensory methods draw upon the interconnectedness of place, memory, imagination, affect, social cues, and embodied knowledge to represent a more complex portrait of any given site, as Sarah Pink describes in *Doing Sensory Ethnography*, an approachable and comprehensive guide to one such practice.[23] Sensory methods allow anyone to participate in the process of collecting information about the site based on their own sensory experiences in a place, treating sense-based memories and experiences as a legitimate archive that overlaps with archives held by institutions or in community memory. Opening a dialogue about how interpreters, staff, visitors, and others experience a site provides a wealth of personal insights about space, through methods as simple and cost-effective as a handout with guiding questions or a directed discussion.[24]

Sensory methods present an opportunity to better incorporate the social model of disability—or the redefinition of disability as a condition shaped by socially produced barriers rather than medical conditions—into fieldwork and documentation.[25] Frameworks in disability studies emphasize the critical knowledge that people with disabilities have about dominant social patterns. This knowledge can be drawn out through sensory methods that focus on internal, emotional, or affective sensations stemming from social, external, place-based conditions.[26]

Reframing the documentation process around justice means moving beyond the common collection practices that prioritize vision to consider the knowledge gleaned through alternative senses. Such methods are democracy in action, democratizing ways of knowing.[27] Disability scholarship emphasizes the notion of bodyminds, as unique or distinct entities composed or drawn from multiple sensory inputs, the political values projected on our bodies, and our individual histories.[28] Sensory methods guide one to tune into sounds, smells, visual stimuli, textures, sensations within the body (like anxiety), and awareness of one's own body in space. Most approaches to the senses name only five. However, sensory methodologies underscore the reality that each person has a peculiar chemistry of sensory inputs.

In this framework, disability becomes a concept that gives access to other ways of knowing. By drawing information through a multiplicity of senses, the customary privileging of certain senses is disrupted and the range of senses employed by people with disabilities becomes a basis for design. Simultaneously, this approach redefines the meanings of place and considers more deeply the social and emotional feelings connected to material aspects of the built environment, such as the texture of surfaces, lighting conditions, soundscapes, and signage.

This understanding of sensory methods makes it possible to interrogate historic places, asking such questions as: What forms of physical evidence are present in the building or landscape that reflect historical norms about "able" bodies and minds? How was the original structure, floor plan, array of surfaces, or larger design modified over time, particularly by people with disabilities, to gain greater access to the built environment? With this set of questions, a single researcher can analyze a place through their sensory experience. Yet that singular perspective is not fully aligned with disability justice principles of collective engagement and intersectionality. Sensory methods beg for a diversity of experiences. How might more voices be brought into sensory-based documentation? Group sensory explorations with community partners could be developed to provide a range of multimedia documentation.

COMMUNITY ENGAGEMENT AND PUBLIC PEDAGOGY

Documentation must be in long-term dialogue with community partners; it must also include public engagement in the form of sustainable relationship-building with groups and individuals who are most impacted by the way that historical documentation has implicitly centered normative bodyminds and omitted people with disabilities. Plan storytelling sessions and oral history interviews with community stakeholders, whether groups or individuals—there are often community-led initiatives already in place. Offer an array of channels for discussion, input, contribution, feedback, and revision. Make these relationships sustainable—with ongoing support in the form of access, resources, programming, financial compensation, and acknowledgment. Most of all, the knowledge produced in these relationships must be accessible, in language and in location (online or in a public and physically accessible institution).

Free and open digital access for the purposes of education, advocacy, and research expands the documentation process. Democratically informed documentation, predicated on practices of care and access, can facilitate thoughtfully developed site interpretation. Documentation and interpretation become symbiotic processes building toward meaningful historic site experiences for staff and visitors alike.

INTERPRETATION

Within cultural resource management, interpretation refers to the storytelling of places, objects, and beings. Often conducted by park rangers, docents, and guides, this approach to storytelling goes beyond merely providing information to creating meaningful, participatory experiences. Interpretation can take form through guided tours, programs, exhibits, audio-visual materials and brochures. These varied interpretive forms forge connections between the site and the visitor.

Interpretation allows visitors to actively participate in their site visit: to reflect on why places matter, why particular sites received preservation status and others did not, and how those preservation protections shape visitors' experiences. Therefore, interpretive material should consider visitors' concerns, interests, and the "authority" they bring to the historic site. Effective interpretation is an interactive exchange between visitor and interpreter that integrates visitors' perspective through practices of shared authority, collaboration, and outreach.

Interpretation also holds the potential to attract new visitors through diverse storytelling. Often, these "hidden" stories are already embedded in place, though they may have gone unnoticed by interpretive staff. As historic sites assert the value of diversity, equity, inclusion, and accessibility initiatives, they must attend to the experiences of people with disabilities, past and present, who have shaped the built environment. Disability histories are insufficiently addressed in historic and cultural sites. While accessibility legislation is necessary, it is not enough to simply make places compliant with physical and programmatic accessibility measures. Rather, the inclusion of disability histories will help foster deeper connections with and welcome diverse visitors to historic and cultural sites.

Every historic site, house museum, and national park unit has disability histories to tell. Stories of accessibility and lived experiences of people with disabilities are woven into the fabric of each site's history. Interpreting the lives of historic persons with disabilities can facilitate a sense of empathy and create opportunities for building connections with disabled and nondisabled visitors today. Further, this interpretation can enable change in museum practices, available accessibility resources, and employment opportunities. In so doing, historic sites and parks commit to meaningful acts of inclusion that have the potential to address past injustices at the same time they can diversify audiences.

In 2018 and 2019, Perri Meldon, one of REPAIR's members, collaborated with staff at the Home of Franklin D. Roosevelt National Historic Site (HOFR). Though we in REPAIR may critique HOFR's prominence as a representative site of disability history as being steeped in financial, gender, and racial privilege, preservation practitioners can also benefit from the extant accessibility features that have endured precisely because of FDR's identity and contributions as a former US president. Further, these very privileges reveal in stark relief the discrepancy of available resources for contemporary marginalized people with disabilities.

HOFR exemplifies how historic sites can move beyond compliance alone to integrate the stories of people with disabilities. As a national historic site dedicated to the only president with visible physical disabilities, HOFR employees prioritize making the New York home accessible to a range of visitors. The house museum and surrounding property strive to be models of physical and programmatic accessibility. It already contains many examples of historical accommodations. After his 1921 polio diagnosis, Roosevelt adapted his home for wheelchair use. Roosevelt's staff built ramps, installed railings and handlebars, and minimized thresholds between doorways.[29]

These adaptations are still on view for visitors today. For example, visitors may walk or roll onto the transparent viewing platform that juts into Roosevelt's sunken living room. This platform, compliant with federal accessibility laws including the Architectural Barriers Act of 1968 and the Rehabilitation Act of 1973 as amended, is wide enough to allow multiple people to stand and a wheelchair to rotate with ease. The railing that surrounds it does not exceed the height at which a seated person could see into the living room. The overall design—the railings, columns, and base—mirrors the room's architectural style; therefore, it does not diminish its historic integrity. If visitors peer through the glass beneath them, they will see a replica of the wooden ramp Roosevelt used to descend into the room. This is one of many renovations undertaken by HOFR to simultaneously make the visitor experience accessible and acknowledge how Roosevelt navigated his home. The national historic site thus blends accessibility features, past and present, and interprets them for the visiting public.

These accessibility features document changes in accessibility laws, as well as attitudes toward and provisions available for people with disabilities, across the twentieth and twenty-first centuries. This evolution is rich fodder for interpretive material. Visitors can consider the challenges, struggles, and accomplishments resulting from individuals' actions and movement-led protest while reflecting on the limitations and opportunities available for people with disabilities during Roosevelt's lifetime.

Interpretive opportunities about US disability history abound for historic sites, even with less visible or prominent accessibility features embedded in their built environment. Perhaps the most precious historic accessibility features at HOFR are the most ephemeral, and they can often go undocumented or overlooked. Tourists who have extra time during their visit at HOFR can join a special tour to Top Cottage, a ten-minute drive from the Roosevelt family home. Designed by Roosevelt, Top Cottage was the president's retreat when

Figure 16.2. Photograph of Franklin Delano Roosevelt at Top Cottage. He is sitting in his wheelchair and his dog, Fala, is in his lap. A little girl stands next to him. *Creative Commons Attribution 2.0, Wikimedia Commons.*

he visited his family in New York. Its floors are level and free of thresholds or barriers. Roosevelt could navigate this retreat with ease, without assistance from an aide. When the park guide takes visitors onto the back porch, a docent explains how, in fall and winter, Roosevelt would have peered through the trees toward the family property and the Hudson Valley. In gazing into the green expanse through the backyard, visitors may miss the mound to the right side of Top Cottage's porch. It is now largely eroded and covered with grass, but it's evident that the mound is not natural. That mound is packed soil, an earthen ramp that Roosevelt used to descend from the porch to the backyard. This is no fancy accommodation or mechanism of his day; earthen ramps are vernacular examples of accessibility measures taken by ordinary people who needed alternatives to using the staircase.

Examples like Roosevelt's earthen ramp manifest in all historic sites; interpretive staff need only to think creatively to uncover these stories. Does the archival collection contain walking sticks, self-made braces, or other objects that indicate a person's disability? Are there examples of improvisation (that is, the wooden board that Roosevelt used to descend into the sunken living room) that indicate individual accommodations? How many floors does the historic site have, and how would the surrounding terrain have affected people with disabilities, both in the past and today? Did people in the past receive daily assistance from loved ones and community members at the historic site? Considering this chapter's earlier section on sensory methods, how might a tour that deemphasizes sight and instead encourages other sensory exploration uncover alternative or additional disability stories?[30] No matter how ephemeral these traces may be, material culture and the stories of how people with disabilities navigated the world around them become opportunities to interpret the diverse lives of individuals in the past.

Interpretation of US disability history in historic sites is necessary to recognize disability as a site of civil rights struggle. By exceeding baseline accessibility compliance to include the stories of people with disabilities, cultural sites illuminate the thread from self-made adaptations like Roosevelt's earthen ramp to the indelible mark of universal design in the American built environment today. Compassionate interpretation of the historic experiences of people with disabilities enhances visitors' sense of belonging in public spaces.

These kinds of interpretive interventions aren't built in a day. The disability justice–based performance collective Sins Invalid cites "sustainability" as a key principle, writing, "We pace ourselves, individually and collectively, to be sustained long term. Our embodied experiences guide us toward ongoing justice and liberation."[31] Transformative change in historic preservation is not possible if our work striving for greater accessibility, representation, and equity leads to continual burnout. Pacing ourselves and building supportive networks to nurture justice-based initiatives are integral to creating meaningful, long-lasting change.

SUSTAINING TRANSFORMATION

Faced with systemic barriers, stewards of historic properties might invest in consultation with community partners more knowledgeable than themselves about disability. One-time interventions, such as consultant-driven assessments, certainly can be beneficial. This technique is often used by museums to identify barriers to access and prioritize simple, cost-effective interventions that will enhance accessibility. Assessments of accessibility must be ongoing and progress toward the ideal of justice measured in concrete terms.

Wherever possible, REPAIR endorses forms of collective organizing that position all project partners as learners engaged in dialogue, observation, study, and shared decision making, empowering all involved to become advocates for access. By extending the concept of collective organizing from the political economy into the cultural sphere, it becomes possible to address multiple forms of inequality expressed in the historic buildings and landscapes considered to be the nation's landmarks and treasures. Collective learning and action build ongoing organizational capacity for addressing the challenges inherent in maximizing and sustaining equitable access to historic places. As with other issues of structural inequality, it is critical to engage allies in the project of institutional transformation.

Some projects based at parks or historic sites surely will be initiated by concerned staff and administrators. Others may be led by people with disabilities concerned with preserving their heritage sites and installing modern accessibility measures. In either model REPAIR recommends mutual learning as a way to forge a shared foundation of knowledge about accessibility and disability.[32] In *The Art of Access: A Practical Guide for Museum Accessibility,* Heather Pressman and Danielle Schulz cite "communities of practice" as being integral to the creation of sustainable and collaborative solutions to access barriers. They define "communities of practice" as spaces in which "individuals with interest in learning more deeply about some aspect of their work can come together, formalize their conversations, and intentionally create new knowledge for their field of practice."[33] As a community of practice ourselves, REPAIR believes in this model of collaborative learning. Communities of practice provide a forum for the exchange of ideas and resources, opportunities for mutual aid, and solidarity across identities, disciplines, and skill sets to gain insight into subjects relevant to all engaged members. Scaling up from communities of practice that focus on strengthening access measures at particular historic sites, REPAIR advocates for building networks among those committed to accelerating disability justice in historic preservation.

Building communities of practice dedicated to disability justice work can ultimately facilitate material and intangible reparative efforts in historic preservation as a field. Allies who have dedicated their volunteer time or careers to protecting and interpreting historic places rarely have the bandwidth to absorb the literal and abstract costs of central initiatives to integrate previously underinterpreted histories. Moreover, previously excluded potential community partners should not be asked to lend their insights without receiving direct compensation. REPAIR encourages a collective learning process and shares the disability justice movement's beliefs in compensation as a form of redress, both for systemic exclusion and as appropriate compensation for forms of knowledge essential to redesigning preservation as an equitable and ethical form of cultural work. It is vital to ensure that historic sites concretely support the communities most affected by the stories being told at the site. Particularly if disability stories play a role in making a historic site uniquely worthy of preservation and interpretation, the site has significant ethical responsibilities to disabled people today.

WHAT NEXT?

REPAIR expects to remain learners in the sphere of disability justice. As continual learners, we understand how approaching issues of access in the holistic, justice-oriented ways we and others have outlined may feel daunting. The undertaking is challenging and will require an ongoing collective effort. However, the work may be made sustainable through relationship building with community partners, investment in internal organizational infrastructures capable of fostering accessibility, and acceptance of natural ebbs and flows of productivity corresponding to fluctuations in project contributors' time and energy.

It isn't necessary to reinvent the wheel when striving to create greater accessibility at a historic site. As workers at historic places, we always ask ourselves how particular historic sites and their content may impact visitors and the experiences they take away with them. Building on existing diversity, equity, and inclusion initiatives is always possible, simply by asking how disability perspectives figure into and can shape project plans. These guiding questions are as applicable to issues of accessibility as they are to other equity-based initiatives.

In the process of slow and intentional organizational transformation, it can be difficult to mark indicators of significant change. REPAIR suggests for the following benchmarks as indicators of meaningful progress toward justice:

- When people with a wide range of physical, sensory, and cognitive disabilities can access every meaningful facet of the experiences offered by a historic site.
- When historic sites materially support the communities whose histories are being interpreted.
- When intersectional perspectives are naturally incorporated into the narratives told at a historic place.

- When those most stigmatized by the hierarchies ableism perpetuates are understood to be legitimate interpreters of their experiences.

Through collective dialogue and action informed by issues of accessibility, justice, and ableism, practitioners in historic preservation and heritage conservation can strategize collectively for social change.

NOTES

1. REPAIR stands for Rethinking Equity in Place-based Activism, Interpretation, and Renewal, reflecting the three cofounders' mutual commitment to inclusive historic representation, historic preservation as reparative work, and supporting place-based advocates for justice.
2. Read Donna Graves and Gail Dubrow, "Taking Intersectionality Seriously: Learning from LGBTQ Heritage Initiatives for Historic Preservation," *The Public Historian* 41, no. 2 (2019): 290–316.
3. REPAIR has created a website that features case studies of sites of disability history. The growing project is available at https://www.repairhistory.org/.
4. Juliet Larkin-Gilmore, Ella Gallow, and Susan Burch, "Indigenity & Disability: Kinship, Place, and Knowledge-Making," *Disability Studies Quarterly* 41, no. 4 (Fall 2021), https://dsq-sds.org/article/view/8542/6285.
5. For example, National Museum of African American History & Culture, "Whiteness," accessed August 2, 2022, https://nmaahc.si.edu/learn/talking-about-race/topics/whiteness. Opportunities for direct financial support can be found through, for example, the Twitter hashtags #SettlerSaturday, #MutualAidRequest, #Disability CrowdFund, and #TransCrowdFund.
6. For insights into disability justice as methodology, read Leah Lakshmi Piepzna-Samarasinha and Stacey Park Milbern, "Disability Justice: An Audit Tool," accessed August 5, 2022, https://static1.squarespace.com/static/5ed94da22956b942e 1d51e12/t/6232af2503a09a54615b8d48/1647488823793/DJ+Audit+Tool.pdf; Sins Invalid, "10 Principles of Disability Justice," accessed August 5, 2022, https:// www.sinsinvalid.org/blog/10-principles-of-disability-justice; Sami Schalk, "Critical Disability Justice as Methodology," *Lateral* 6, no. 1 (Spring 2017), https:// csalateral.org/issue/6-1/forum-alt-humanities-critical-disability-studies-method ology-schalk/. For historic preservation-focused resources, read MASS Action, "Readiness Assessment," https://static1.squarespace.com/static/58fa685dff 7c50f78be5f2b2/t/59dcdcfb017db28a6c9d5ced/1507646717898/MASS+Ac tion+Readiness+Assessment_Oct17+%281%29.pdf; MASS Action, "Toolkit," last modified September 2017, https://static1.squarespace.com/static/58fa685dff 7c50f78be5f2b2/t/59dcdd27e5dd5b5a1b51d9d8/1507646780650/TOOL KIT_10_2017.pdf; and Sarah Marsom, "#DismantlePreservation," accessed August 10, 2022, https://www.sarahmarsom.com/dismantle.
7. Marsom, "#DismantlePreservation."
8. Alison Kafer, *Feminist, Queer, Crip* (Bloomington and Indianapolis: Indiana University Press, 2013), 6.

9. Perri Meldon, "Interpreting Access: A History of Accessibility and Disability Representations in the National Park Service" (Master's thesis: University of Massachusetts Amherst, 2019).

10. Thomas C. Jester and Sharon C. Park, *Making Historic Properties Accessible, Technical Preservation Sources*, accessed August 3, 2022, https://www.nps.gov/tps/how-to-preserve/briefs/32-accessibility.htm. The National Park Service has subsequently refined the organization's accessibility goals: National Park Service, "Our Commitment to Accessibility," accessed August 10, 2022, https://www.nps.gov/subjects/accessibility/index.htm.

11. US Department of Justice, Civil Rights Division, "Guidance on Web Accessibility and the ADA," accessed March 18, 2022, https://www.ada.gov/resources/web-guidance/.

12. National Park Service, "Accessibility & Universal Design Standards," last modified October 22, 2021, https://www.nps.gov/dscw/ds-accessibility-universal-design.htm.

13. For more insight into accessible design, see Prime Access Consulting, accessed September 21, 2022, https://www.pac.bz/.

14. For further information about accessible websites, consult the Web Content Accessibility Guidelines (WCAG), an international set of standards for website accessibility: WCAG, W3C, accessed August 16, 2022, https://www.w3.org/WAI/standards-guidelines/wcag/. Other helpful resources include "Accessibility Checklist," Elsevier, accessed August 16, 2022, https://romeo.elsevier.com/accessibility_checklist/, and "Access Guide," accessed August 16, 2022, https://www.accessguide.io/.

15. "Voluntary Product Accessibility Template," General Services Administration, accessed August 16, 2022, https://www.section508.gov/sell/vpat/; Brian McNeilly and Sina Bahram, "How to Read a VPAT: Assessing Accessibility Conformance Reports," MW2019: MuseWeb, January 31, 2019, https://mw19.mwconf.org/paper/how-to-read-a-vpat-assessing-accessibility-conformance-reports.

16. axe, deque, accessed August 11, 2022, https://www.deque.com/axe/; WebAIM, accessed August 11, 2022, https://webaim.org/.

17. The International Association of Accessibility Professionals includes organizations doing this type of work.

18. Read Anne Derry, H. Ward Jandl, Carol D. Shull, and Jan Thorman, "Guidelines for Local Surveys: A Basis for Preservation Planning," *National Register Bulletin* 24 (1977). The 1977 bulletin was revised by Patricia L. Parker in 1985.

19. National Park Service, "Full List of Theme Studies," last modified June 28, 2022, https://www.nps.gov/subjects/nationalhistoriclandmarks/full-list-of-theme-studies.htm. Particularly relevant case studies include *American Latino Heritage* (2013); *LGBTQ America: A Theme Study of Lesbian, Gay, Bisexual, Transgender, and Queer History* (2016); and *Finding a Path Forward: Asian American Pacific Islander National Historic Landmarks Theme Study* (2018).

20. Since 2011, Frank Kameny's residence has been listed on the National Register of Historic Places. Katie Batza, "LGBTQ and Health," in *LGBTQ America: A Theme Study of Lesbian, Gay, Bisexual, Transgender, and Queer History*, ed. Megan E. Springate (Washington, DC: National Park Service, 2016), 22-1–22-26.

21. For examples of these interactive approaches, read Ned Kaufman, *Place, Race, and Story: Essays on the Past and Future of Historic Preservation* (New York: Routledge, 2009); Andrew Hurley, *Beyond Preservation: Using Public History to Revitalize Inner Cities* (Philadelphia: Temple University Press, 2010); Antoinette Jackson: *Speaking for the Enslaved: Heritage Interpretation at Antebellum Plantation Sites* (Walnut Creek, Left Coast Press, 2012).

22. For more on the framework of "sensory orientation," see Russell Rosen, "Sensory Orientations and Sensory Design in the American DeafWorld," *The Senses and Society*, no. 7 (November 2012): 366–73.

23. Sarah Pink, *Doing Sensory Ethnography* (Los Angeles: SAGE Publishing, 2015).

24. Dara Culhane and Denielle Elliott, *A Different Kind of Ethnography: Imaginative Practices and Creative Methodologies* (Toronto: University of Toronto Press, 2016).

25. National Institutes of Health, "Human Rights Model of Disability," accessed 20 September, 2022, https://www.edi.nih.gov/blog/communities/human-rights-model-disability

26. Merri Lisa Johnson and Robert McRuer, "Cripistemologies: Introduction," *Journal of Literary & Cultural Disability Studies* 8, no. 2 (2014): 127–47.

27. Tanya Titchkosky, *The Question of Access: Disability, Space, Meaning* (Toronto: University of Toronto Press, 2011).

28. The term "bodymind" rejects the Western dualism setting "body" and "mind" as disconnected opposites, instead emphasizing how "body" and "mind" are part of an indivisible whole. Sami Schalk, *Bodyminds Reimagined:(Dis)ability, Race, and Gender in Black Women's Speculative Fiction* (Durham: Duke University Press, 2018).

29. The Home of Franklin D. Roosevelt is a remarkable extant example of individual adaptations to the built environment. That the house and its collections are so well intact demonstrates efforts to commemorate the four-term president immediately following his 1945 death. However, such homes also represent historic preservation's tendency to preserve sites dedicated to wealthy white men. While we can today praise the historic integrity of the property and its contents, we cannot untether its preservation from the gendered, racialized, and socioeconomic dimensions that undergird US historic preservation.

    Likewise, we cannot separate Roosevelt's attitudes on disablement from the time during which he lived. Three years after FDR's polio diagnosis, the United States passed the Johnson-Reed Act of 1924, which restricted immigration of certain communities. The law favored entry of northern and western European immigrants over those from southern and eastern Europe. Asians, meanwhile, were banned entirely. Throughout the early twentieth century, a fear of "yellow peril" spread across the United States, fueled by FDR's own sentiments as expressed in legislation like Executive Order 9066, the forced relocation of Japanese Americans to internment camps. FDR's own beliefs about disability cannot be disentangled from the eugenic and xenophobic sentiments pervasive throughout the time he lived. For more on these histories, read Matthew Frye Jacobson, *Whiteness of a Different Color: European Immigrants and the Alchemy of Race* (Cambridge: Harvard University Press, 1999) and Mae Ngai, *Impossible Subjects: Illegal Aliens and the Making of Modern America* (Princeton: Princeton University Press, 2004).

30. Historically, Western museums have prioritized sight in a hierarchy of senses. This emphasis on sight has contributed to encouraging and discouraging certain

museum practices. For example, look, but don't touch; don't speak loudly; don't bring food into the museum. By diminishing use of the other senses, museums have also become spaces that dictate what a society considers "civil" behavior. These notions of civility, as conveyed by Euroamerican institutions, become bound with "other"-ing non-Western cultures and determining who does and does not belong. For more on the history of museums and senses, read Elizabeth Edwards, Chris Gosden, and Ruth B. Phillips, eds., *Sensible Objects: Colonialism, Museums and Material Culture* (New York: Berg, 2006).

31. Sins Invalid, "10 Principles of Disability Justice."
32. Nancy J. Evans, Ellen M. Broido, Kirsten R. Brown, and Autumn K. Wilke, eds., *Disability in Higher Education: A Social Justice Approach* (San Francisco: Jossey-Bass, 2017); Jay Dolmage, *Academic Ableism: Disability and Higher Education* (Ann Arbor: University of Michigan Press, 2017); "Welcome," Critical Disability Studies Collective at the University of Minnesota, accessed August 10, 2022, https://cdsc.umn.edu/.
33. Heather Pressman and Danielle Schulz, *The Art of Access: A Practical Guide for Museum Accessibility* (Lanham, MD: Rowman & Littlefield, 2021), 25.

Appendix A

Resources

The resources included here are meant to support you in your efforts to make your historic site more inclusive and accessible. Included in this appendix are some of the practical resources contributors to this volume have used in their own work. Along with the sources found in the bibliography, these resources will provide you with a broad base of support in your accessibility and inclusion work.

ACCESS AUDIT

- *ADA Readily Achievable Barrier Removal Checklist for Existing Facilities*, US Department of Justice, https://www.ada.gov/racheck.pdf.
- *Checklist for Existing Facilities*, Institute of Human Centered Design, https://www.adachecklist.org/doc/fullchecklist/ada-checklist.pdf.
- *Renewing the Commitment: An ADA Compliance Guide for Nonprofits* by Irene Bowen, https://search.issuelab.org/resource/renewing-the-commitment-an-ada-compliance-guide-for-nonprofits.html.

DIGITAL CONTENT

- "Create Accessible Content," University of Minnesota, https://accessibility.umn.edu/what-you-can-do/create-accessible-content.
- "Guidelines for Image Description," Cooper Hewitt,
- https://www.cooperhewitt.org/cooper-hewitt-guidelines-for-image-description/.
- *Inclusive Digital Interactives: Best Practices + Research*, a collaboration of Access Smithsonian, Institute for Human Centered Design and MuseWeb, https://access.si.edu/sites/default/files/inclusive-digital-interactives-best-practices-research.pdf.

- *Web Accessibility Initiative*, World Wide Web Consortium, https://www.w3.org/WAI/.
- YouTube DIY captioning, https://support.google.com/youtube/answer/2734796?hl=en.

DISABILITY LAWS AND REGULATIONS

- "About IDEA Individuals with Disabilities Education Act," US Department of Education, https://sites.ed.gov/idea/about-idea/.
- "ADA Resources for Museums, Arts and Cultural Institutions," ADA National Network, https://www.adainfo.org/sites/default/files/Arts-Museums-Cultural-Inst-ADA-Resources-4-12-12.pdf.
- "ADA Requirements for Historic Properties," *STRUCTURE Magazine*, https://www.structuremag.org/?p=7540.
- "ADA Requirements: Wheelchairs, Mobility Aids, and Other Power-Driven Mobility Devices," US Department of Justice, https://www.ada.gov/opdmd.htm.
- "A Guide to Disability Rights Laws," US Department of Justice, https://www.ada.gov/cguide.htm.
- "Factsheet Highlights of the Final Rule to Amend the Department of Justice's Regulation Implementing Title III of the ADA," US Department of Justice, https://www.ada.gov/regs2010/factsheets/title3_factsheet.html.
- Information and Technical Assistance on the Americans with Disabilities Act, US Department of Justice, https://www.ada.gov/law-and-regs/.
- Maintaining Accessibility in Museums, US Department of Justice, https://archive.ada.gov/business/museum_access.htm.
- "Making Historic Properties Accessible," National Park Service, https://www.nps.gov/orgs/1739/upload/preservation-brief-32-accessibility.pdf.
- Publications and videos, ADA National Network, https://adata.org/national-product-search?keys=&type=All&tid=All.
- "What Historic Sites Have Learned After 25 Years with ADA," Engaging Places LLC, https://engagingplaces.net/2015/07/28/what-historic-sites-have-learned-after-25-years-with-ada/.

INCLUSIVE DESIGN

- *ADA Standards for Accessible Design*, 2010, https://www.ada.gov/law-and-regs/design-standards/2010-stds/.
- *Audio Description and Captioning Guide*, New York City Major's Office for People with Disabilities, https://www1.nyc.gov/assets/mopd/downloads/pdf/MOPD-Audio-Description-and-Caption-Guide.pdf.

- *Design for Accessibility: A Cultural Administrator's Handbook* produced by the National Assembly of State Arts Agencies, https://www.arts.gov/sites/default/files/Design-for-Accessibility.pdf.
- *Inclusive Digital Interactives: Best Practices + Research*, a collaboration of Access Smithsonian, Institute for Human Centered Design and Muse-Web, https://access.si.edu/sites/default/files/inclusive-digital-interactives-best-practices-research.pdf.
- *Making History Accessible Toolkit for Multisensory Interpretation* by Intrepid Museum + NYU Ability Project, https://www.intrepidmuseum.org/education/education-accessibility/IMLS-grant-images/Making-History-Accessible-(1).pdf.
- *The Multisensory Museum: Cross-Disciplinary Perspectives on Touch, Sound, Smell, Memory, and Space* by Nina Levent
- A Planning Guide for Making Temporary Events Accessible to People with Disabilities, ADA National Network, https://adata.org/guide/planning-guide-making-temporary-events-accessible-people-disabilities.
- *Smithsonian Guidelines for Accessible Exhibition Design* by Smithsonian Accessibility Program, https://www.sifacilities.si.edu/sites/default/files/Files/Accessibility/accessible-exhibition-design1.pdf.

JOURNALS AND PUBLICATIONS

- *Accessible America: A History of Disability and Design* by Bess Williamson (2020).
- *The Art of Access: A Practical Guide for Museum Accessibility* by Heather Pressman and Danielle Schulz (2021).
- *Building Access: Universal Design and the Politics of Disability* by Aimi Hamraie (2017).
- "Creating Communities of Wellness" by Kristy Van Hoven, *Museologica Brunensia* 7, no. 1 (2018): 19–24, https://digilib.phil.muni.cz/handle/11222/.digilib/138732.
- *Demystifying Disability: What to Know, What to Say, and How to Be an Ally* by Emily Ladau (2021).
- *A Disability History of the United States* by Kim Nielsen (2012).
- *Diversity, Equity, Accessibility, and Inclusion in Museums*, edited by Johnnetta Betch Cole and Laura Lott (2019).
- *Effective Diversity, Equity, Accessibility, Inclusion, and Anti-Racism Practices for Museums* by Cecile Shellman (2022).
- *Everyone's Welcome: The Americans with Disabilities Act and Museums* by John Salmen (1998).
- *The Inclusive Historian's Handbook*, https://inclusivehistorian.com/.

- "The Local History Museum, So Near and Yet So Far" by Catherine Kudick, *The Public Historian* 27, no. 2 (Spring 2005): 75–81.
- *Mind, Body, Spirit: How Museums Impact Health and Wellbeing* by Jocelyn Dodd and Ceri Jones (2014), https://southeastmuseums.org/wp-content/uploads/PDF/mind_body_spirit_report.pdf.
- *Programming for People with Special Needs: A Guide for Museums and Historic Sites* by Katie Stringer (2014)

SOURCES OF FREE PUBLIC DOMAIN MUSIC

- Free Music Archive, https://freemusicarchive.org/.
- Free Public Domain Music, https://www.freemusicpublicdomain.com/.
- FreePD, https://freepd.com/.
- Musopen, https://musopen.org/.
- Open Music Archive, http://www.openmusicarchive.org/.
- Pixabay, https://pixabay.com/music/.

Bibliography

ADA National Network. "Accessible Parking." Accessed September 20, 2022. https://adata.org/factsheet/parking.

———. "National Product Search." Accessed October 15, 2022. https://adata.org/national-product-search?keys=&type=All&tid=All.

———. "An Overview of the Americans with Disabilities Act." Accessed September 16, 2022. https://adata.org/factsheet/ADA-overview.

———. "What Is the Americans with Disabilities Act (ADA)?" Accessed January 12, 2022. https://adata.org/learn-about-ada.

"ADA Title III Technical Assistance Manual." Accessed September 20, 2022. https://www.ada.gov/reachingout/title3I4.html.

Adair, Bill, Benjamin Filene, and Laura Koloski, eds. *Letting Go? Historical Authority in a User-Generated World.* Philadelphia, PA: The Pew Center for Arts & Heritage, 2011.

Administration of Community Living. "About Community Living." Last modified September 29, 2020. https://acl.gov/about-community-living.

AI-Media. "The Difference Between d/Deaf and Hard-of-Hearing." Accessed September 7, 2022. https://www.ai-media.tv/ai-media-blog/the-difference-between-d-deaf-and-hard-of-hearing-2/.

All Access Disneyland: Magical Planning with Special Needs. "About." Accessed May 28, 2020. https://allaccessdisneyland.com/about/.

Alzheimer's Association. "Michigan Chapter Social Engagement Programs." Accessed September 7, 2022. https://www.alz.org/gmc/helping_you/social_engagement.

Ambrose, Timothy, and Chrispin Paine. *Museum Basics.* Second edition. New York: Routledge, 2006.

America250. "About." Accessed January 2, 2022. https://america250.org/about/.

American Alliance of Museums. "DEIA Definitions." Accessed January 2, 2022. https://www.aam-us.org/wp-content/uploads/2018/04/AAM-DEAI-Definitions-Infographic.pdf.

———. "Diversity, Equity, Accessibility and Inclusion." November 30, 2017. https://www.aam-us.org/programs/diversity-equity-accessibility-and-inclusion/#:~:text=Diversity%20and%20Inclusion%20Policy%20Statement,people%20and%20museums%20we%20represent.

———. "Museum Facts & Data." Accessed January 3, 2022. https://www.aam-us.org/programs/about-museums/museum-facts-data/.

———. "Museums and Trust." Accessed January 5, 2022. https://www.aam-us.org/2021/09/30/museums-and-trust-2021/.

American Association for State and Local History. "AASLH Statement of Standards and Ethics." Accessed January 2, 2022. http://download.aaslh.org/AASLH+Statement+of+Standards+and+Ethics+-+Revised+2018.pdf.

———. "National Visitation Report Summary 2019." November 2019.

———. "Small Museums." Accessed March 29, 2022. https://aaslh.org/communities/smallmuseums/.

American Historical Association. "Historians in Historic Preservation." Accessed October 10, 2022. https://www.historians.org/jobs-and-professional-development/career-resources/careers-for-students-of-history/historians-in-historic-preservation.

Anti-Defamation League. "A Brief History of the Disability Rights Movement." Accessed January 3, 2022. https://www.adl.org/education/resources/backgrounders/disability-rights-movement.

Ark, V. T., E. Liebtag, and N. McClennen. *The Power of Place: Authentic Learning through Place-Based Education*. ASCD, 2020.

Bahram, Sina. "I Know Why the Caged Bird Sings: Freeing Museums from Behind the Glass." Filmed November 2015 in Minneapolis, Minnesota. MCN Ignite video, 6:26. https://www.youtube.com/watch?v=h44hDbfUlo0.

Bahram, Sina, Corey Tompson Design, and Melanie Fales. "Inclusive Design: and Accountability: A Methodology of Museums for All Shapes and Sizes." American Alliance for Museums Annual Meeting, Boston, Massachusetts, May 21, 2022.

Baldwin, Nancy Ikeda. "Nancy Ikeda Baldwin." Interview by Lu Ann Sleeper. February 27, 2013. Oral History Center, UC Berkeley Library. https://digicoll .lib.berkeley.edu/record/218926?ln=en.

Barco. "Please Don't Touch: The Rise of Coronaproof Museum Technology." *Blooloop* (blog). N.d. https://blooloop.com/museum/opinion/post-covid -museum-technology/.

Batza, Katie. "LGBTQ and Health." In *LGBTQ America: A Theme Study of Lesbian, Gay, Bisexual, Transgender, and Queer History*, edited by Megan E. Springate. Washington, DC: National Park Service, 2016.

Beatty, Bob. "Running the Numbers on Attendance at History Museums in the US." *Hyperallergic*, March 1, 2018. https://hyperallergic.com/429788/run ning-the-numbers-on-attendance-at-history-museums-in-the-us/.

Beck, Larry, and Ted Cable. *Interpretation for the 21st Century*. Chicago: Sagamore Publishing, 2002.

Blinn, Sean. *Advocating for Your Organization with Local Government*. Nashville, TN: American Association for State and Local History, 2020.

Briney, Amanda. "An Overview of Historic Preservation." *ThoughtCo.*, January 23, 2020. https://www.thoughtco.com/historic-preservation-and-ur ban-planning-1435784.

Burkholder, Pete, and Dana Schaffer. "A Snapshot of the Public's Views on History: National Poll Offers Valuable Insights for Historians and Advocates." *Perspectives on History*, August 30, 2021. https://www.historians.org /publications-and-directories/perspectives-on-history/september-2021/a -snapshot-of-the-publics-views-on-history-national-poll-offers-valuable -insights-for-historians-and-advocates.

Burn, Sylvia. "Requirements to Create Accessible Audio and Visual Media." US Department of the Interior, September 7, 2017. Accessed July 14, 2022. https://www.doi.gov/sites/doi.gov/files/uploads/ocio_directive _2017-003_requirement_to_create_accessible_audio_visual_media _-_signed_07sep17_2_2_0.pdf.

Burns, Adam. *Railroad Museums: A Complete Guide.* Revised June 25, 2022. Accessed on June 29, 2022. https://www.american-rails.com/museums.html.

Caldwell, Ben, Michael Cooper, Loretta Reid, and Gregg Vanderheiden. "Web Content Accessibility Guidelines." December 11, 2008. Accessed July 14, 2022. https://www.w3.org/TR/WCAG20/.

Centers for Disease Control and Prevention. "Data & Statistics on Autism Spectrum Disorder." Accessed May 28, 2023. https://www.cdc.gov/ncbddd /autism/data.html.

———. "Disability & Health Data System." Accessed January 3, 2022. https:// www.cdc.gov/ncbddd/disabilityandhealth/dhds/index.html.

———. "Disability Impacts All of Us Infographic." September 16, 2020. https://www.cdc.gov/ncbddd/disabilityandhealth/infographic-disability -impacts-all.html.

———. "What Is Autism Spectrum Disorder?" Last modified March 31, 2022. https://www.cdc.gov/ncbddd/autism/facts.html.

Cleaver, Joanne, *Doing Children's Museums: A Guide to 265 Hands-On Museums.* Charlotte, VT: Williamson Publishing, 1992.

Colorado Railroad Museum. "Conservation By Design for the Colorado Railroad Museum, Golden CO. Interpretive Master Plan." Internal document. December 2020.

Commission on Wartime Relocation and Internment of Civilians. *Personal Justice Denied: Report of the Commission on Wartime Relocation and Internment of Civilians.* Seattle: University of Washington Press, and Washington, DC: Civil Liberties Public Education Fund, 1997.

Corbett, Katharine, and Howard Miller. "Shared Inquiry into Shared Authority." *The Public Historian*, 28, no. 1 (February 2006): 15–38.

Crane, Jennifer L. "Forebears and Museums Both Provide Adventures in History." *The BestTimes*, September 2011, 28.

———. "Special Needs Overview: Information and Accommodations for the Museum Setting." Presentation at the Johnson County Museum, Shawnee, Kansas, January 2009.

Critical Disability Studies Collective at the University of Minnesota. "Welcome." Accessed August 10, 2022. https://cdsc.umn.edu/.

Cross, Jody E., and Nedda E. Moqtaderi. "A Landscape History of Mt. Cuba." *Mt. Cuba History Project*, no. 10 (2004): 326.

Culhane, Dara, and Denielle Elliott. *A Different Kind of Ethnography: Imaginative Practices and Creative Methodologies.* Toronto: University of Toronto Press, 2016.

Davies, Dave. "Meet the 7 Most Popular Search Engines in the World." Search Engine Journal. March 3, 2021. https://www.searchenginejournal.com/seo-guide/meet-search-engines/.

Department of Veteran's Affairs. "VA History in Brief." Accessed January 3, 2022. https://www.va.gov/opa/publications/archives/docs/history_in_brief.pdf.

Derry, Anne, H. Ward Jandl, Carol D. Shull, and Jan Thorman. "Guidelines for Local Surveys: A Basis for Preservation Planning." *National Register Bulletin* 24 (1977).

Described and Captioned Media Program. "Captioning Key—Text." *Described and Captioned Media Program.* Accessed June 1, 2022. https://dcmp.org/learn/captioningkey.

DeWitt, John. L. *Final Report: Japanese Evacuation From the West Coast, 1942.* Washington, DC: US Government Printing Office, 1943. https://collections.nlm.nih.gov/catalog/nlm:nlmuid-01130040R-bk

Dichtl, John. "Most Trust Museums as Sources of Historical Information." AASLH, August 12, 2020. https://aaslh.org/most-trust-museums/.

Disneyland. "Disneyland Park Guide for Guests with Disabilities." Accessed on May 28, 2022. https://disneyland.disney.go.com/media/dlr_nextgen/SiteCatalog/PDF/Disneyland_Disabilities_Guide_09112015.pdf.

Dolmage, Jay. *Academic Ableism: Disability and Higher Education.* Ann Arbor: University of Michigan Press, 2017.

Duke, Amy, and Jennifer L. Crane. "The Museum Experience for Special Populations." Presentation at the Greater Kansas City Coalition for Museum Learning, Shawnee, Kansas, March 2013.

Edwards, Elizabeth, Chris Gosden, and Ruth B. Phillips, eds. *Sensible Objects: Colonialism, Museums and Material Culture.* New York: Berg, 2006.

Evans, Nancy J., Ellen M. Broido, Kirsten R. Brown, and Autumn K. Wilke, eds., *Disability in Higher Education: A Social Justice Approach.* San Francisco: Jossey-Bass, 2017.

"Executive Order 9066: Resulting in Japanese-American Incarceration (1942)." National Archives and Records Administration. https://www.archives.gov/milestone-documents/executive-order-9066.

Falk, Cynthia G. "Accessibility." *The Inclusive Historian's Handbook*, April 1, 2019. https://inclusivehistorian.com/accessibility/.

Frisch, Michael H. *A Shared Authority: Essays on the Craft and Meaning of Oral and Public History.* Albany: State University of New York Press, 1990.

Galveston Railroad Museum. "Visit." Accessed May 20, 2022. https://galvestonrrmuseum.org/visit/.

Gender Decoder. "About This Tool." Accessed March 22, 2022. http://gender-decoder.katmatfield.com/about.

Goldhagen, Sarah Williams. *Welcome to Your World: How the Built Environment Shapes Our Lives.* New York: Harper, 2017.

Graves, Donna, and Gail Dubrow. "Taking Intersectionality Seriously: Learning from LGBTQ Heritage Initiatives for Historic Preservation." *The Public Historian* 41, no. 2 (2019): 290–316.

Ham, Sam H. *Interpretation: Making a Difference on Purpose.* Wheat Ridge: Fulcrum Publishing, 2013.

Hammond, Paul. "Recommended Practices for Railway Museums." Heritage Rail Alliance, April 25, 2019. https://heritagerail.org/wp-content/uploads/2019/10/HRA_Toolkit_April_25_2019_FINAL.pdf.

Harris, Donna Ann. *New Solutions for House Museums: Ensuring the Long-Term Preservation of America's Historic Houses.* Second edition. Lanham, MD: Rowman & Littlefield, 2020.

Heritage Consulting, Inc. Final Heritage Tourism Assessment and Interpretive Plan for the Jacobus Vanderveer House. Philadelphia, July 2013.

Heritage Rail Alliance. "Frequently Asked Questions." Accessed May 10, 2022. https://heritagerail.org/faq/

Hirano, Ron M. "Ronald M. Hirano." Interview by Lu Ann Sleeper, June 6. 2013. Oral History Center, UC Berkeley Library. https://digicoll.lib.berkeley.edu /record/218949?ln=en.

Holmes, Hannah Takagi. "An Oral History with Hannah Holmes." Interview by Arthur Hansen, Lawrence de Graaf Center for Oral and Public History, California State University Fullerton, August 27, 1981.

Holt Morgan Russell Architects. Jacobus Vanderveer House Historic Structure Report. Princeton, New Jersey, July 2001.

Hurley, Andrew. *Beyond Preservation: Using Public History to Revitalize Inner Cities.* Philadelphia: Temple University Press, 2010.

Inazu, John. "Beyond the Legality of Executive Orders." *The Hedgehog Review*, February 16, 2017. https://hedgehogreview.com/web-features/thr/posts /beyond-the-legality-of-executive-orders.

Institute for Museum and Library Services. "Museum Data Files." November 2018. https://www.imls.gov/sites/default/files/museum_data_file_docu mentation_and_users_guide.pdf.

International Council for Museums. "Museum Definition." Accessed May 25, 2022. https://icom.museum/en/resources/standards-guidelines/muse um-definition/.

Jackson, Antoinette. *Speaking for the Enslaved: Heritage Interpretation at Antebellum Plantation Sites.* Walnut Creek: Left Coast Press, 2012.

Jacobson, Matthew Frye. *Whiteness of a Different Color: European Immigrants and the Alchemy of Race.* Cambridge: Harvard University Press, 1999.

Jandl, H. Ward. *Rehabilitating Interiors in Historic Buildings Identifying and Preserving Character-Defining Elements.* Accessed May 14, 2023. https://www.nps .gov/orgs/1739/upload/preservation-brief-18-interiors.pdf.

Jester, Thomas C., and Sharon C. Park. *Making Historic Properties Accessible.* Washington, DC: US National Park Service, Heritage Preservation Services, 1993. https://www.nps.gov/tps/how-to-preserve/briefs/32-accessibility .htm

Johnson, Merri Lisa, and Robert McRuer. "Cripistemologies: Introduction." *Journal of Literary & Cultural Disability Studies* 8, no. 2 (2014): 127–47.

Kafer, Alison. *Feminist, Queer, Crip*. Bloomington and Indianapolis: Indiana University Press, 2013.

Kaufman, Ned. *Place, Race, and Story: Essays on the Past and Future of Historic Preservation*. New York: Routledge, 2009.

Keim, Laura C. "Why Do Furnishings Matter?" In *Reimagining Historic House Museums: New Approaches and Proven Solutions*, edited by Kenneth C. Turino and Max Van Balgooy, 207–16. Lanham, MD: Rowman & Littlefield, 2019.

Kluth, Paula, and Patrick Schwarz. *"Just Give Him the Whale!": 20 Ways to Use Fascinations, Areas of Expertise, and Strengths to Support Students with Autism*. Baltimore: Paul H. Brookes Publishing Co., 2008.

Lacke, Susan. "Historic Shouldn't Mean Inaccessible: Preservation and the ADA." Accessibility.com, October 19, 2020. https://www.accessibility.com/blog/historic-shouldnt-mean-inaccessible-preservation-and-the-ada.

Lackoi, K., et al. *Museums for Health and Wellbeing: A Preliminary Report, National Alliance for Museums, Health and Wellbeing*. London: The National Alliance for Museums, Health and Wellbeing, 2016.

Ladau, Emily. "Developing Sensory Tools for Interpreting Historic Sites." Presentation, December 10, 2019.

Larkin-Gilmore, Juliet, Ella Gallow, and Susan Burch. "Indigenity & Disability: Kinship, Place, and Knowledge-Making." *Disability Studies Quarterly* 41, no. 4 (Fall 2021): https://dsq-sds.org/article/view/8542/6285.

Library of Congress. "Ansel Adams's Photographs of Japanese-American Internment at Manzanar" (digital collection). Library of Congress. https://www.loc.gov/collections/ansel-adams-manzanar/about-this-collection/.

Library of Congress. "Audio Description Resource Guide." National Library Service for the Blind and Print Disabled (NLS). Accessed September 17, 2022. https://www.loc.gov/nls/about/services/reference-publications/guides/audio-description-resource-guide/.

Linenthal, Edward, and Tom Engelhardt. *History Wars: The Enola Gay and Other Battles for the American Past*. New York: Holt Paperbacks, 1996.

The Living New Deal. "Historic Sites Act." Accessed October 10, 2022. https://livingnewdeal.org/glossary/historic-sites-act-1935/.

Lonetree, Amy. *Decolonizing Museums: Representing Native America in National and Tribal Museums.* Chapel Hill: University of North Carolina Press, 2012.

Manzanar Committee. "Manzanar National Historic Site Wins Prestigious Award For Barracks Exhibit" (news release). *Manzanar Committee.* April 14, 2016. https://manzanarcommittee.org/2016/04/14/manzanar-barracks-oah-award/.

Marks, John Garrison, and W. Maclane Hull. "Visitation at Historic House Museums." AASLH, January 9, 2020. https://aaslh.org/visitation-at-historic-house-museums/.

Marsom, Sarah. "#DismantlePreservation." Accessed August 10, 2022. https://www.sarahmarsom.com/dismantle.

MASS Action. "Readiness Assessment." https://static1.squarespace.com/static/58fa685dff7c50f78be5f2b2/t/59dcdcfb017db28a6c9d5ced/1507646717898/MASS+Action+Readiness+Assessment_Oct17+%281%29.pdf.

MASS Action. "Toolkit." Last modified September 2017. https://static1.squarespace.com/static/58fa685dff7c50f78be5f2b2/t/59dcdd27e5dd5b5a1b51d9d8/150764.

Matterport. "Add Tags to Your Space." Last modified July 6, 2022. Accessed July 14, 2022. https://support.matterport.com/s/article/Create-a-Mattertag-Post?language=en_US#reorder-new-tags.

——. "Capture Services." Last modified September 19, 2022. Accessed September 19, 2022. https://matterport.com/capture-services.

——. "Create and Use Deep Links." Last modified May 22, 2022. Accessed July 14, 2022. https://support.matterport.com/s/article/How-to-Connect-Two-or-More-Spaces-with-Mattertags-and-Deep-Links?language=en_US.

——. "High Resolution 360º Cameras." Last Modified September 19, 2022. Accessed September 19, 2022. https://matterport.com/cameras/360-cameras.

——. "Highlighted Reel & Guided Tour in Workshop 3.0." Last modified April 7, 2022. Accessed July 14, 2022. https://support.matterport.com/s/article/Highlight-Reel-und-gefhrte-Tour-in-Workshop60272?language=en_US.

——. "How Do I Create a Video of My Matterport Space." Last modified July 1, 2022. Accessed July 14, 2022. https://support.matterport.com/s/article/How-do-I-create-a-video-of-my-Matterport-Space?language=en_US.

——. "How to Transfer a Space Between Organizations." Last modified June 24, 2022. Accessed July 14, 2022. https://support.matterport.com/s/article/How-To-Transfer-a-Space-Between-Organizations?language=en_US.

——. "Introducing 3D Showcase for iOS." Last Modified July 19, 2022. Accessed July 19, 2022. https://matterport.com/blog/introducing-3d-showcase-ios.

——. "Keyboard Shortcuts for 3D Showcase & Workshop." Last modified April 7, 2022. Accessed July 14, 2022. https://support.matterport.com/s/article/Keyboard-Shortcuts-for-3D-Showcase-Workshop?language=en_US.

——. "Meet the World's Leading Spatial Data Platform." Last modified 2022. Accessed July 14, 2022. https://matterport.com/.

——. "No Space Out of Reach." Last Modified September 19, 2022. Accessed September 19, 2022. https://matterport.com/3d-camera-app.

——. "Scanning Outside & Paths to Guest Houses." Last modified June 23, 2022. Accessed July 14, 2022. https://support.matterport.com/s/article/Scanning-Outside-Paths-to-Guest-Houses?language=en_US.

——. "Supported 360 Spherical Cameras." Last modified April 13, 2023. https://support.matterport.com/s/article/Supported-360-Spherical-Cameras?language=en_US&categfilter=&parentCategoryLabel=.

McNeilly, Brian, and Sina Bahram. "How to Read a VPAT: Assessing Accessibility Conformance Reports." MW2019: MuseWeb, January 31, 2019. https://mw19.mwconf.org/paper/how-to-read-a-vpat-assessing-accessibility-conformance-reports.

Meek, Drew. "Displays Inside Railroad Equipment vs. the ADA." Railway Preservation News, February 26, 2006. Accessed April 9, 2022. http://rypn.org/forums/viewtopic.php?f=1&t=30329.

Meldon, Perri. "Interpreting Access: A History of Accessibility and Disability Representations in the National Park Service." Master's thesis, University of Massachusetts Amherst, 2019.

Mita, Travis. "An Oral History with Cheryl Gertler and Travis Mita." Interview by Arthur A. Hansen. Oral History # 528. Transcript. Japanese American. Center for Oral and Public History, California State University Fullerton, Fullerton, California, May 5, 2002. https://cdm16855.contentdm.oclc.org /digital/collection/p16855coll4/id/12413/rec/1.

Moore, Jennifer, Adam Rountrey, and Hannah Scates Kettler. "3D Data Creation to Curation: Building Community Standards for 3D Data Preservation." American Library Association, 2022. Accessed July 14, 2022. https://www .ala.org/acrl/sites/ala.org.acrl/files/content/publications/booksanddigi talresources/digital/9780838939147_3D_OA.pdf.

Mount Vernon. "Ann Pamela Cunningham." Accessed October 10, 2022. https://www.mountvernon.org/library/digitalhistory/digital-encyclopedia /article/ann-pamela-cunningham.

Mt. Cuba Center. "Core Values." Internal/Institutional Document, September 2018.

——. "History." September 2022. https://mtcubacenter.org/about/history/.

——. "Strategic Plan 2016–2020." Internal/Institutional Document, 2015.

Nakada, John. "John Nakada Interview." Interview by Richard Potashin, July 23, 2010. Audio, 02:13:21. Densho Digital Repository. https://ddr.densho.org /narrators/532/.

National Deaf Center on Postsecondary Outcomes. "The Deaf Community: An Introduction." *National Deaf Center on Postsecondary Outcomes.* Accessed June 28, 2022. https://www.nationaldeafcenter.org/sites/default/files /The%20Deaf%20Community-%20An%20Introduction.pdf.

——. "Why Captions Provide Equal Access." *National Deaf Center on Postsecondary Outcomes.* Accessed June 10, 2022. https://www.nationaldeafcenter .org/sites/default/files/Why%20Captions%20Provide%20Equal%20Ac cess.pdf.

National Endowment for the Arts. "Blue Star Museums Frequently Asked Questions." Accessed on May 10, 2022. https://www.arts.gov/initiatives /blue-star-museums/frequently-asked-questions.

National Institutes of Health. "Human Rights Model of Disability." Accessed September 20, 2022. https://www.edi.nih.gov/blog/communities/human -rights-model-disability.

National Museum of African American History & Culture. "Whiteness." Accessed August 2, 2022. https://nmaahc.si.edu/learn/talking-about-race /topics/whiteness.

National Park Service. "Accessibility—Manzanar National Historic Site (U.S. National Park Service)." *Manzanar National Historic Site.* Accessed May 30, 2022. https://www.nps.gov/manz/planyourvisit/accessibility.htm.

———. "Accessibility Service—Evaluation and Transition Plan Overview Manzanar." November 2017, p. 8. http://npshistory.com/publications/manz /accessibility-self-eval.pdf.

———. "Accessibility & Universal Design Standards." Last modified October 22, 2021. https://www.nps.gov/dscw/ds-accessibility-universal-design.htm.

———. "America's First National Historic Site." Accessed October 10, 2022. https://www.nps.gov/sama/index.htm.

———. "Directions." Last modified June 1, 2022. Accessed July 14, 2022. https:// www.nps.gov/cari/planyourvisit/directions.htm.

———. "Full List of Theme Studies." Last modified June 28, 2022. https://www .nps.gov/subjects/nationalhistoriclandmarks/full-list-of-theme-studies.htm.

———. "Historic American Buildings Survey." Accessed October 10, 2022. https://www.nps.gov/hdp/habs/.

———. "How to List a Property." Accessed September 10, 2022. https://www .nps.gov/subjects/nationalregister/how-to-list-a-property.htm.

———. "Magnolia Plantation." Last modified November 6, 2021. Accessed July 14, 2022. https://www.nps.gov/cari/learn/historyculture/magnolia-planta tion-history.htm.

———. "National Historic Preservation Act." Accessed October 10, 2022. https://www.nps.gov/subjects/historicpreservation/national-historic-pres ervation-act.htm.

———. "NPS History—Manzanar Japanese Garden Tour Guide." November 2017. Accessed June 1, 2022. http://npshistory.com/brochures/manz/garden-tour.pdf.

———. "Manzanar National Historic Site." *Manzanar National Historic Site.* Accessed June 4, 2022. https://www.nps.gov/manz/planyourvisit/upload/Manzanar_National_Historic_Site.txt.

———. "Manzanar National Historic Site Museum Management Planning Team." 2011. http://npshistory.com/publications/manz/mmp-2011.pdf.

———. "Our Commitment to Accessibility." Accessed August 10, 2022. https://www.nps.gov/subjects/accessibility/index.htm.

———. "Remembering Manzanar." 21:51. Accessed May 15, 2022. https://www.youtube.com/watch?v=Spo1Khmp2U4&ab_channel=ManzanarNPS.

———. "The Secretary of the Interior's Standards for the Treatment of Historic Properties." Accessed May 14, 2023. https://www.nps.gov/orgs/1739/secretary-standards-treatment-historic-properties.htm.

———. "THINGS TO DO Explore Manzanar Block 14 Exhibits." Accessed May 15, 2022. https://www.nps.gov/thingstodo/explore-manzanar-block-14-exhibits.htm.

———. "Your Dollars At Work." *Manzanar National Historic Site.* Updated May 14, 2020. https://www.nps.gov/manz/learn/management/yourdollarsatwork.htm.

National Trust for Historic Preservation. "Saving Americas Historical Sites." Accessed October 10, 2022. https://savingplaces.org/saving-americas-historic-sites#.YOSgZezMJAc.

Nelson, Lee H. *Architectural Character: Identifying the Visual Aspects of Historic Buildings as an Aid to Preserving Their Character.* Accessed May 14, 2023. https://www.nps.gov/orgs/1739/upload/preservation-brief-17-architectural-character.pdf.

New England ADA Center ADA Title II Action Guide for State and Local Governments. "Home." Accessed October 15, 2022. https://www.adaactionguide.org/index.php/.

———. "Resources." Accessed February 26, 2020. https://www.adaactionguide .org/resources#.

Ngai, Mae. *Impossible Subjects: Illegal Aliens and the Making of Modern America.* Princeton: Princeton University Press, 2004.

Nielsen, Kim E. *A Disability History of the United States.* Boston: Beacon Press, 2012.

Norris, Linda. "Authenticity Is a Lie." *The Uncatalogued Museum* (blog), July 11, 2016. https://uncatalogedmuseum.blogspot.com/2016/07/authenticity -is-lie.html.

Piepzna-Samarasinha, Leah Lakshmi, and Stacey Park Milbern. *Disability Justice: An Audit Tool.* Accessed August 5, 2022. https://static1.square space.com/static/5ed94da22956b942e1d51e12/t/6232af2503a09a54615 b8d48/1647488823793/DJ+Audit+Tool.pdf.

Pink, Sarah. *Doing Sensory Ethnography.* Los Angeles: SAGE Publishing, 2015.

Pressman, Heather, and Danielle Schulz. *The Art of Access: A Practical Guide for Museum Accessibility.* Lanham, MD: Rowman & Littlefield, 2021.

Prince, Carl. *Middlebrook: The American Eagle's Nest.* Somerville, NJ: Somerset Press, 1958.

Railroaddata.com. "Tourist Railroads and Railway Museums International." Accessed June 29, 2022. https://railroaddata.com/rrlinks/Tourist_Rail roads_and_Museums_International/.

———. "Tourist Railroads and Railway Museums USA." Accessed June 29, 2022. https://railroaddata.com/rrlinks/Tourist_Railroads_and_Railway_Muse ums_USA/.

Railway & Locomotive Historical Society, Inc. "History of the Railroad & Loco-motive Historical Society." Accessed June 30, 2022. https://rlhs.org/WP /indexphp/history-of-the-rlhs/.

Reynolds, Paul. "Matterport Space Search Now Available." Matterport. Last Modified July 19, 2022. Accessed July 19, 2022. https://matterport.com /blog/matterport-space-search-now-available.

Rosen, Russell. "Sensory Orientations and Sensory Design in the American DeafWorld." *The Senses and Society*, no. 7 (November 2012): 366–73.

Rosenberg, Francesca. "What Does It Mean to Be an Accessible Museum?" *Medium*, November 16, 2017. https://stories.moma.org/what-does-it-mean-to-be-an-accessible-museum-9e9708254dc9.

Rosenzweig, Roy, and David Thelen. *The Presence of the Past*. New York: Columbia University Press, 2000.

Ruiz, Randolph R. "Displays Inside Railroad Equipment vs. the ADA." Railway Preservation News, October 19, 2006. Accessed April 9, 2022. http://rypn.org/forums/viewtopic.php?f=1&t=30329.

"Runaway from Prescriber." *Pennsylvania Gazette*, January 11, 1770.

Sakurai, Richard. Interview by Richard Potashin, July 24, 2010. Audio, 02:22:13 Densho Digital Repository. https://ddr.densho.org/narrators/536/.

Salmen, John P. S. *Everyone's Welcome: The Americans with Disabilities Act and Museums*. Washington, DC: American Alliance of Museums, 1998.

Sandell, Richard. *Museums, Society, Inequality*. London: Routledge, 2002.

Schalk, Sami. *Bodyminds Reimagined:(Dis)ability, Race, and Gender in Black Women's Speculative Fiction*. Durham: Duke University Press, 2018.

———. "Critical Disability Justice as Methodology." *Lateral* 6, no. 1 (Spring 2017). https://csalateral.org/issue/6-1/forum-alt-humanities-critical-disability-studies-methodology-schalk/.

Section508. "Integrating Accessibility into Agency Diversity, Equity, Inclusion and Accessibility (DEIA) Implementation Plans." Last modified December 20, 2021. Accessed July 14, 2022. https://www.section508.gov/manage/deia-guidance/.

———. "Voluntary Product Accessibility Template." Accessed August 16, 2022. https://www.section508.gov/sell/vpat/.

Seidel, John. "The Archaeology of the American Revolution: A Reappraisal & Case Study at the Continental Army Cantonment of 1778–1779, Pluckemin, New Jersey." PhD dissertation, University of Pennsylvania, 1987.

Sekel, Clifford, Jr. "The Continental Army in Winter Encampment at Pluckemin, New Jersey. December, 1778–June, 1779." Master's thesis, Wagner College, 1972.

Sen, Arijit, and Lisa Silverman, eds. *Making Place: Space and Embodiment in the City*. Bloomington and Indianapolis: Indiana University Press, 2014.

Shrikant, Aditi. "How Museums Are Becoming More Sensory-Friendly for Those with Autism." *Smithsonian Magazine*, January 5, 2018. https://www.smithsonianmag.com/innovation/how-museums-are-becoming-more-sensory-friendly-for-those-with-autism-180967740/.

Silverman, Lois. *The Social Work of Museums*. New York: Routledge, 2009.

Sins Invalid. "10 Principles of Disability Justice." Accessed August 5, 2022. https://www.sinsinvalid.org/blog/10-principles-of-disability-justice.

Smithsonian Accessibility Program. "Smithsonian Guidelines for Accessible Exhibition Design." Accessed October 18, 2022. https://www.sifacilities.si.edu/sites/default/files/Files/Accessibility/accessible-exhibition-design1.pdf.

Star Institute. "Understanding Sensory Processing Disorder." Accessed October 20, 2022. https://www.spdstar.org/basic/understanding-sensory-processing-disorder.

Steamtown National Historic Site Pennsylvania. "Steamtown National Historic Site Announces Accessible Exhibit Improvements." November 20, 2019. Accessed April 9, 2020. https://www.nps.gov/stea/learn/news/steamtown-national-historic-site-announces-accessible-exhibit-improvements.htm.

Stromberg, Kirk. "Matterport Capture App for Android Is Officially Here!" Matterport. Last modified July 19, 2022. Accessed July 19, 2022. https://matterport.com/blog/matterport-capture-app-android-officially-here.

Swan, Deanne W. "The Effect of Informal Learning Environments on Academic Achievement during Elementary School." Paper presented to the American Educational Research Association, Philadelphia, Pennsylvania, 2014. https://www.imls.gov/blog/2014/04/children-who-visit-museums-have-higher-achievement-reading-math-and-science.

Szalavitz, Maia. "Making Connections." *Popular Mechanics*, November 18, 2015. https://www.popularmechanics.com/culture/a18227/subway-sleuths-mta-autism-program/.

Tilden, Freeman. *Interpreting Our Heritage*. Chapel Hill: University of North Carolina Press, 2007.

Titchkosky, Tanya. *The Question of Access: Disability, Space, Meaning*. Toronto: University of Toronto Press, 2011.

Trepanier, Gabrielle. "Ingenium Accessibility Standards for Exhibitions." 2018. https://accessibilitycanada.ca/wp-content/uploads/2019/07/Accessibility-Standards-for-Exhibitions.pdf.

Turino, Kenneth, and Max van Balgooy. *Reimagining Historic House Museums: New Approaches and Proven Solutions*. Lanham, MD: Rowman & Littlefield, 2019.

Ukai, Nancy. "The Mihara Braille Board." *50 Objects* (blog). Accessed May 5, 2022. https://50objects.org/object/the-mihara-braille-board/.

——. "Nameplates." *50 Objects* (blog). Accessed August 7, 2021. https://50objects.org/object/nameplates/.

——. "Takato Hamai's Crutches." *50 Objects* (blog). Accessed August 10, 2019. https://50objects.org/object/takato-hamais-crutches/.

US Access Board. "ADA Accessibility Guidelines." N.d. https://www.access-board.gov/adaag-1991-2002.html#4.1.7.

——. "Architectural Barriers Act." Accessed July 25, 2022. https://www.access-board.gov/law/aba.html#:~:text=The%20ABA%20stands%20as%20the,August%2012%2C%201968%20be%20accessible.

——. "Section 508 (Federal Electronic and Information Technology)." N.d. Accessed July 14, 2022. https://www.access-board.gov/law/ra.html#section-508-federal-electronic-and-information-technology.

US Census Bureau Public Information Office. "Nearly 1 in 5 People Have a Disability in the U.S., Census Bureau Reports—Miscellaneous—Newsroom—U.S. Census Bureau." US Census Bureau, May 19, 2016. Accessed January 3, 2022. https://www.census.gov/newsroom/releases/archives/miscellaneous/cb12-134.html.

US Department of Education. "A History of the Individuals with Disabilities Education Act." Last modified January 11, 2023. https://sites.ed.gov/idea/IDEA-History.

———. 504, Rehabilitation Act of 1973." Accessed September 14, 2023. https://www.dol.gov/agencies/oasam/centers-offices/civil-rights-center/statutes/section-504-rehabilitation-act-of-1973.

US Department of Health, Education, and Welfare. Office for Civil Rights. *Rehabilitation Act of 1973*. Washington, DC, 1973.

US Department of Justice. "Guidance on Web Accessibility and the ADA." Accessed March 18, 2022. https://www.ada.gov/resources/web-guidance/.

———. "Laws, Regulations, & Standards." Accessed July 25, 2022. https://www.ada.gov/2010_regs.htm.

US Department of the Interior. "Accessibility Statement." N.d. Accessed July 14, 2022. https://www.doi.gov/accessibility.

US Department of the Interior. National Park Service. "National Register Bulletin: How to Apply the National Register Criteria for Evaluation." 1997. https://www.nps.gov/subjects/nationalregister/upload/NRB-15_web508.pdf

Unrau, Harlan D. *The Evacuation and Relocation of Persons of Japanese Ancestry During World War II: A Historical Study of the Manzanar Relocation Center*. US Department of the Interior, National Park Service, 1996. https://www.nps.gov/parkhistory/online_books/manz/hrs16d.htm.

Vespa, Jonathan. "The Graying of America: More Older Adults than Kids by 2035." Center for Disease Control and Prevention, March 13, 2018. Accessed January 3, 2022. https://www.census.gov/library/stories/2018/03/graying-america.html.

———. "The U.S. Joins Other Countries with Large Aging Populations." Census.gov, March 13, 2018. Accessed January 3, 2022. https://www.census.gov/library/stories/2018/03/graying-america.html.

Vespa, Jonathan, Lauren Medina, and David M. Armstrong. "Demographic Turning Points for the United States: Population Projections for 2020 to 2060." US Census Bureau, last modified February 2020. https://www.cen

sus.gov/content/dam/Census/library/publications/2020/demo/p25-1144
.pdf., 25-1144.

Web Accessibility Initiative. "Web Content Accessibility Guidelines (WCAG)
Overview." 2005. Last modified June 30, 2022. https://www.w3.org/WAI
/standards-guidelines/wcag/.

WebAIM. "Alternative Text." Accessed October 24, 2022. https://webaim.org
/techniques/alttext/.

Weil, Stephen. "From Being About Something to Being for Somebody: The
Ongoing Transformation of the American Museum." *Daedalus* 128, no. 3
(Summer 1999).

Williamson, Bess. *Accessible America: A History of Design and Technology*. New
York: New York University Press, 2019.

Withers, A. J., Liat Ben-Moshe, Lydia X. Z. Brown, Loree Erickson, Rachel da
Silva Gorman, T. L. Lewis, Lateef McLeod, and Mia Mingus. "Radical Disabil-
ity Politics." In *Routledge Handbook of Radical Politics*, 178–93. Oxfordshire:
Routledge, 2019.

Wong, Margie Y. "Margie Y. Wong." Interview by Richard Potashin, January
21, 2011. Audio, 01:54:38. Densho Digital Archives. https://ddr.densho.org
/narrators/598/.

Wood, Keith. "Manzanar National Historic Site Hosts Record 105,307 Visitors
in 2016." *Manzanar Committee* (blog), January 26, 2017. https://manzanar
committee.org/2017/01/25/manzanar-visitors-2016/.

The Workshops Rail Museum. "Accessibility." Accessed May 20, 2022. https://
theworkshops.qm.qld.gov.au/.

Index

AASLH. *See* American Association for State and Local History

AAM. *See* American Alliance of Museums

accessibility, 53, 58, 59, 60, 62; audit, 18, 20, 23-25, 28, 32n4, 239, *see also*, Transition Plans; definition, 3, 8; digital, 171, 220-223; financial, 46-47, 49; mental, 168; physical, xvii, 3-4, 7, 11, 15, 24, 28-29, 33, 58-59, 98, 117, 121-122, 137, 142, 144-145, 165, 169, 219, 223, 228-229, 233; programmatic, xvii, 14, 28, 33, 185, 228-229; sensory, 174; socio-economic, 171; supports, 30, 40, 73, 76, 88, 135, 147; *See also* visual aids

accessibility programming, 83-96

ADA. *See* Americans with Disabilities Act

ADA-compliant: furnishing, 210; railings, 200; ramps, 200; slopes, 200, 203, 205; Adaptive redesign, 204; Aging population, 153

advisory committee or group, 19, 25, 89, 135-137, 143, 146

alt text, 31, 44, 100, 109-110, 223

Alzheimer's Association, 19, 92-94, 96n5

Alzheimer's disease. *See* dementia

American Alliance of Museums, 3, 5, 53, 121

American Association for State and Local History, xiii, 3, 37

American Sign Language (ASL), xv, 91-92, 131, 141, 147, 185-187, 193

Americans with Disabilities Act, xvii, 1, 3, 7-8, 9n26, 11, 14-15, 18, 20n1, 24-28, 35, 38, 48, 53, 58-59, 59, 62n7, 117-118, 125, 152, 165, 170, 193, 199-200, 202-203, 210, 219, 239-241; Accessibility guidelines, 15; Minimum requirements, 14; Title I, 11; Title II, 11, 18, 24-26, 58, 152; Title III, 11-12, 16, 24-25, 203, 240

Architectural Barriers Act of 1968, 6-7, 53, 229

ASL. *See* American Sign Language

autism, 9n8, 40, 68, 70n5, 72-82, 88-91, 96n3, 96n4, 135-138, 143-144, 174; autism advisory group, 89, 135-137, 143, 146; people on the autism spectrum as an audience, 88-91; specialized interest, 72-73, 80; staff training, 88-89

audience. *See* visitors

authenticity, 35-36, 40-42, 47-49

barrier removal, 15-19, 24, 64, 203, 239

barriers: attitudinal, 135; communication, 16, 24, 29, 130-131; digital, 171; language, 131; physical, 130, 141-143; sensory, 130, 134, 141, 144; visual, 131; financial, 46, 135

bias. *See* Discrimination

blind or low vision, 30-31, 44, 46, 75, 84-88, 99, 123, 131-132, 146, 184, 186-187; people who are blind or have low vision as an audience, 84-88

61, 84; touch tours, 46, 83–88, 96n2, 132, 170; virtual tours, 15, 43–44, 49, 97–111, 122
transition plans, 18, 23–26, 28, 84, 185
trust in museums, 5, 8, 155, 161

universal design, 59, 68, 121, 140, 142–143, 153, 200, 231, 235n13, 240–241

video, 42–43, 49, 122, 142, 145–146, 160, 185–186, 223, 240; accessibility, 43–44; camera
options, 102–103; music, 43, 50n16
viewshed, 208, 211, 213
visitor center, 55, 59–60, 178–179
visual vocabulary, 134–137
virtual programming, 84, 86–95, 92, 93–95, 122
visitation, 5, 200–201; impacts on children, 5
visitors, 35–36, 39, 42, 45–47, 204; circulation, 200–202; demographics,

38; developing and finding new. 39, 48
visual aids, 45, 73, 76, 89–90, 135, 137, *See also*, visual vocabulary. verbal description, 131–132; in video, 186; virtual verbal description tour, 86–88, 145. Vocational Rehabilitation Act. *See* Architectural Barriers Act and Rehabilitation Act of 1973

website, 29–31, 39–40, 44, 119, 124–25, 186, 191, 220–223; accessibility, 44, 50n19, 102, 235n14
wayfinding, 119, 132, 146, 202
well-being, 164, 170
Washington, George, 54, 55, 61
Wentz, Peter, 53, 57, 60
wheelchair accessible. *See* accessibility, physical
working with the community. *See* advisory committee or group
World War II, 177, 179–184

About the Editor

Heather Pressman (she/her) is an educator with a passion for accessibility and inclusion. She believes that everyone has the right to access and enjoy cultural experiences regardless of their abilities or disabilities. Heather currently serves as the director of learning and engagement for the Molly Brown House Museum, where she works to expand access, despite the physical challenges of a more than 130-year-old historic house. She got into this work because she saw through her friend's experience how much people with disabilities were missing out on in museums and at historic sites. Heather holds a master's degree in museum studies from Johns Hopkins University, where she teaches "Accessibility in the Museum." She coauthored *The Art of Access: A Practical Guide for Museum Accessibility* (Rowman & Littlefield, 2021).

About the Contributors

Charlotte Barrows is a registered landscape architect and associate with Nelson Byrd Woltz. She has been working at Mt. Cuba Center since 2018. She holds a bachelor of science in architecture with honors from the University of Virginia and a master's in landscape architecture from the Harvard Graduate School of Design. Charlotte recently authored a chapter "Photographs as Tools for Restoring the Historic Landscape of Olana" for *Active Landscape Photography: Diverse Practices* (Routledge Press, 2023) edited by Anne C. Godfrey.

Sean Blinn (he/him) is an independent museum professional based in New Jersey. He has worked on projects for museums, libraries, and galleries throughout the northeastern United States and has presented at professional conferences across the United States and in Europe. Mr. Blinn is a member of the board of directors of the Mid-Atlantic Association of Museums and has served as an appointed member of numerous local government historic preservation and planning commissions. He holds a master's in museum studies from Johns Hopkins University, a master's in political science from Binghamton University, and a bachelor's in political science from Haverford College.

Caroline Braden is the accessibility manager at The Henry Ford in Dearborn, Michigan. She has presented on accessibility at national and regional museum conferences and published an article for the University of Michigan's Working Papers series titled "Welcoming All Visitors: Museums, Accessibility, and Visitors with Disabilities." In 2016, Caroline received the John F. Kennedy Center for the Performing Arts Leadership Exchange in Arts and Disability (LEAD) Award for Emerging Leaders. She holds a bachelor's in anthropology, a master's in educational studies, and a museum studies graduate certificate from the University of Michigan.

Jennifer Crane is a patient access educator at Children's Mercy Hospital in Kansas City. She earned a BSE in elementary education from Emporia State

University. She taught special education in Texas and Kansas, then worked as education curator at the Johnson County Museum in Shawnee, Kansas. She holds an MET from MidAmerica Nazarene University and a master's in history from the University of Missouri–Kansas City. Ms. Crane wishes to thank Dr. Massimiliano Vitiello of the University of Missouri–Kansas City and Anne Jones of the Johnson County Museum for their generous help and encouragement with the writing of this chapter.

Sarah Kirk (she/her) is a curator passionate about eighteenth-century American culture and creating accessible educational opportunities at historic sites. Sarah was diagnosed with ADHD when she was thirteen years old and uses her daily struggles to inspire the equitable learning opportunities she designs. She is the curator of the Old Barracks Museum, where she manages the museum collection and creates accessible exhibits in the 260-plus-year-old building. Sarah holds a master's in museum studies from Johns Hopkins University and a bachelor's in history from Temple University.

Jennifer Lauer is a landscape designer at Nelson Byrd Woltz, where her focus area is historic preservation and cultural landscape interpretation in the public realm. Her recent work has included public historic sites such as the John and Alice Coltrane Home, Middleton Place, Sylvester Manor, and the Crowninshield Garden at the Hagley Museum. She has assisted with construction administration for the Mt. Cuba Center Comprehensive Landscape Plan since 2021. Jennifer holds a bachelor of arts in environmental studies with honors from Allegheny College and a master's in landscape architecture from SUNY College of Environmental Science and Forestry (SUNY-ESF).

Charlotte J. Martin has over ten years of experience working in museum education and accessibility. She is director of access initiatives at the Intrepid Museum, where she and her team develop specialized programs and resources and collaborate across the institution to embed accessibility in programming, training, customer service, design, infrastructure, and hiring. Charlotte has presented at conferences around the world and worked and consulted at a variety of museums. She previously served as president of the NYC Museum Educators Roundtable. Charlotte has an MAT in museum education from George Washington University and a bachelor's in history of art from Yale University.

Selena Moon is an independent scholar and writer based in Minnesota. Her research interests include Japanese American mixed race and disability history. She received her bachelor's in history from Smith College and master's in history from the University of Massachusetts Amherst.

About the Contributors

Elizabeth J. Nosek has been using the stories found in museum collections to engage visitors for over thirty years. Her love of museums and their use of informal education to build bridges between people found her working in a variety of museums from Delaware to Hawai`i before taking up her position as curator of education and exhibits at the Colorado Railroad Museum. Nosek holds degrees in cultural anthropology from Hamline University and history museum studies from the Cooperstown Graduate Program. She is the author of several articles on guest service and museum education for the *Docent Educator* and *ALHFAM Bulletin*. Nosek is also the author of *Interpretive Master Planning: A Framework for Historical Sites* (Rowman & Littlefield, 2021).

Megan S. Reed is a cultural heritage preservationist who joined the National Park Service's National Center for Technology and Training in the summer of 2021 after nearly ten years of working in various historical parks across the National Park Services and in Presidential Libraries within the National Archives. She joined the NCPTT documentation team as part of the center's ongoing research program to document the Slave and Tenant Farming Housing project. She has a background in archaeology, museum collection management, and 3-D LiDAR laser scanning.

REPAIR Collective Biography: In 2019, Gail Dubrow (professor of architecture, landscape architecture, history, and public affairs and planning at the University of Minnesota), Laura Leppink (alumnus of UMN's Heritage Studies and Public History master's program), and Sarah Pawlicki (PhD candidate in history at UMN) cofounded REPAIR: Disability Heritage Collective. REPAIR stands for Rethinking Equity in Place-based Activism, Interpretation, and Renewal, reflecting the three cofounders' mutual commitment to inclusive historic representation, historic preservation as reparative work, and supporting place-based advocates for justice. The collaborative project has subsequently grown to include collaborators Chelsea Wait (PhD candidate in architecture at the University of Wisconsin–Milwaukee), Morgan LaCasse (graphic designer and illustrator), Shana Crosson (spatial technology consultant), and Perri Meldon (PhD candidate in American studies at Boston University). We have listed contributing authors in alphabetical order by last name. Each author provided nuanced commentary on chapter sections primarily written by other members of the authorship team.

Sara Thomson is the special education and access manager at the New York Transit Museum, managing access programs for children through adults. She also advises on accessibility for all programming and across all museum departments. Sara previously worked for nine years at a school for children with multiple disabilities, and she interned and volunteered at multiple museums with a focus on accessibility. Sara was a steering committee member of the Museum, Arts and Culture Access Consortium in New York City. She received a master's in museum studies from the Johns Hopkins University and a bachelor's in history from Clemson University.

Kristy Van Hoven is a museum scholar studying the health and wellness benefits of museum participation and the museo-medical partnerships that support healthy communities from within the museum sector. She has worked in historic homes, museum foundations, medical museums, and with care teams in the hospital setting. In her leadership roles she works to ensure patients, caregivers, and families get to experience museum collections and experience the stories of their communities not just inside the museum but beyond the gallery walls.